The Art of
Maintaining a Florida
Native Landscape

Ginny Stibolt

Illustrations by Marjorie Shropshire

For Barbara
Green gardening matters!
Ginny Stibolt

University Press of Florida
Gainesville / Tallahassee / Tampa / Boca Raton
Pensacola / Orlando / Miami / Jacksonville / Ft. Myers / Sarasota

VIVA FLORIDA 500
1513–2013

A Florida Quincentennial Book

Text copyright 2015 by Ginny Stibolt
Illustrations copyright 2015 by Marjorie Shropshire
All rights reserved
Printed in the United States of America on acid-free paper

This book may be available in an electronic edition.

20 19 18 17 16 15   6 5 4 3 2 1

Library of Congress Control Number: 2015933805
ISBN 978-0-8130-6131-3

The University Press of Florida is the scholarly publishing agency for the State University System of Florida, comprising Florida A&M University, Florida Atlantic University, Florida Gulf Coast University, Florida International University, Florida State University, New College of Florida, University of Central Florida, University of Florida, University of North Florida, University of South Florida, and University of West Florida.

University Press of Florida
15 Northwest 15th Street
Gainesville, FL 32611-2079
http://www.upf.com

This book is dedicated to the native plant enthusiasts who volunteer for native plant societies across the country. Because of their hard work, the societies are able to provide education, outreach, and eco-activism to promote native plants and help protect local ecosystems. As a result, more gardeners across the country are now asking for and using native plants in their yards to attract birds, butterflies, and other pollinators.

Contents

Preface

Thanks to my involvement with the Florida Native Plant Society (FNPS) for the past eight years, I no longer garden the way I used to. Except for my edible gardens, I purchase only natives, and these days not so many of those, since my landscape has become more self-sustaining. I have reduced the size of the lawn established by the previous owner of our house and replaced it with a mixture of meadows and wooded areas. While I've done a lot of research in the writing of this book, many of the techniques shared here are personal, hard-learned lessons. I've combined the science of botany with commonsense ideas to rethink what the ideal landscape might look like and which ecosystem services it can offer.

The general public has preconceived notions about how landscape plants should look—both in the store and in the ground. While there are certainly exceptions, some of the ideas are formed by several influences:

- Garden centers resell plants that big suppliers such as Bonnie Plants produce to look good on the shelves—often in full bloom. What happens after the plants are sold doesn't seem to be an important factor in their business plans.
- Garden TV shows, websites, and magazines that depict instant landscaping makeovers and perfect gardens with no weeds, no wear and tear, and no plants that don't "pop."
- The all too common practice of disposable seasonal plantings, especially in public spaces—pansies in the winter, thirsty impatiens in the summer, and mums in the fall.

In addition to seasonally planted garden beds, many homeowners are also expected (or required) to maintain weed-free and always-green lawn. Artificially supported turfgrass requires herbicides, insecticides, fungicides, and extra irrigation to keep it going. Even so, when this whole campaign to thwart Mother Nature's abhorrence of monocultures fails, the homeowners start the whole process again by killing everything and resodding. Isn't this the definition of insanity—doing the same thing over and over and expecting a different result? And so it is with lawn care—trying to impede the tendency of species diversification is an expensive and uphill battle. (I have included guidelines for more sustainable freedom lawns in chapter 8.)

Managing the perfect turfgrass lawn and always-blooming garden edges requires a lot of work, time, and money. Those garden centers do not weep when the plants you buy need to be replaced the next season, because they are grown to produce the most sales, not necessarily to be successful in customers' landscapes. As a result, many gardeners are trained to plant for today and not for the future. Annuals forced to bloom early have completed their life cycles and may not make the effort to keep blooming after the stress of transplanting. Perennials forced to bloom early may also fail to adjust to "normal" garden care. Many people get discouraged and say they have a black thumb, but in most cases, it's not really their fault—they've been set up for failure to enhance the profits of garden centers and their suppliers.

So when we native plant enthusiasts start talking to people who are used to the instant landscapes and the pretty-on-the-shelf plants, we have a lot of talking to do. First is changing people's minds about what is attractive. Fortunately, more examples of native gardens across the nation are getting attention, such as the highly publicized High Line Park in Manhattan. And then we need to talk to people about the longevity of their new plants and the fact that natives are best planted when in dormancy, when they may not be particularly attractive.

Sometimes in our enthusiasm about how native landscapes are more sustainable and have a different type of beauty, we may overpromise the ease of care. This sets up another situation where people often fail. Those new to natives, on being promised a "no-maintenance" landscape, just plop them into the ground and ignore them, thinking that since they're natives, they'll do fine in their home climate, but often those neglected plants die. They may be native, but they are not made of plastic or cement! Any plant needs attention during its establishment period and also during stressful times after that.

I wrote this book to help people manage their expectations of what it's really like to live with a native (or mostly native) landscape in a typical urban/suburban neighborhood. Yes, a native landscape does need maintenance, especially during the establishment phase, but so much less than one with seasonally planted exotics. The timing and extent of the maintenance is also so much more flexible.

A native landscape works best if it's planted for the future, so you won't necessarily get that instant landscape, because the success rate of trees and shrubs is much higher if you start with small plants. You'll need to wait for them to fill in, but you space them out to accommodate their mature sizes. I've provided some strategies to make the waiting more entertaining and more beautiful than a broad expanse of mulch.

So come with me on this adventure. Whether you're getting ready to take that first step into native gardening or have already started, we'll have some fun learning to appreciate "The Real Florida." If you live in other parts of the country, except for the specific choices of plants, most of what is discussed here will apply anywhere, and your landscape can be authentic to your region. No matter where we live, we don't want it to look like Anywhere, U.S.A.

The idea for this book came from several sources: a conversation I overheard between Jake Ingram, a retired landscape architect, and a fellow FNPS member agreeing that several good books on Florida native plants were available, but none covering their long-term care; an idea by Meredith Babb, my editor at University Press of Florida, that we might need a book on Florida invasives; and background chatter on various blogs and Facebook posts by people having trouble keeping their newly planted natives alive, or disappointed with their new natives because they were not instantly beautiful.

Half the royalties from this book will be paid automatically to the

Florida Native Plant Society to further support their important work. As mentioned above, my association with the FNPS has changed the way I think about gardening. The society is filled with smart and dedicated members who work hard to promote the "Real Florida" in many ways: outreach to the public, funding of research and conservation, participation in land management reviews, and recognition of good native landscape design. Regarding land management reviews, FNPS participates in the Land Management Review teams of the Florida Department of Environmental Protection (as mandated by Chapter FS 259, Florida Statutes) as the conservation member of an eight-member team. On each state land reviewed, an FNPS member provides ecological expertise and works to promote the preservation and conservation of the native plants and native plant communities of Florida.

Thanks to the staff at the University Press of Florida for their hard work and expertise in putting together this book. Thanks to the people who read the manuscript or parts of it at various stages—Steve Woodmansee, Anne Cox, Roger Hammer, Jim Reveal, Shirley Denton, and Sue Dingwell.

The photographs are mine, and thanks go to Marjorie Shropshire for her beautiful illustrations—they add clarity to the text.

And last, thanks go out to everyone who is trying to create more authentic landscapes by using and promoting the use of local native plants. I hope this book will be helpful in managing native landscapes in your own yard, and on public and private lands in your community.

Check out my blog to find updates, events, speaking engagements, and reviews: www.GreenGardeningMatters.com.

Green Gardening Matters,
Ginny Stibolt

1

Introduction to Natives
and Their Ecosystems

Since the 1950s the typical dream home landscapes have included large and meticulously cared-for lawns. For many reasons, more people are jumping off the lawn-care cycle of constant need of water, fertilizer, and pesticides by replacing some or all lawn with groupings of native plants. But some native plant enthusiasts may overpromise the benefits of natives with their easy-care message. By all means let's get started, but with our eyes open.

Using Florida as an Example

This book includes broad strategies for planting landscapes with native or mostly native plants, from the design process to long-term maintenance. While Florida plants and native ecosystems are used as examples, these methods can be translated to any planting zone. The key (wherever you are) is, "Right plant, right place."

Native plant myths—only partially true

- They don't need watering once established, so you can stop irrigating.
- They don't need fertilizer, so soil doesn't matter.
- They don't need pesticides, so you can stop using poisons.
- And they don't need ongoing maintenance, so you can save time and money.

Doesn't this sound great? No irrigation, no fertilizer, no pesticides, and no maintenance. Sure, but these promises are too broad for urban/suburban environments. The goal of this book is to help you define a realistic plan for turning your yard into a working ecosystem featuring native plants that support butterflies and birds, and then to develop a plan of action for ongoing care. Mother Nature will thank you.

Municipal or Public Lands

While this book covers issues dealing with homeowners' properties, much of what is discussed here is also applicable to community associations, schools, cities, towns, and counties that maintain land. When public agencies or land managers move beyond what they've always done in the past by replacing high-maintenance lawns with more natural areas planted with natives, they can reduce pollution and set a good example for their citizens, plus they can save time and money.

One reason that it may be hard to change is that municipal workers know how to "mow and blow" all those lawns and roadsides on a weekly basis, and maybe lawn contractors already have a deal to apply pesticides and fertilizers. This book provides guidelines and strategies to help both land managers and their workers adjust to the more specific maintenance requirements of native landscapes. In the end, if these strategies are applied, there will be less water pollution from pesticide and fertilizer runoff and less air and noise pollution as use of lawn maintenance equipment is reduced.

Which Plants Are Native?

Most people on this continent consider plants to be native if they were established in a locale before the Europeans arrived. This is not an entirely satisfactory definition because native plant ranges continue to change as seeds are carried naturally by wind, bird, and tide; also, indigenous people developed and moved plants. However, a pre-European timeline is easy to verify, because early European botanists scoured the New World looking for plants to collect. Most of these specimens were sent back to Europe for identification and classification, so we know a good deal about the flora back then. Since this definition is the most used, it's the one this book will use.

The reason natives are so important is that they have adapted to a specific place over a period of time sufficient to develop complex and essential relationships with the physical environment and other organisms in a given ecological community. When our landscapes emulate the native habitats of the region with the right mix of well-established plants growing in soil that would naturally be in that place, they will then support wildlife and require less outside help from us. In most cases urban/suburban sites won't become true wildlands because they are part of a tended garden space, but they can become authentic landscapes for the area.

The other part of a definition of native is whether a plant is a regional native or endemic to an area or a particular ecosystem. For instance, the eastern dune sunflower (*Helianthus debilis*) occurs natu-

Dune sunflowers create a wonderful ground cover for hot, dry spots. If you're on Florida's east coast, plant the eastern dune sunflower (*Helianthus debilis*), but on the Gulf coast, choose the west coast dune sunflower (*H. debilis* subsp. *vestitus*) or the cucumber-leaf sunflower (*H. debilis* subsp. *cucumerifolius*).

rally in the eastern coastal areas of Florida, but it also grows well in sandy soils that are inland. It would be considered a regional native in inland habitats, but native purists would not consider it native there, and many worry about planting it on Florida's west coast, because it could damage populations of the less abundant west coast dune sunflower (*H. debilis* subsp. *vestitus*). So be aware of other close relatives of natives that you plant.

In most cases and unless you're re-creating or restoring a wildland with only indigenous natives that would have been growing there before the Europeans arrived, easy-to-grow regional natives may be a reasonable choice, especially if they are as hardy as that beautiful and tough dune sunflower.

Also, plant provenance is important. Red maple (*Acer rubrum*) is native to the eastern United States and north into the eastern Canadian provinces, but if you try to grow a maple bred from Quebec stock in South Florida, it will leaf out and bloom eight weeks too late in the spring, it will lose its leaves too early in the fall, it has adapted to freezing soil in the winter, and it will thus be quite likely to fail. It's important, when purchasing plants, that they are derived from local stock. The best way to ensure this is to shop at local nurseries that specialize in native plants. This way you'll be getting plants that won't be surprised by local seasonal fluctuations.

Finding Appropriate Natives

Although native plants have increased in popularity, it's still unlikely you'll be able to wander into your local big box store to find a wide selection of locally grown natives. These stores may have a few of the most commonly planted natives such as magnolias, live oak, and maybe some native bunching grasses, but they are usually supplied by a nationwide distributor that may obtain their trees in bulk from distant sources. Plus, many of the native plants they do offer may be native cultivars (cultivated varieties) such as a Little Gem Magnolia (*Magnolia grandiflora* 'Little Gem'), a smaller, slow-growing, and more compact version of the wild plant. Many ecologists don't consider cultivars to be true natives, serving the same functions in the ecosystem as the unnamed wild species. On the other hand, you may need a smaller, more compact version to fit a tight spot in your landscape, so maybe the cultivar of a native offers a better choice for the local ecosystem than an exotic.

You'll want to develop a relationship with a local nursery specializing in natives for most of your plants. Well-informed nursery employees can make suggestions based on the experiences of local clients and work with you as you implement each stage of your planned landscape installation. Running a native nursery is a difficult business. Many customers expect that plants will be inexpensive and "pop" just like the faux plants in the big box stores that are bred to look good for retail displays and thrown out when they fade.

Many native plants have dormant periods when they don't look that attractive in a pot, but native plant nurseries don't throw them away, because they know they will leaf out and put on new growth the next season. Some natives take a long time to germinate and grow very slowly—it may take several years for them to grow to a size that will make an impact in the landscape—as a result, they won't be cheap to buy. But, if a native is the right plant for your space, it will live to its full life expectancy, which makes it an overall bargain. Carefully selected and properly planted natives won't need to be replaced again and again.

The website of the Florida Association of Native Nurseries (FANN, www.plantrealflorida.org) offers a tool for finding specific plants and nearby member nurseries. Also, the Florida Native Plant Society (www. fnps.org) has chapters across the state, and many hold regular native plant sales as part of their outreach. In other states, join and support your local native plant society for inside information on contacting local native vendors. The website of the American Horticulture Society includes a page listing all the native plant societies, at ahs.org/gardening-resources/societies-clubs-organizations/native-plant-societies.

Arguments for Native Plants

Native plants provide a sense of place. Sadly, in much of the country, the gardens look pretty much the same no matter where you go, because adaptable exotic plants, such as Asian azaleas, crape myrtles, begonias, impatiens, mums, pansies, and zinnias, are widely sold and planted, while plants native to each region are not. If you shop only in big box stores, your landscape will probably end up looking like Anywhere, U.S.A.

Doug Tallamy has made the case for using native plants in every landscape, no matter how small, in his iconic 2007 book *Bringing Nature Home*. He says that planting natives in small landscapes may not re-create ancient ecosystems, but it does provide enough biodiversity to support some of what's left of our wildlife. He maintains that native plants form the basis for ecosystems and without them there will be fewer butterflies and fewer pollinators. Without those bugs, there will be fewer birds, frogs, lizards, and other insect predators.

One of the promised benefits of a native landscape is that native plants don't require pesticides and that somehow they've learned to resist the native bugs. In reality, many native insects prefer native plants to exotics, and in fact, some of them cannot exist without their specific larval foods. For instance, the caterpillars of Florida's state butterfly, the zebra longwing (*Heliconius charitonius*), require passionflower leaves (*Passiflora* spp.), preferably growing in partial shade, for food. So your native vines may be well chewed, while the exotics might not be eaten at all.

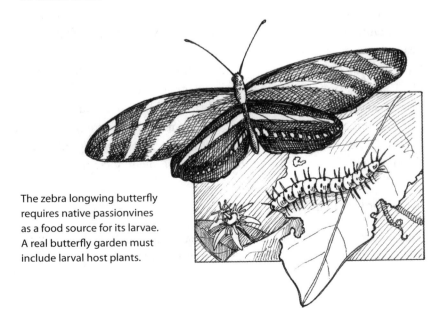

The zebra longwing butterfly requires native passionvines as a food source for its larvae. A real butterfly garden must include larval host plants.

Bugs

Entomologists classify true bugs as those belonging to only one order of the insects, the Hemiptera. Members of this order have sucking mouthparts, and many are significant garden pests such as aphids.

Informal use of the term "bug" refers to various members of the arthropod phylum (animals with exoskeletons) that include the six-legged insects; the eight-legged spiders, mites, and scorpions; the crustaceans such as sowbugs and pillbugs; and the many-legged centipedes and millipedes. With apologies to the entomologists, this book uses the informal terminology.

What changes when you plant native ecosystems? It's your attitude toward those bugs. You will want to plant enough larval host plants so the caterpillars can be sustained. True butterfly gardeners cheer when caterpillars eat their plants! And when you support ongoing populations of various bugs (both prey and predator), your yard will also attract more small birds and they in turn will attract larger predatory birds and so on. At this point you would never poison the bugs you've worked so hard to attract, so in a way, the promise of native landscapes not needing pesticides is correct, but for entirely different reasons.

Know Your Natives

Before you start planting, learn what is native in your region by reading books and searching online resources, signing up for master naturalist courses, and joining your local native plant society chapter. Attend seminars, go on field trips, help on workdays, attend meetings, and go to conferences. (To find a master naturalist program, see the website of the Alliance of Natural Resource Outreach and Service Programs: www.anrosp.org).

Also, learn to identify plants that are known to be invasive in your region, so you'll know what needs to be removed from your landscape first. If you buy plants from garden centers in Florida, some of the plants labeled "Florida-friendly" are natives, but many are not, so be on guard. Unfortunately, you may also find invasives for sale.

This book provides examples of native plants in various discussions of maintenance, but it is not a plant-list book. Several good books and other resources for Florida gardeners, listed in resources, will help you identify native plants already growing in your yard and to choose suitable additions to expand your habitats. Also, just because a plant is native to your location and would grow well in your yard does not automatically make it a good choice. An obvious example of an unwanted native is poison ivy (*Toxicodendron radicans*), a lovely plant with shiny leaves that turn bright red in the fall and white berries that birds and other wildlife love to eat. But you probably don't want it in a suburban landscape where people are likely to rub up against it. Also some fussy native plants have specific requirements to grow and are unlikely to thrive on most urban/suburban properties, so choose plants that grow readily in many different habitats for the best success.

Irrigation for Natives

Here in Florida, native plants have adjusted to the five-month wet season (aka hurricane season—from June through October), the seven-month dry season during the cooler months, and all the variations within this basic pattern. In other sections of the country, the pattern of rainfall is different, but the principle is the same. Normally, natives (once they are established) flourish in their native habitats with only the rainfall for irrigation. That being said, in severe droughts even well-established natives in their natural environments might suffer dieback and not recover.

Your yard is not a native ecosystem—it's only an imitation. Plus, many native plants are not naturally drought tolerant, and some, such as the cardinal flower (*Lobelia cardinalis*), require a consistently moist site with rich soil and will die if you plant them in a dry, sandy, sunny location. You'd do better to plant the drought-tolerant Indian blanket (*Gaillardia pulchella*) there. So do your research and select only the best plants for the various microclimates in your landscape.

The promise that native plants don't need irrigation is only partially true. If you are comparing the care of an established native landscape to a lawn or to a bed of thirsty impatiens, then yes, natives, once they're established in appropriate habitats, require much less irrigation. On the other hand, even though it's natural for native plants to die prematurely in extreme drought conditions out in wild areas, you probably don't want that to happen in your landscape. Many gardeners plan for supplemental irrigation to preserve their native habitats during extreme droughts.

Ecosystems in Your Yard

An ecosystem is complex interrelationship of organisms (plants, animals, fungi, and bacteria) and the substrate where they live and die. Healthy soil is an ecosystem, but a yard's landscape with its plants and animals is part of a larger ecosystem that also encompasses the soil; your yard is also part of the neighborhood ecosystem.

Soil Ecosystems

Healthy soil is a complex ecosystem consisting of microorganisms such as bacteria, fungi, and microscopic worms, and macroorganisms such as earthworms, ants, insect larvae, salamanders, millipedes, centipedes, and more. The soil also provides habitat to native bees and wasps, gopher tortoises, moles, voles, and snakes. (Moles are carnivorous mammals—not rodents—that eat insect larvae and worms, while voles are rodents that eat underground plant parts.)

Before humans disturbed Florida's native ecosystems, the native soils provided sufficient nutrients for the plants or they would not have grown there. When you try to establish a new native plant community in a disturbed site, such as a former lawn, an agricultural site, or fill material, you may have some soil building to accomplish until your plants can fend for themselves. Sometimes it's not easy to discern the soil type of your property, but it's worth the effort in your quest for native habitats. Elevation and topography indicate potential soil type as well as historic hydrology. In Florida, older homes tend to be located in areas that were "high and dry," plus the soil in older neighborhoods has had a chance to recover from the initial shock of development, especially if there is good tree canopy. On the other hand, many newer homes in Central and South Florida have been built on former wetlands. If you're inland but still required to carry flood insurance, your property's soil is probably material used to fill an original wetland.

You may have a rough idea of the state of your soil because of previous planting successes and failures. Before you start planting, it's important to know about your soil and the various microclimates in your landscape. Get your soil tested at your local extension office, and while you're there, ask for a detailed soil map of your region to get a rough idea of the type of soil expected to occur there naturally. When you know what type of soil you have and whether remediation is necessary to support natives, then you can decide what natives would flourish there. While some native plants are highly adaptable and will grow just about anywhere, others require a specific soil type. It's probably a good idea to avoid fussy plants with very specific habitat needs in our highly modified urban/suburban ecosystems.

It's been shown that synthetic fertilizers are not good for the web of soil inhabitants needed to support native plants. But the soil may need to be improved in other ways, such as compost topdressing or organic mulching, so your plants have adequate nutrients and microorganisms. Soil building for native landscapes could be a multiyear process, continuing until your plants are mature enough to provide adequate leaf and litter drop to serve as their own mulch. On the other hand, many native ecosystems occur where the soil is naturally poor. If poor soil is the history of your area, your strategies will be different. So the promise of no fertilizers for natives may or may not be true, but avoid synthetic fertilizers in any case.

Landscape Ecosystems

Many people plant natives because they wish to attract birds and butterflies. Inviting wildlife into your yard means you'll need to create an ecosystem that provides food, shelter, and water for your guests. The first thing to do is to stop using broad-spectrum, landscape-wide pesticide applications to allow your bugs and their predators (birds, frogs, bats, and lizards) to reach a balance. The predators' populations will vary depending on the abundance of their prey—the more bugs you have, the larger your bird population. Cats and dogs severely damage the delicate balance of predator and prey. Remove these subsidized predators, especially cats, from your landscape.

A functioning ecosystem should have a wide variety of flower types, berries, seeds, and nuts. Plant the larval food for various butterflies; many of them have specific requirements. Hummingbirds are attracted to flowers for their nectar, especially red or orange tubular ones, but they will also visit many other types of flowers, plus they eat small bugs, especially when rearing young. Work to create a selection of native berry-bearing shrubs and trees, because berries and seeds are important food for many songbirds, particularly when they are migrating. To provide food for wildlife, let some of your flowers go to seed and allow some meadow areas to remain uncut at least until late winter.

Build structure in your landscape for wildlife. Birds and butterflies need places to nest and hide from predators and shelter for protection from wind and rain. Create areas where vegetation grows from the ground to high in the trees. Use a combination of different-sized shrubs, vines, and trees. Vertical layering simulates the natural ecotones or edges between different habitats such as between meadow and forest, and it provides shelter for many types of wildlife.

In addition, it's important to leave snags (standing dead tree trunks) and downed trees or logs in place. In wildlands this happens without human help, but in urban/suburban areas, your design would probably allow snags to remain only in the back or hidden behind some neater or more civilized landscape plantings. You may even "plant" a vertical log or two somewhere in your yard for cavity-nesting birds and high perching birds such as hawks that use the vertical standing wood. These planted logs are more useful to secondary cavity nesters if you predrill various-sized holes into them. Native bees and wasps can use the smallest holes as nests, while birds can use the larger holes.

The website of the National Wildlife Federation provides information on designing habitat for wildlife and a process for certifying your landscape (as well as church yards, schoolyards, and whole communities) as habitat: www.nwf.org.

A goal for your native landscape is to provide enough habitat services to support a top predator such as this wonderful hawk.

One mark of a successful ecosystem in an urban/suburban environment is whether it supports top predators such as hawks and owls. It may take several years of habitat building before this happens, but it's fun and educational to witness the progression toward a working ecosystem each season.

Keep a Record

Establishing native ecosystems in your landscape will be a multiyear process. It's important to keep a log of your activities. A logbook doesn't need to be fancy, and you don't need to be a talented artist to make it work, but it will be invaluable as the years go by. Use it to sketch plant arrangements in wildlands or other places where you admire the landscape. You can record ideas for your own native landscape, keep a detailed list of when and where you purchased plants or other supplies, and later, record how well they did, including the failures. Keep a list of plants that you want or need, so at a nursery or native plant sale you'll have a starting point for needed plants.

Take photos of each phase of your landscaping to record your progress. Later, when you wish to tell the story of how you transformed the property from unsustainable lawn to lovely native ecosystems, you'll have a visual record. See chapter 11 for ideas on how to tell your story.

The "No-Maintenance Landscape" Is a Myth

Compared to a lawn and a formal landscape with shrubs pruned into gumdrop or lollipop shapes, a well-designed native landscape, once it's established, will require much less ongoing maintenance. Depending on the arrangement, the maturity of the native habitat, and the neighborhood, you may find that your work sessions in the yard, including weeding, pruning, and mulching, will range from monthly for newly planted landscapes to once or twice a year for mature plantings.

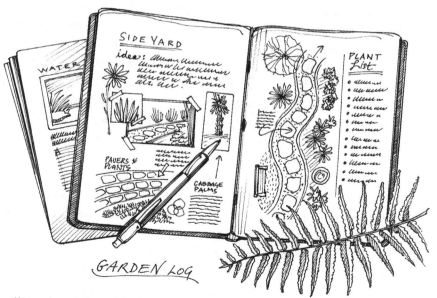

Keep a log of plans with plant lists. Also, record planting details: plant sources, planting dates, and how well they did. This detailed information will be invaluable in subsequent stages of developing your native landscape.

2

Planning Native Plant Projects

A good way to get started with native landscaping is to visit nearby parks or wildlands. Try to find areas that seem to emulate your soil type, geography, and landscape situation. Look for a mix of trees and shrubs similar to those growing in your neighborhood and maybe even on your own lot if it's big enough. In some highly developed areas, this may not be easy to do, but try to find something as close in type and appearance as you can. Take photos or make sketches in your logbook and take note of how native or near-native landscapes arrange themselves. In the parks, the rangers may have done some editing of the natural landscapes; if possible, talk to them to see what they've planted or removed and why. One of the things you'll notice is that Mother Nature does not create symmetrical landscapes—balanced, yes, but there are rarely straight lines or perfectly matched specimens. Depending on ecosystem, you may also notice that most plants in groupings include only one or two species, with only a smattering of other types.

One of the more important objectives for your visits is to develop a list of likely trees, shrubs, perennials, and annuals that occur together and might be appropriate for your landscape. Learn as much as you can about their adult sizes and how long they take to reach maturity, what soils they like, how long they'll live, and likely companion plants. While this book is not a landscape design book, per se, if you don't prepare and plan well, maintaining your native landscape could become much more difficult to manage.

Develop an Overall Landscape Plan

If you can afford it, hire a landscape architect or a native garden designer to help with your overall plan for natives. This step will save money in the long run because people trained in this field know the questions to ask, will be familiar with plants that work well for your area, will help determine whether you'll have a drainage issue, and should create a scale drawing of your property. Note: Many landscape architects are not schooled in native plants, so be sure to choose one who has been successful with native plant installations.

If you choose not to hire a professional to help with your plan, many online resources and books are available with information on how to begin. You will need a scale graphic of your property. If you don't have a lot survey, you can search for an aerial view of your property and capture the screen as a graphic, print it out, and use it to make your notes. In this first stage of planning, determine which direction your house and other buildings are facing and mark north with an arrow on the map. This is important to know because some plants do better with only morning sun, while others are adapted to hot afternoon exposure. Knowing the orientation of the property means that you can predict the sun's path in summer and winter and plan around it.

Even though your goal may be to minimize any evidence of a gardener's hand in your native landscape, it will not become a true wildland. Your overall plan and plant selections should be influenced by your study of regional natural landscapes, but in an urban/suburban environment, it must also accommodate the human use of the land. When developing planting patterns, leave space for access paths for weeding, mulching, and manual irrigation during the establishment phase and during extended droughts. Also, leave enough space between buildings and plants—even small herbaceous plants should be at least 2 feet from buildings.

Your selected plants should be the appropriate size and shape for the space available without a lot of trimming and hacking. For instance, it would be unwise to plant a live oak (*Quercus virginiana*) in a small front yard of only 20 by 40 feet. It may look fine for the first decade, but eventually it will outgrow that space and become a maintenance

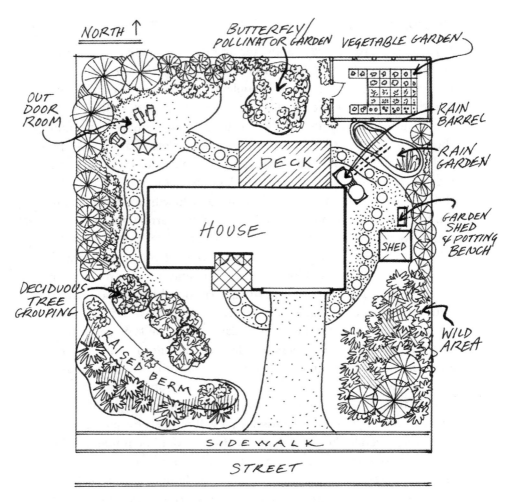

NORTH ↑

BUTTERFLY/
POLLINATOR GARDEN   VEGETABLE GARDEN

OUT
DOOR
ROOM

RAIN
BARREL

RAIN
GARDEN

DECK

HOUSE

GARDEN
SHED
& POTTING
BENCH

SHED

DECIDUOUS
TREE
GROUPING

WILD
AREA

RAISED BERM

SIDEWALK

STREET

LANDSCAPE PLAN

Create a plan for your whole landscape even though
you might be able to work on only one space at a time.

nightmare. Its roots will eventually destroy sidewalks, the driveway, and maybe even the foundation of the house. Its massive branches will overhang the street and the roof. It would need to be trimmed back on a regular basis and in the process would end up looking awful. A better choice for a small space would be a trio of river birches (*Betula nigra*) planted toward one end of the yard—not in the dead center of the space. Likewise, keep utilities in mind. Don't plant trees under or near power lines or on top of underground infrastructure such as septic systems, water or gas mains, irrigation pipes, or buried cables. If you don't know what's under the ground in your landscape, call 811, or in Florida, go to the sunshine 811 website (www.sunshine811.com) to request an evaluation. Other states have similar programs.

Even with all your planning and consideration of the mature sizes of your plants, sometimes Mother Nature can surprise you with an unexpected growth pattern that forces a change of plan. For instance, a sweet bay magnolia (*Magnolia virginiana*) planted in a damp spot might send up a bunch of suckers that form a nice thicket, but if you hadn't taken that into account in your plan, the plants next to the magnolia might be crowded out. Since the suckering will continue, it might be more sustainable to move the neighboring plants to other locations, even if they are fairly large by the time this happens. In another situation, maybe a saw palmetto (*Serenoa repens*) planted itself near a path and will overtake that space if allowed to grow. The two most sustainable choices in this case are to either move the shrub before it grows too large, or reroute the path to a new location that will allow the palmetto to expand to its full glory. If you allow both the palmetto and the path to remain in place, the need to cut back the sharp fronds to keep the path clear will be never ending—a maintenance nightmare.

Before you start any actions, take photos from various vantage points, including from curbside and from the inside of your house. Repeat the photography sessions in various seasons so you have an unbiased record of your existing landscape. Then as you start work on various projects, take more detailed photos of the designated area before, during, and after your work to record the process. When you look at the photos later, you may be able to catch awkward plant juxtapositions, or other trouble spots that might not be so obvious in person. See chapter 11 for tips on taking good landscape photos.

You may find that sketching your landscape from various directions will allow you to slow down enough to determine the dominant features and see an overall design that you might not notice in a quickly snapped photo. Even if you don't have "talent," you can draw some ovals and curves to represent the plants and planting areas. Then keep notes of how your present landscape will be transformed through the planned stages to a more natural and native-rich habitat.

Dividing up Your Projects

Once you have a long-term landscape plan or vision, it's often a good idea to develop your native landscape over several years—one project at a time. As you make progress in your plantings, the overall plan may change, but your initial vision will still guide the process.

A multistaged landscape installation has several advantages:

- It keeps the projects small enough so it doesn't overwhelm the available labor—not only for preparations and planting, but also for the initial irrigation and maintenance tasks needed to ensure the long-term survival of new plants.
- It is easier to budget for plants and supplies for one section of the landscape or for only a couple of special projects.
- Gradual change, in stages, doesn't shock the community or the neighbors, and this is particularly important for people who live under the watchful eye of an HOA—a homeowners association.
- You can plant the eventual tallest trees in the first stages to give them a head start, then come back a few years later to plant understory trees and shrubs when the initial trees are large enough to cast some shade, but still small enough that their root systems have not spread too widely.
- Most important, by the third or fourth wave of plantings, you'll have gained enough experience to adjust your methods. You'll have seen which native plants are doing well on your property and which ones have struggled. You'll also be able to judge how well your soil preparation, irrigation, mulching, and weed eradications have worked. You can then modify the next stages of your landscaping accordingly.

What to Keep?

There may be some trees, shrubs, and perennials already growing on your property that you'll wish to keep, either permanently or temporarily, as part of the naturalization process. Deciding what to keep may be one of the most important parts of developing your overall landscape plan. Of course, you'll remove exotic invasive plants, but natives, native cultivars, or non-invasive exotics that are growing well in spots that fit into your plan could all be candidates for inclusion. Select the trees that are in the best shape and in the most logical places for your landscape plan, but when given a choice, give preference to natives that are less common in your neighborhood to promote diversity.

The big advantage of keeping existing trees and shrubs is that they are established and may already be providing some good shade and habitat value for your property's ecosystem. Your landscape plan will need to accommodate them and their root systems.

Evaluating Existing Trees

It's a good idea to have a certified arborist evaluate the trees you wish to keep and answer any questions you may have about them as well as the shrubs. Even if you hire a landscape architect to help with planning

---

Tree Evaluation List

An experienced certified arborist will have a lot of information to offer as to what trees to keep and which ones to remove to move your landscape plan forward. It's best to arrange for more than one evaluation, because these are important decisions and opinions may differ. You may have to pay for these assessments, so make the best use of your investment by being ready for these visits.

Here is a list of suggested questions for the arborist:

- What is the genus and species of each tree? Which trees are invasive, common, uncommon, or desirable in some way, including the right size for the space? Ask for a written list of tree species.

continued

- Ask for recommendations on which trees to keep and which to remove based on the following features:

  Long-term ongoing care. In other words, will it require repeated pruning for crossed branches, water sprouts or suckers, will it need repeated heavy irrigation, or is it susceptible to a known disease?

  Species diversity on your property and in the neighborhood;

  Wildlife habitat value;

  The ability to mingle with other trees and shrubs in its vicinity, including its sensitivity to new plantings within its drip line.

- For trees that are close enough to damage buildings, driveways, or other heavily used areas if they fall, ask about their wind resistance factors:

  Are the trunks sound?

  Are the roots likely to disrupt the sidewalks, drives, septic tanks, or other underground infrastructure?

  Do the canopies need to be lightened to improve wind resistance and what would be the pruning plan? Would topping be part of the trimming? (If the answer to this is yes, find another arborist.)

- For unwanted trees located away from human infrastructure objects, ask about alternative methods for removal such as topping or girdling, which will save money and also leave snags for habitat.

- Ask if you can keep the chips of your removed trees.

- Of course you'll ask about insurance, ask to see their certification papers, and ask about payment options if you hire them to work on your trees. It's usually not a good idea to pay the total due up front.

your landscape transformation, he or she will probably recommend an arborist to evaluate the trees. Take good notes so you know what you have and what you can expect from them in the future. See box on page 19 for a list of suggested questions.

Sometimes Mother Nature does not plant trees with enough space to grow. You will need to decide which trees to keep based on your plan, possible danger if they are likely to fall, and ongoing upkeep.

Keep in mind that removing major limbs will slow the growth of a tree and put stress on the tree's vitality, so remove as few as possible to accomplish the reason for the trim. A trim should not be more than 20 percent of the tree, and when the arborist is finished, it should not be obvious that the tree has been pruned. Some types of trees develop crossing branches and water sprouts that weaken their structures and are improved by trimming, but others such as conifers rarely need corrective pruning. The trimming will increase the sunlight within their drip lines and make them more wind tolerant. In some cases, you may wish to limb-up (remove low branches) selected trees with low-growing branches to open up the area, but keep in mind that when you do this, it reduces the habitat value of that tree and may increase the maintenance chores—weeds may become a problem with the increased light and visibility.

Topping and hat-racking are bad ideas for landscape trees and will shorten their life spans; unless the top has already been damaged in a storm, don't top trees you wish to keep. Note: many fruit trees are pruned in this manner to keep the fruit within easy reach, but in most other cases, just say no to topping.

The vast majority of tree roots are located within the top foot of the soil, and the average root spread is four times farther from the trunk than the tips of the branches. In a natural environment the roots of neighboring trees and shrubs intermingle, but if you wish to plant some additional shrubs, understory trees, or other plants near your existing trees, you'll be invading an established root zone. When planting understory plants, dig carefully and adjust the locations of the planting holes as you run into large roots. Some trees are relatively tolerant of disturbance around their roots, while others, such as flowering dogwood (*Cornus florida*), won't do well at all with digging and foot traffic on and around its root system—learn about tolerance of your saved trees and tread carefully within their drip lines and beyond. Do not add soil over roots to even out the terrain, and if you plan to use a mulch to keep down the weeds, keep it thin—2 or 3 inches maximum with no mulch touching the trunk. Use chunky mulch because roots need air in the soil around them.

Dealing with Existing Shrubs

After you decide which trees to keep, you'll need to figure out what to do with your shrubs. Get rid of shrubs that are known to be invasive in your region and ones that are doing poorly. Remove these shrubs sooner, rather than later, even if they are in an area that you're not ready to replant with natives yet. If shrubs are not invasive or diseased, leave them in place while you research their habits and habitat values to see which ones to favor in your landscape plans.

As with the trees, choose the shrubs that look the best, fit into your plan, and add the most habitat value. If possible, keep the native shrubs of various sizes and those that are the most unusual in your neighborhood. If you can, spend at least a full year observing the trees

Foundation Shrubs

Most foundation shrubs are planted too close to buildings and too close together in an effort at instant-impact curb appeal, plus many of these shrubs are exotic species. If your foundation plantings have been in place for more than a decade, the shrubs have probably outgrown their spaces or have been sheared into gumdrop shapes or compact hedges. Should these boring foundation plants be retained, used elsewhere, or trashed? Some people replace the foundation shrubs entirely with a grouping of bunching grasses or a cottage-type garden filled with native perennials and self-seeding annuals that won't outgrow the space, but fill it nicely with lots of color, butterflies, and pollinators. That being said, dense shrubbery offers excellent cover for some types of wildlife, so maybe you should continue to trim them and leave them in place. Or maybe you're in a fire-prone area where you'll want to remove all tall plants from under the eaves to decrease the likelihood of a house fire. There is no one correct answer for all situations.

If the shrubs are native, they may be a great addition to a wilder section of your landscape. Prepare them for transplanting by root-pruning them at least 4 weeks ahead of time so they have time beforehand to grow new roots close to the main canes. See chapter 5 for more details on transplanting and root pruning.

One option for overgrown shrubs that are desirable, slow growing, and relatively healthy is to transplant half of them to other locations and severely trim back the remaining shrubs, maybe even down to the ground. This way they'll have a chance to grow back in a more natural and easier-to-maintain shape. While the space will look empty until they grow back, you could fill it in with containers or temporary, quick-growing plants such as bunching grasses, wildflowers, or vine-covered trellises. It's also a possibility that when cut back to the ground or transplanted, those shrubs will never fully recover and may die, but you won't know that right away, so it might be easier to start with new young plants. As with all gardening, plans don't always work out and good gardeners have learned to go with the flow.

and shrubs to see how they fit in with the other existing vegetation and pay attention to what they look like and how much sun they receive in each season.

Unlike the trees, you can trim most shrubs yourself with a heavy-duty lopper, bow saw, or even a shovel, for shrubs that send out new stems (canes) from their roots. But just because you're able to trim the shrubs, that doesn't mean they all need to be whacked into submission. If shrubs have been repeatedly pruned back, try letting them grow out to see what they look like. For instance, beautyberry (*Callicarpa americana*) has a lovely arching pattern and can grow to be quite large depending on where you live, but it's a common practice in Florida to chop it back each year to 18-inch stubs. When converting a shrub like this to a more natural growth pattern, some judicious pruning of excess canes will probably be needed. It may take a couple of years to rehabilitate a shrub into a more natural shape, but it's worth the effort, because naturally shaped shrubs are so much easier to maintain.

Shrubs play a vital role in creating good habitat value for your landscape. Many shrubs have a dense growth pattern so they provide good cover for wildlife and good screening in your landscape design. Plus, you can select a collection of shrubs that provide a year-round supply of berries and flowers for birds. Native shrubs add character to any landscape and will play a large role in making your landscape authentic.

Selecting Vines

Vines typically make up a large portion of the curtain of vegetation from the ground to the canopy in the ecotones at the edges of wooded areas. This vegetation creates important habitat values for many types of wildlife as shelter and places to raise young. Vines growing on trellises or arbors can fill empty spots in a newly planted landscape where the trees and shrubs are planted far enough apart to allow for their adult growth. Vines can convert plain-Jane fences into a solid mass of blooms or berries that are attractive to butterflies, hummingbirds, and humans. Some vines make a wonderful, thick ground cover, but fast-growing vines can overtake the landscape, and ones that are woody can deform small trees.

This dogwood (*Cornus florida*) was strangled by a vine and became deformed as it tried to grow around it. Regular removal of woody vines would have prevented this.

When deciding on which vines to keep, choose the ones with the most habitat value and maybe mix different species together so that as a group some will look good most of the time. Keep in mind that some of the vines could be temporary in your overall plans. Most perennial vines in an urban/suburban landscape will need to be controlled with yearly trimming, but you can choose species that are not too exuberant to reduce your maintenance chores.

What to Do with Existing Herbaceous Plants

The nonwoody plants offer the most flexibility in your existing landscape. Whether annuals or perennials, these plants are in some ways the easiest to work with, in that you can move them or replant them in various parts of your landscape. Your relationship with these plants is not a long-term commitment as with trees or shrubs, but without them, your landscape would be barren indeed. On the other hand, many of our noxious weeds are herbaceous plants, so as a group they may create a major challenge in your landscape until they mature to the point when disturbed areas are reduced.

One of the important reasons for observing your landscape through-out a whole year before starting to make major changes is that many herbaceous plants die back for part of the year. Most, like the golden-rods (*Solidago* spp.), spotted beebalm (*Monarda punctata*), and snow squarestem (*Melanthera nivea*) die back during the winter, while oth-ers, like meadow garlic (*Allium canadense*) and Florida betony (*Stachys floridana*), die back in the summer.

Designing with herbaceous plants can be challenging because most of them put on a show and then fade into the background or become "messy." You need to think about the year-round appearance of your landscape. Many herbaceous plants have lovely foliage with interest-ing textures, and of course, with ferns you'll never have blooms. From a design perspective it's a good idea to group a bunch of one type of plant in an appropriate area, and then next to that area to plan for a drift of another species with a different texture and different bloom time. Avoid an unnatural checkerboard arrangement or having a little bit here and a little more over there because this could be too busy for most landscape designs. If you're working with perennials, it's easier to keep plants in place from one year to the next, but with annuals and self-seeding perennials, your plants will be on the move. Learn what the seedling stage looks like and pull out or transplant those that are growing where you don't want them. You may find that after a few years, you'll get used to the chaotic plant placement, but to start, it's probably best to keep your landscape organized so it looks as though a plan is being followed, especially around the edges where the plants are the most visible. See chapter 7 for more on edges.

Microclimates

One of the first projects you'll need to tackle as you develop your over-all plan is to locate the various microclimates around the landscape. This way you'll be able to choose the most appropriate plants for each

Regulations on Moving or Removing Plants

If your property includes a wetland or shoreline, laws are in place that regulate the removal or trimming of certain plants. You need a permit to remove or trim back mangroves (*Avicennia germinans, Rhizophora mangle*, and *Laguncularia racemosa*), and sea oats (*Uniola paniculata*) may not be removed from dunes. Many other wetland and dune species are also regulated.

Find out what regulations are in effect before you begin any removal project. Rare or endangered plants should not be removed from your property, to help support their populations. Some municipalities have regulations on tree removal from private properties depending on size of the trees and their placement in the landscape. While invasive plants need to be removed ASAP, there are often regulations against transporting these plants.

You may not remove plants from parks, roadsides, or properties (public or private) without permission whether they are rare or not. Purchase native plants from reliable nurseries and look for the label "nursery-propagated," as opposed to "nursery-grown," which does not necessarily rule out that plants might have been dug from the wild.

particular condition. Are there wet spots or planned wet spots? Often one clue to persistent dampness is a cover of moss over the soil or wetlands plants volunteering in that space. Where are the hot, sunny areas, and are they made hotter by nearby rocks, cement, or asphalt? Are there patches of clay soil or very sandy soil? Are there areas where tree roots have spread out? Do you have windy areas or sheltered spots? Gauge the sunny and shady areas in both summer and winter—there will be significant seasonal differences. All of these factors are important for the well-being of your plants.

If an irrigation system is already in place, and you plan on keeping it, map out where the pipes are and the location of irrigation zones, including overlaps and areas that are not covered. Plan your landscape so that plants with similar needs or habitat types are grouped together by irrigation zone. For instance, if creating a meadow, make sure that it lies, as much as possible, in one or two irrigation zones so the irrigation routine can be designed to support that ecosystem during installation, and later, for ongoing care.

The use of municipal or well water for landscape irrigation is a huge drain on our natural aquifers. Saving water is an important reason for converting to more natural landscape using native plants.

As you reduce irrigation, some of the wet conditions in and around sprayers or in overlapping areas will change accordingly. Plan ahead for this and other microclimate changes in existing microhabitats as lawn or hardscape is reduced.

Now that you know your conditions, learn enough about the native plants to know where they will thrive now and into the future as they mature. Your plan could be general when you start the process, with labels such as drought-tolerant ground cover or medium-sized, deciduous tree, but eventually you'll need a detailed list of plants for each set of projects or native habitats. See appendix I for a list of suggested native plants for Florida and southeastern states and resources for books and websites where you can find the details of specific plants.

Grouping Plants

After you decide what to keep in your landscape and what to remove, work on removal so new plants have the best chance for survival. Once the site is prepared, avoid plopping single specimen trees or shrubs throughout the landscape with vast open areas or lawn between them. Using your research in parks and wildlands, create groupings of probable companions that could have grown together there before human interventions.

There are several reasons to plant natives in groupings or groves of compatible natives that emulate what Mother Nature would do. The following are some possible groupings for natives in an urban/suburban landscape.

Groves of Compatible Trees

Plant groupings of trees with shrubs and understory ground covers that all grow well in the same environment. Likely places for planting

Your yard is not an arboretum, so avoid the single-specimen plantings. Use groupings of compatible plants for the health of the plants and to reduce the need for ongoing maintenance.

groves would be various corners of your property where the trees have enough room to grow to full size—horizontally and vertically: watch for overhead wires. If you're in a fire-prone situation, the canopy of groves should be at least 30 feet from any building. The tree collection could consist of a few or single understory species with one specimen of a compatible taller tree or three full-sized trees with groupings of tall shrubs as an understory. See chapter 9 for more on groves.

Vines with Showy Flowers

Vines can scramble up and over a fence, pergola, or trellis. Trumpet creeper (*Campsis radicans*), cross vine (*Bignonia capreolata*), and coral honeysuckle (*Lonicera sempervirens*) will attract hummingbirds, while the passionvines (*Passiflora* spp.) serve as larval food for various butterflies and nectar for bees and butterflies. If you want fast, showy results in your native landscape, vines work well.

Butterfly or Pollinator Gardens

These popular gardens can take many forms since many nectar and pollen plants are available for bees and butterflies. A grouping of butterfly plants will be most attractive to butterflies and pollinators, plus it will have the most impact in the landscape. Not only will you have a

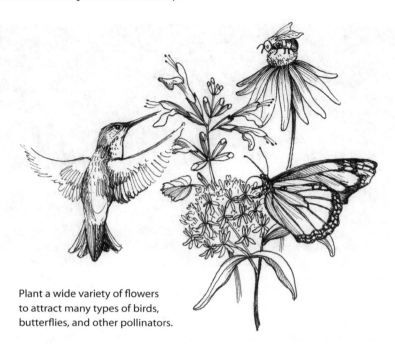

Plant a wide variety of flowers to attract many types of birds, butterflies, and other pollinators.

wide variety of showy flowers, but also you'll also have all those beautiful butterflies decorating your garden. Plants that supply nectar could be herbaceous plants (annuals and perennials) or flowering shrubs and trees. Several ingredients make up a successful butterfly garden: (1) no broad-spectrum insecticides; (2) lots of sun exposure; (3) a mixture of flower structures, and in Florida, there should be something blooming year-round; and (4) larval food plants, because without the caterpillars there will be no butterflies. If the butterfly garden is front and center of your yard, you may wish to locate the herbaceous larval plants in a separate, more out-of-the-way place where eaten foliage would not be so noticeable.

Rain Gardens

Rain gardens or bioswales can be planted in natural or manmade swales that collect rainwater from roofs, driveways, or other impervious surfaces. The idea behind rain gardens is to eliminate or greatly reduce stormwater runoff from your property. Some of the trapped water will be absorbed by the plants, while the rest will percolate into the soil and, it is hoped, help to refresh the aquifer below. Plants with greater leaf area will absorb more water through transpiration. Ideally, the rain garden system should be large enough to absorb most of the rainwater in three days most of the time, but Florida's heavy rains can quickly fill your garden, so plan for overflows directed away from buildings.

Suitable rain garden plants must thrive during periods of both inundation, which is obvious, and drought so they can make it through dry periods without special irrigation. It's best to use mostly perennial and woody plants for long-term stability and for easier maintenance. For more information and a list of rain garden plants for Florida, see chapter 10.

Shoreline Plantings

Wetland plants at the edges of a pond or waterway provide a buffer and habitat between waterways and other landscaped areas. Many times plants such as ferns, pickerelweed, rushes, sedges and grasses will grow there naturally, but if not, be sure to plant some, and by all means replace the lawn next to the water or wetland with a buffer area filled with hardy plants that can adjust to soggy conditions; if the level of the water is prone to change, the plants need to adjust to both soggy and dry conditions. These buffer areas are extremely important for the health of waterways and ponds, whether natural or artificial, because they soak up excess nutrients and stabilize the shoreline.

Wetland plants at the water's edge and emergent plants in the water provide beautiful landscape features and essential habitat values for beneficial wildlife. See chapter 10 for more details.

Outdoor Features

In addition to planning your landscape around existing buildings with their overhead and underground infrastructure, you may wish to incorporate other outdoor features, or hardscapes into the plan, including play areas, outdoor cooking spots, paths, a patio, garden shed, compost piles, vegetable gardens, sculpture pieces, signs, decorative boulders, or water features. (Note: If you do a lot of outdoor cooking on a grill, make sure that it's away from highly flammable plants such as palmetto.) You may also wish to plan for privacy from neighbors, the street, or other unattractive feature. Curving paths through a native landscape with occasional stopping points furnished with a bench, a small shelter, or pergola add to the "planned landscape" appearance even if the native plants look kind of "wild." Plan for a low-growing buffer between high-use areas and the "wilder" habitats—maybe plant some neat arrangements of short bunching grasses along pathways or at the edges of patios or sitting areas.

Even though your landscape design is outdoors, consider how it will look from inside through the windows and from outdoor living spaces such as patios and lanais. Too often, a 20-year-old house will have old, overgrown foundation plants, and all you can see outside the windows are the ugly backs of these shrubs. Work your landscape arrangements so that you can enjoy the best parts from inside. Maybe you can locate a concentration of butterfly nectar flowers just outside your kitchen window, or create a water feature designed to attract birds with a slow drip powered by a solar pump just outside a screened porch.

Plant Natives, But Be B-R-A-S-H

B—Have a border. A border provides a sense of order. This can be an area of mowed lawn or shrubs.

R—Recognize the rights of others. The rights of others are very important, and being arrogant won't win over the opposition.

A—Advertise. Advertise by putting up a small sign. Tell people why you are planting as you are.

S—Start small. Start small—there is a lot to learn about your site. "Sneak up" on your neighbors and gradually increase the size of your "natural" beds around trees, turning them into a native landscape with paths of lawn.

H—Humanize. Humanize by having paths, artifacts, walls—things that give a "tended and intended" look.

The B-R-A-S-H concept was created by attorney Bret Rappaport and is used here with his permission. For more information on weed laws and a variety of natural landscaping topics, consult the Wild Ones Handbook—available at www.wildones.org.

Rainwater Management

Be sure to plan for rainwater flow in your landscape plan. As sustainable gardeners, we should strive to retain as much rainwater as possible on our properties. In addition, we should use permeable surfaces for patios, paths, and driveways wherever possible. We can plan for this by installing a series of rain barrel systems and by directing overflow to pipes under pathways or into sloping swales leading away from buildings and high-use areas.

You might want to build a large-capacity drywell to absorb the water quickly. The final destination of the overflow could be a rain garden, pond, or seasonal pond in an area where it will not damage foundations, driveways, or other structures.

Energy-wise Landscaping

It's a good idea to plan for energy savings with wise placements of plants. Trees will cool the air around them, not just because of their shade, but also because they move a great deal of water up from the soil into the air. A full-grown oak tree will transpire more than 400 gallons of water into the air on a hot summer day. When this happens, the air is cooled because the evaporation process absorbs heat from the surrounding area. (The same principle is in effect when you sweat—as moisture evaporates, your skin is cooled.) A mass of trees and shrubs can cool your landscape by 10 or more degrees during hot weather, making the surrounding area more comfortable for you and your family—plus your air conditioner will have less work to do when the air surrounding your house is already cooler.

You can use outside plants to moderate the temperature inside your house in other ways. You could plant deciduous trees on the south or western side of the house far enough away so they don't hang over the roof, but close enough to provide shade in the summer, and then in the winter when the leaves are gone, the solar energy can help heat the house. Be sure to account for seasonal changes in the angle of the sun when calculating distances—shadows will be much longer in the winter months; however, if you're in a fire-prone area, the tree canopies need to be at least 30 feet from buildings to maintain a clear area.

Shading the air conditioner condenser can make it more efficient in the summer, but if it also serves as a heat pump in the winter, use deciduous trees and shrubs to do this. Make sure that fallen leaves and other tree trash do not collect inside the compressor unit. You may wish to cover it with fine netting or screening so the leaves can't get in but airflow is unimpeded.

If your building is subject to persistent onshore winds, you could plant groves of tough, salt-tolerant trees and shrubs on the windward side to break up the wind flow. Plant the groves far enough away to minimize possible damage from high winds. This will not only make the areas around the house safer and more comfortable, it will also reduce both your heating and cooling bills.

Privacy Landscaping

In an urban/suburban environment your property is likely to be surrounded by neighbors, roads, and alleyways. In South Florida, you see many hedges made of severely trimmed weeping fig trees (*Ficus benjamina*), and practically anywhere else in the country you'll encounter privet hedges, which are usually the invasives: Chinese privet (*Ligustrum sinense)* and glossy privet (*L. lucidum*). Those hedges are a lot of work to maintain—weeping figs are large fast-growing trees in frost-free zones and the privets can also grow to twenty feet or more. Another problem with a monoculture hedge (fig, privet, or otherwise), is that it could be more vulnerable to damaging infestations. A much better option is to use a variety of evergreen native shrubs and small trees with different textures and various blooming times—it will become a hedgerow sized to its location. This way it will need much less care, plus it would be much more interesting visually and have much higher habitat value. Plus, if one of the species has a pest problem one year, the others will still be healthy—you will have "hedged your bets." For much more about hedgerows, see chapter 9.

The Waiting Game

The temptation when refurbishing the landscape is to purchase the biggest trees you can afford for an instantaneous effect, but this is rarely a good use of your money. Older nursery trees and shrubs will have been treated harshly to keep the roots small enough to fit into a pot, and so with much of the root system lacking, they will require a lot more care for a much longer time until they adapt to their new spot, and some may never recover from the shock of being grown in a container for so many years or being dug up from a field. When you use relatively young specimens, they adapt quickly with a lot less care and will start growing much sooner. In fact, a small sapling will soon catch up in size to that larger specimen you paid so much more for. Either way, it will be at least several years before the new native landscape matures enough to fulfill all the needs of your original plan, whether privacy, shade, or habitat.

It's important to plant those small trees and shrubs with enough room to accommodate their adult sizes. In other words, don't plant so your landscape looks good today, but plant for the future. If you crave a fuller landscape right away use, some bunching grasses between your trees and shrubs, or you could install some temporary trellises or arbors with fast-growing vines. In a few years remove the vines to make room for the trees as they mature.

If you're not looking for shade, another way to fill the empty areas between trees and shrubs is to go for a meadow-type of look by starting with lots of showy wildflowers and bunching grasses. Once the trees and shrubs gain enough size, the temporary meadow will gradually change in character with the increased shade and greater root competition from the trees. As this begins to happen, you may wish to transplant some of the long-lived perennials to sunnier locations. See more about creating and managing meadows in chapter 8.

A Well-Designed Landscape Will Be Easier to Maintain

When you plan ahead to include the right plants for each area of your landscape, your maintenance chores will be lessened over the years, but they won't go away entirely. If you hire landscapers to do maintenance, make sure they are informed of your plans, can identify the plants, and don't treat the natives like weeds.

3

Invasive Exotics

Invasive exotic plants have cost us billions of dollars—both public and private moneys. One of the very good reasons for planting only native plants is to avoid adding to this huge problem. In this book, the terms "invasive" and "aggressive" are not used interchangeably. *Invasive* is used to describe only the exotic plants included in invasive plant lists of the Florida Exotic Pest Plant Council (FLEPPC), while *aggressive* is used to describe any exuberant plant—exotic or native. FLEPPC is a nonprofit organization that does research on invasives (www.fleppc.org).

Invasive Definition

With some exceptions, most of today's invasive plants were purposefully imported with good intensions, but if a plant has been determined to be invasive, it has already negatively affected native habitats far into wild areas. These plants invade in several ways: their seeds are carried by birds or other animals, wind, or water into native ecosystems; once established, their rampant growth may cover everything in sight displacing a significant portion of the native flora. Some invasives, such as Australian-pines (*Casuarina* spp.), are allelopathic and exude a type of chemical that poisons or impairs neighboring plants and/or prevents seed germination.

Because of their ability to reproduce, spread, and outcompete natives, invasives have been shown to rapidly displace or degrade the native habitat. The invasive label is not given lightly, but proven through extensive fieldwork in undeveloped areas. You may not guess that a plant is invasive by its behavior in your yard. For instance, heavenly-bamboo (*Nandina domestica*) has been widely planted in nontropical landscapes in southeastern states and seems relatively well behaved within a landscape setting, but its berries are carried by birds far and wide into native areas. It has been on FLEPPC's Category I invasive list for Florida for many years.

The problem with invasives is that native habitat destruction will continue to increase unless we all act. Remove invasives from your yard, don't purchase them, and educate the store management when you see invasives for sale. Be part of the solution; don't be part of the problem. When you create the priority list of what to do, removing invasive plants needs to be at the top.

As of 2013, FLEPPC lists 76 Category I invasive plant species as the most invasive in the state. It also lists 75 potentially invasive plants as Category II. These lists change over time as more plants are found doing damage to the native ecosystems in Florida's wildlands. Most other states have similar EPPCs that maintain invasive plant lists, and the USDA plant database (plants.usda.gov/) lists where each plant may be invasive. While other states' invasive plants are not the same as Florida's, the problems are just as serious and methods of eradication are similar.

Find out what plants are invasive in your area and learn to recognize invasives in all stages of growth. Monitor your whole property, and maybe even your neighborhood for invasive plants. To prevent regrowth in your neighborhood and also in your landscape, become an activist by organizing or participating in community workdays to remove invasives from parks or other shared lands. Attend educational presentations or field trips that emphasize the invasives commonly planted in the neighborhood. For these neighborhood-wide activities, it's a good idea to work in cooperation with your county or other municipal organizations. If you need an expert to come into your neighborhood, work with groups such as the local native plant society, master gardeners, or master naturalists on invasive workdays. You'll learn a lot and help to reduce the spread of invasives in your neighborhood. The majority of homeowners simply have no idea that a problem exists.

Keep after the invasives on your property so they will be less likely to reestablish from new seeds that are brought in by bird or wind or from fragments of root or rhizome. When they do sprout up again, get them while small and before they set seed if possible—procrastinating will only make the problem worse.

In addition, invasive waterweeds can take over natural ponds and exclude native plants—some are so rampant that they cause dead zones in the water that kill fish and other wildlife. Large aquatic ecosystems are the responsibility of various governmental agencies, but homeowners with small ponds on their properties may be on their own. Water hyacinth (*Eichhornia crassipes*) and hydrilla (*Hydrilla verticillata*) are the best known waterborne invasives, but there are several others to worry about as well. These invasives may be carried to a pond by wildlife such as waterbirds or turtles. An infestation can start with just a few pieces of plant material. Water hyacinths can be easily removed because they are large and not rooted; after pulling them out, use them in your compost pile. But other waterweeds can be extremely difficult to eradicate, so quick action is required. Check with local authorities to see if they can help or if there are regulations pertaining to local ponds.

Water hyacinths are easy to remove from a small pond because they are large and not rooted to the bottom. Add the removed plants to your compost pile—they provide good, nutrient-rich humus.

It's possible that the best nonherbicide treatment for hydrilla or other small invasive waterweeds in a pond or lake is sterilized (triploid) Asian grass carp (*Ctenopharyngodon idella*). In Florida, you'll need a permit from the Florida Fish and Wildlife Conservation Commission (www.myfwc.com), and in the process you'll need to build fish barriers

Invasive Plants Most Likely to Be in a Florida Yard

This short list of invasives, with eradication methods and suggested "alter-natives," is just a small sample of some domesticated plants that have gone wild and caused harm to our native areas. Many of these plants are still widely sold and planted. So let's get to work!

After removal of any invasive, do not leave it in your yard waste; otherwise, it could spread wherever the county's yard waste compost is used. You can dispose of it with the trash so it goes to a landfill, or use the plants in your brush piles or compost unless there are seeds or berries. Bag the seeds and throw them in the trash. Some people burn these weeds, but don't burn Brazilian pepper or other members of the poison ivy family, as you don't want to produce toxic smoke that could affect anyone who inhales it. Before burning, check to see if you need a permit and then burn on a damp, no-wind day.

For good-sized trees close to buildings, you'll probably need an arborist to remove them. You may wish to have the arborist paint the cambium layer (just inside the bark) with an herbicide to kill the roots. While the arborist is on site, the workers may also be able to help with some of the invasive shrubs that need chipping. Ask for the wood chips to use as path mulch, especially if there are visible seeds, so you can watch out for new sprouts.

If trees are away from places where they can damage something, you can girdle them by removing a 3- or 4-inch strip of bark around the circumference at the base of the trunk, or top it at 10 or 15 feet tall. Neither of these methods will kill a tree right away and there will be sucker growth for a year or so, but it will die and then become a snag in the landscape.

at pond outlets so they cannot escape. While these fish eat the water-weeds preferentially, they will live for several years and can clean out desirable native plants as well, so proceed with caution.

For more information on Florida's invasive plants with photos for identification, see the website of the Florida Exotic Pest Plant Council (www.fleppc.org) and the Atlas of Florida Vascular Plants (www.florida.plantatlas.usf.edu). Use the USDA plant database (www.plants.usda.gov) to find resources for other states.

Common Landscape Invasives in Florida

Silktree or mimosa (*Albizia julibrissin* Durazz): A small and often multi-stemmed tree with beautiful, pinkish, silky-looking flowers. It's in the legume family (Fabaceae), which means it can grow in poor soils. It reseeds prolifically and the seeds remain viable for a several decades. Since it's small and the wood is soft, you may be able to remove its trunks yourself with only a bow saw. After removal, it will sucker, so you'll need to cut back the suckers quickly or apply herbicide to the cut surface and any new suckers.
Alter-natives: Eastern redbud (*Cercis canadensis*); white fringe-tree (*Chionanthus virginicus*); Walter's viburnum (*Viburnum obovatum*); and in South Florida, coco-plum (*Chrysobalanus icaco*).

Scratchtroat or (locally) coral ardisia (*Ardisia crenata* Sims.), also shoebutton (*Ardisia elliptica* Thunb.): The berries of these evergreen shrubs or small trees have been planted by birds in wild areas. Learn to identify the foliage so when you see it on your property, you can pull it out before it grows too large and before it develops berries. If berries are present, put them in a bag so they can't fall during the extraction process. If they are too large to pull or dig, saw the trunks and either remove the suckers or hit them with herbicide.
Alter-natives: Marlberry (*Ardisia escallonioides*); wax myrtle (*Morella cerifera*); Coontie (*Zamia integrifolia*).

Asparagus-fern (*Asparagus aethiopicus* L.): This evergreen perennial has been widely planted, but it has become invasive, especially in South Florida. It's not the crop and it's not a fern, but a flowering plant in the lily family (Liliaceae) with white flowers and red fruit.

Birds eat the fruit, which are then deposited elsewhere, and it also spreads vegetatively. It's best to dig it up before the fruit appear to keep birds from spreading them.

Alter-natives: Coastal verbena (*Glandularia maritima*); coontie (*Zamia integrifolia*); coral bean (*Erythrina herbacea*); cinnamon fern (*Osmundastrum cinnamomea*).

Camphortree (*Cinnamomum camphora* (L.) J. Presl): This large evergreen tree with shiny leaves reseeds prolifically. It looks nice so people leave it alone thinking it might be a holly, but when you crush a leaf, you can smell the pungent mothball odor. Pull it up while small, or if too large, an arborist will be needed. After it has been cut down, it will sucker, so remove the suckers or treat them with herbicide.

Alter-natives: Hollies (*Ilex* spp.); southern magnolia (*Magnolia grandiflora*); eastern redcedar (*Juniperus virginiana*).

Coco-yam or (locally) wild taro (*Colocasia esculenta* (L.) Schott): This moisture-loving perennial was brought to Florida as a crop, but it has become a widespread pest. It usually spreads via seed, but it can bunch and spread via roots. Any piece will grow new plants, so dig out as much as you can; when it regrows, you may need to apply herbicide. If it's in or right next to water, use only herbicides approved for aquatic environments. It's recommended that you hire a licensed professional for aquatic eradications. Don't replant the area with natives for at least several months to make sure it's really gone.

Alter-natives: Rattlesnakemaster (*Eryngium aquaticum*); scarlet rosemallow (*Hibiscus coccineus*); blue mistflower (*Conoclinium coelestinum*); Carolina redroot (*Lachnanthes caroliana*).

Shrubverbena (*Lantana strigocamara* R. W. Sanders (also referred to as *L. camara*)): Butterflies and other pollinators love the flowers on this shrub, so it has been widely sold for butterfly gardens. All parts of this plant are poisonous to pets, but birds distribute the seeds from its berries into wild places. It also hybridizes with native lantana species, which disrupts native habitats even more. So while there are sterile cultivars with no berries, the cross-pollination may still continue to do damage. The wood is soft and easy to cut back, but it will continue to sucker unless you remove the roots or use herbicide on the new suckers.

Alter-natives: American beautyberry (*Callicarpa americana*); marlberry (*Ardisia escallonioides*); spotted beebalm (*Monarda punctata*); snow squarestem (*Melanthera nivea*).

Chinese privet (*Ligustrum sinense* Lour.) Also glossy privet (*L. lucidum* W. T. Aiton): These exotic privets have been widely planted as hedges because they take to trimming and also sucker to fill in gaps. They escaped from cultivation very soon after introduction as birds carried their seeds into wild areas. They become large shrubs or small trees and grow in dense thickets in the wild areas. The best way to treat them is to cut them down and either dig out the roots or treat the stumps with herbicide. It will probably be a multiyear project to remove a large population because they sucker profusely. **Alter-natives: Florida swampprivet (*Forestiera segregata*); American strawberry bush (*Euonymus americanus*); and for Central and South Florida, twinberry (*Myrcianthes fragrans*) and coco-plum (*Chrysobalanus icaco*).**

Japanese honeysuckle (*Lonicera japonica* Thunb.): This evergreen vine has invaded most of the eastern states. As is the case with many vines, herbicide is not very effective because they can root at every node. The best strategy for this type of vine is to pull as much as you can from trees and shrubs and also from along the ground. For vines that are too high to reach, cut them to separate them from the ground. Dig up the roots where you can and cut the rest. When they regrow, dig again or treat with herbicide, or both. It will probably take more than one year to get rid of them. **Alter-natives: Trumpet honeysuckle (*Lonicera sempervirens*); passionflower (*Passiflora* spp.); evening trumpetflower (*Gelsemium sempervirens*).**

Heavenly-bamboo (*Nandina domestica* Thunb.): This widely planted evergreen shrub has plenty of berries that birds love to eat, but it is poisonous to humans, pets, and even birds in some cases. It may appear to be a normal plant in your yard, but it's highly invasive in Florida. Dig out the shrub with as much of the root mass possible. It's likely to resprout, so remove the new sprouts quickly or apply herbicide. **Alter-natives: Gallberry (*Ilex glabra*); American beautyberry (*Callicarpa americana*); blueberries (*Vaccinium* spp.); and for South Florida, coco-plum (*Chrysobalanus icaco*).**

Britton's wild petunia or (locally) Mexican petunia (*Ruellia simplex* C. Wright): This invasive, perennial forb is still widely sold because people like its purple, season-long flowers. It's a tough plant and will thrive in marginal conditions, so it may take several sessions of removal by digging or herbicide treatments, or both. Any piece of the root left in the soil can sprout, so be vigilant and don't plant anything you care about near its removal site for at least two years. Some sterile cultivars are available, but these are not recommended.
Alter-natives: Standingcypress (*Ipomopsis rubra*); blazing-stars (*Liatris* spp.); spotted beebalm (*Monarda punctata*).

Chinese tallowtree or (locally) popcorntree (*Sapium sebiferum* (L.) Dum. Cours.): This medium-sized tree has white fruit eaten by birds and then carried to wild areas. Its heart-shaped leaves produce good fall color. It is so vigorous that if you try to girdle it, new bark will form over the gap. It was imported by Ben Franklin for making candles, but it has run amok.
Alter-natives: Winged elm (*Ulmus alata*); chickasaw plum (*Prunus angustifolia*); flatwoods plum (*Prunus umbellata*).

This Chinese tallow tree (*Sapium sebiferum*) grew bark over a girdling cut. If you girdle it, be sure to make a gap of at least 3 inches.

Brazilian-pepper or (locally) Florida-holly (*Schinus terebinthifolia* Raddi): If you are unlucky enough to have this invasive large shrub to medium-sized tree growing on your property, you need to know that it's in the poison ivy family (Anacardiaceae) and contains the same oil that is poisonous to touch—urushiol. Some people even have allergic reactions when this plant is blooming, and it's been found to poison some birds that overindulge in its berries. So remove with care and don't burn it, because the smoke is toxic and could cause allergic reactions in anyone who breathes in the smoke. If you can, remove as much of the root mass as possible because it sprouts readily from any root fragments that are left. Another method of removal is to cut down the main trunks and then apply herbicide to the cambium layers (just inside the bark) of the stumps. When sprouts grow, get rid of them quickly before they get too large. Keep in mind that if you allow the sprouts to grow for long periods, the root system will regain its strength. So keep an eye out for sprouts and treat them sooner rather than later.

You may use the branches in a stick pile or in your compost, but handle that compost with your poison ivy gloves. Be aware that the sticks become very brittle and sharp with age.

Alter-natives: Any of the several native hollies (*Ilex* spp.); sparkleberry (*Vaccinium arboreum*); persimmon (*Diospyros virginiana*); and in South Florida, seagrape (*Coccoloba uvifera*).

Creeping oxeye or wedelia (*Sphagneticola trilobata* (L.) Pruski): This beautiful but aggressive ground cover is only on the Category II list (as of 2013), so it has not significantly invaded wild areas, but if it's left unchecked in your landscape, especially a meadow area, it will cover everything in less than a year. If this happens, there is no substitute for rolling it back like a rug and pulling up as many of the roots as possible. After a few weeks, check for new growth, and check every other month for the next year or two. It is knocked back by a hard frost but will grow back from the roots.

Alter-natives: Turkey tangle fogfruit (*Phyla nodiflora*); dune sunflower (*Helianthus debilis*); starrush white-top (*Rhynchospora colorata*); Indian blanket (*Gaillardia pulchella*).

Chinese wisteria (*Wisteria sinensis* (Sims) Sweet), in more northern regions Japanese wisteria (*Wisteria floribunda* (Willd.) DC.): These

When removing wedelia (*Sphagneticola trilobata*) that has taken over a whole area, roll it back like a carpet, pulling out as many roots as you can. The more roots you get now, the less you'll have later.

vining garden favorites with their pendulous, fragrant lavender flower clusters have been widely planted from the Mid-Atlantic southward to north central Florida. They are legumes, so they grow well in poor soils. As with many vines, herbicide is not that effective for established plants, so pull them up from the ground and remove as much of the growth from trees and trellises as possible, especially if there is hanging fruit. When it resprouts, pull again or treat new growth with herbicide. If the size of the stem is significant, you may need to saw it off and treat the cambium layer with herbicide.
Alter-natives: American wisteria (*Wisteria frutescens*); trumpet honeysuckle (*Lonicera sempervirens*); evening trumpetflower (*Gelsemium sempervirens*).

4

Site Preparation and Landscape Editing

Editing includes both preliminary and ongoing removal of unwanted plants, especially exotic plants that have become invasive in your region, and then the planting of desired plants. Editing also includes the pruning of desirable plants that have become too large or dominant in the landscape. While maintenance of a native landscape is necessary, the extent of the chores and timetable for completing them is much more flexible than for a rigid, artificial landscape where every errant sprout or weed looks out of place.

When you decide to plant natives, your preparation method will depend on the conditions of the site and your overall landscape plan. Before you start planting your new natives and maybe even before removing unwanted plants, you'll need to address any drainage issues. See chapter 10 for various strategies dealing with moist habitats.

Removal of Unwanted Plants

After determining which plants to keep as part of your planned landscape as discussed in chapter 2, the next step is to remove unwanted plants from the area. If you have invasives or other aggressively spreading weeds in the planting area, it's best to accomplish their removal as completely as possible before installing any new plants.

**Complete removal of unwanted plants is crucial
to the success of your native plant installations!**

This site preparation has to be the first step because if aggressive weeds are allowed to persist, trying to remove them later from between newly planted natives is likely to disrupt their roots, or herbicide traces could spread beyond the targeted plants. Also, the ongoing maintenance of removing forever-resprouting weeds would discourage even the most ardent native plant enthusiast.

In addition to the plants known to be invasive in your region, there are other types of plants you may wish to remove.

Some Other "I-Don't-Want-It" Plants

High-Maintenance Turfgrass in a Lawn

Just think of all the money you could save and all those poisons that would not be absorbed into the environment if you drastically reduced the size of your lawn and more sustainably managed the lawn that remains. See chapter 8 for strategies on turning a monoculture turf lawn into a "freedom lawn" or meadow.

Native Plants That Inflict Pain or Itchiness

Examples include sand spur (*Cenchrus* spp.), stinging nettles (*Urtica* spp.), poison ivy (*Toxicodendron radicans*), and catbriers (*Smilax* spp.).

Aggressive Plants (Even If Native)

These are plants that tend to envelop whole areas, such as annuals like beggar ticks (*Bidens alba*) or perennials with persistent tubers or rhizomes like Florida betony (*Stachys floridana*) and scorpion-tail (*Heliotropium angiospermum*). Also, if you have mature trees on your property, you may find that their abundant seedlings or root suckers will have become weeds as well.

Other Exotics That Don't Fit Your Plan

These plants may not have become invasive yet, but many, like the crape myrtle (*Lagerstoemia indica*), are so overplanted that replacing them with underrepresented natives will create more diversity in your yard and in your neighborhood. The timing of their removal is more flexible than that of other unwanted plants. You may wish to keep them through the first few years of naturalizing, but when their replacements are large enough to make an impression, remove these boring exotic plants.

Depending on the nature of the unwanted plants and the size of

The ridged tubers of Florida betony (*Stachys floridana*) look like rattlesnake tails. If you leave any of these tubers in the soil, they will grow back even through a thick layer of mulch. On the plus side, the tubers are edible—use like radishes.

the project, various methods can be employed to eradicate them; as discussed in chapter 3, you may want to bring in a certified professional to remove the most noxious weeds requiring integrated weed management—a combination of, or sequential use of, several methods for removal. Some herbaceous plants are easily removed and can just be pulled out or smothered with a deep layer of organic mulch, but others that have deep rhizomes require several separate attacks over a couple of seasons to eradicate. Removal of unwanted trees and shrubs requires different strategies than for herbaceous weeds; this may be a more strenuous or expensive exercise to start, but woody plants are usually easier to manage in the long run. When selecting control methods for any of the plants, remember that the purpose of this procedure is to prepare space for new native plants and also to preserve native species and their communities. Your ultimate goal is to build functioning ecosystems in your landscape.

Removing Large Trees

In your quest for a native/naturalistic landscape, it's best to retain as many mature trees (native or not) as possible, because they cool the area and provide good habitat values, but remove invasive species quickly.

Herbicides

Many people oppose using herbicides because of the expense and collateral damage to surrounding ecosystems. If you are managing a small lot without too many pervasive and noxious weeds, then preparing a site for native plants can probably be accomplished with only physical removal (hand-weeding for small sites or soil scraping for larger sites), solarization, or smothering of unwanted plants. Site preparation of larger properties or ones that have become totally infested with invasives or other aggressive and persistent weeds would probably include at least some herbicide use for complete removal. Some scientists think that the ecological risks of herbicide use such as glyphosate for focused, short-term eradication efforts are small compared to the ongoing threat of invasives, but others warn that we really don't know the long-term effects of herbicides in ecosystems, especially aquatic habitats. That said, prudent use of herbicides can save a lot of time and effort in site preparation.

Research the choices of herbicides available and choose the best ones for various situations. For instance, the best herbicide for preventing seed germination will be different fomr ones used against established plants, and the best ones for terrestrial use may be harmful to aquatic animals. Some herbicides are popular for turf management because they work only on broad-leaved plants and not grasses. When purchasing herbicides, **read and follow the instructions on the labels**. Do not second-guess those instructions. More is not better.

Pay close attention to what you are spraying and be as selective as possible when applying any type of herbicide. To be as conservative as possible, cut or dig out the plant first, and then spray only the regrowth. Avoid spraying during rainy or windy days. Since most herbicides disrupt plant metabolism in some way, they work best on vigorously growing plants. If a plant is dormant or half-dead, an application of herbicide will be much less effective because little metabolic activity is occurring. Another thing to keep in mind is that most herbicides are systemic,

continued

so if you apply herbicide to a tree sucker or root sprout, it's possible you'll kill the whole tree.

Also, protect yourself from coming in contact with the herbicide. Wear gloves (maybe latex or rubber gloves under cotton gardening gloves), long sleeves, long pants, and maybe a facemask. Once you are done, wash those clothes and keep the herbicide gloves separate from your general gardening gloves.

Herbicides sold at retail operations are usually premixed with other chemicals that help the base chemical be more effective or efficient. The secondary chemicals are usually surfactants that reduce surface tension, break down the wax on leaves, or help the herbicide stick to the leaves. Consider the effects of these secondary ingredients in addition to the main herbicide. For instance glyphosate, a broad-spectrum herbicide, is the main ingredient in several commercial products such as RoundUp®, Rodeo®, and Aquamaster®, but each of these products contains different formulations of secondary products that makes each of them a better choice for one situation, such as an aquatic environment, but not for another.

Preemergent herbicide deters seed germination. One of the best known is corn gluten, a powder applied to the soil and watered in. This will not poison existing plants, and later as it decomposes in the soil, it becomes a nitrogen-rich nutrient. Synthetic chemical formulas are available that also deter germination. Either way, you'd use this to reduce your weeding chores in an established landscape and not in an area you intend to seed in the near future. Note: by using a preemergent herbicide, you will miss out on native plants that may have planted themselves in your landscape.

So-called homemade herbicides such as boiling water, soap, salt, and vinegar will kill plants, but they may also kill everything in the soil including earthworms, beneficial bugs, and microbes. These homemade remedies are unregulated, not well tested, and could have more detrimental long-term effects on your soil ecosystems than commercial herbicides that kill only plants. Boiling-hot water will certainly kill (by cooking) any plant material it's poured on; it will also kill all the soil inhabitants and any other roots in the area. If you put vinegar in a spray bottle and spray a thicket of weeds, you will also kill all the toads that are hiding among them. The vinegar's acidity may also kill most of the microorganisms in the soil and make nutrients in the soil less available for the next plantings there for at least the next several weeks. Pouring salt on a plant will kill it and most of the microbes in the soil, plus a salty soil may inhibit growth of future plants. The salt residue is likely to last longer than other products. There are many times when just pulling a bunch of weeds and then quickly mulching the disturbed soil is the best choice.

Here are a few resources on herbicides, their toxicity to you and the ecosystems in which they are used, and their effectiveness for killing various types of plants. Keep in mind that the strategies for large landholders such as The Nature Conservancy will be different from yours for your own suburban property. Large landholders often need to be more aggressive with herbicide use because they might not revisit that area for two years or more. You, on the other hand, have ready access to your landscape and can quickly take care of new sprouts from a stump or the new growth that emerges from a piece of root that you may have missed.

- From the Florida Extension Service: edis.ifas.ufl.edu/fr345, edis.ifas.ufl.edu/wg209, plants.ifas.ufl.edu/.
- From The Nature Conservancy: www.wilderness.net/toolboxes/documents/invasive/Weed Control Methods Handbook.pdf.
- From the Pesticide Information Center: npic.orst.edu/
- From the Florida Exotic Pest Plant Council: www.fleppc.org/Misc/HerbicideAdvice.pdf.

More references are listed in resources; also see the sidebar on solarization on page 57.

In addition, if a native tree is unsound and growing in a location where it could damage the infrastructure including buildings, hardscape structures (driveways, sidewalks, or patios), overhead wires, and underground pipes, then removal may be necessary. In a case where an otherwise satisfactory tree that is common in your neighborhood is crowding out a more desirable or rarer tree, you may want to remove it or at least have some of its branches pruned back to allow better growth of the less common tree. Encouraging diversity of your woody plants will increase the habitat value of the property as a whole even if it's a small lot.

In most cases, as discussed in chapter 2, you'll need an arborist for large tree removal and pruning in urban/suburban neighborhoods that are close to buildings and high-use areas, but there may be other strategies if the tree is located in a rarely used area and won't damage anything of value when it falls. The arborist could just top the tree and apply an herbicide on the cut. This action may cause the tree to send up suckers from its base that you could then trim back repeatedly or treat with an herbicide. This will kill the tree within a couple of years and you'll be left with a snag, a habitat for birds and other wildlife. Another strategy is to girdle the tree by removing three or four inches of bark and sapwood (cambium) from all around the trunk. You will have created an interruption of the phloem cells so nutrients cannot be transported from the roots to the upper portion of the tree or the reverse. Again, this may not kill the tree right away and some trees will regrow bark over the gap to restart the flow. Watch this tree for suckers and regrowth and maintain the gap in the bark until the tree dies. (Girdling does not work for palms because their nutrient and water transport tissues are located throughout the trunk. Topping a nonclumping palm species will kill it because all its growth takes place from its heart at the apex.)

When you have a tree removed, several issues must be resolved. If the arborist is chipping the wood on-site, ask for the load of chips—what could be more appropriate for mulching your landscape than your own trees? But if it's an allelopathic tree like an Australian-pine, use that mulch only for pathways and areas where you don't want anything to grow. Whenever possible within your landscape plan, leave the logs on the ground and the stumps in place. Some people will grind the stump to below the soil level to make way for a landscape feature, but you may wish to leave as much height to stumps as is practical for the arborist and reasonable for your landscape. To integrate the stumps and snags into the landscape, plant vines at the base or make it into a planter by drilling into the wood, digging out some of the wood, inserting some soil into the top, and then planting it with something that will cascade down. Deadwood logs and stumps support many different critters. If the stump has been cut flush with the ground, you could pile soil and mulch on top of it to create a mound in your landscape. If the mound is in a sunny location, plant it with a wide variety of native butterfly plants. Eventually the stump will decompose, but if it's buried, it will happen faster because the soil teems with microbes, worms, and other organisms that run the decomposition process. Meanwhile you get to enjoy the butterflies.

Once a tree has been removed, topped, or girdled, it may send up suckers at its base and even from shallow roots nearby. Your sucker strategy will depend on the reasons for taking out the tree. If it is an invasive species, all the suckers should be destroyed as soon as possible so the root mass cannot regain any strength from new growth. If the tree was removed because it was structurally unsound, then maybe one or more suckers could be encouraged if they are growing in a reasonable location for your landscape plan. You'll need to be careful about encouraging only the ones you want and pulling the rest of them out—if you pull the suckers rather than cutting them, you'll also

STUMPS & SNAGS

Wherever possible, incorporate stumps, snags, and logs into your landscape to support a wide variety of wildlife.

destroy the growth bud, while cutting them just encourages regrowth. Don't use herbicide in this case, because it could kill the whole tree including the suckers you're trying to encourage.

Removing Shrubs and Small Trees

The decision of which shrubs and small trees to remove will be made during the design process, but when a shrub or small tree is to be removed, it sometimes works best if you prune away the side branches and just leave two or three feet of the trunk or one of the main canes of a shrub. That way the trunk can be used for leverage as you dig into the root-ball. First tip it one way while you dig out the roots on the opposite side and then push the trunk another way and dig away on the side opposite from that direction. It's easier with two people, but you can accomplish even a difficult removal by yourself if you make good use of crowbars, pick mattocks, or other prying tools. Remember that your shovel is not a pry bar so don't put too much strain on it. It's important to remove as many of the roots as possible to reduce potential regrowth. This process will be greatly complicated if the plant to be removed is in the midst of a thicket of plants you wish to keep. In this case, dig out the main root at the base, but don't completely disrupt the soil and other roots. If sprouts grow from the roots that were left behind during the initial removal, very carefully treat them with herbicide or cut them back as soon as possible.

If the tree or shrub to be removed is actually a shoot from a surface root of a larger tree or shrub that you want to keep in the landscape, work to pull it from the root to remove the bud where it was formed. If you simply prune it back to the root, this will be a recurring chore because of the bud tissue in the root, and depending on the tree, it could be as often as once a year. It's not good for the health of trees to remove surface roots, but shrubs are usually less sensitive, so you could prune the roots back to reduce the number of suckers. It's best to do this a little at a time to minimize harm to the main shrub.

Removing Vines

Several of Florida's worst invasive plants are vines, including air-potato (*Dioscorea bulbifera*), Japanese and Old World climbing ferns (*Lygodium japonicum* and *L. microphyllum*), Japanese honeysuckle

(*Lonicera japonica*), and kudzu (*Pueraria montana* var. *lobata*), to name just a few. Obviously, if you have invasive vines, they need to be removed sooner rather than later. Herbicides often don't work well for most vines, so repeated physical removal and gathering of fruits is the standard procedure for removal. Some communities hold an annual air-potato roundup with fun prizes for the largest "potato" found.

Many fast-growing vines, even natives, can present a tough maintenance problem when growing in the wrong spaces. An aggressive vine can completely smother and deform a small tree in a couple of years; some can climb to the tops of mature tall trees and begin to shade out the canopy in the area. Some vines are easier to control than others. For instance, an established catbrier (*Smilax* spp.) thicket at the base of a tree will have tough, woody rhizomes and may also have developed grapefruit-sized tubers intermingled with and below the tree roots, making them very difficult to remove. If you simply cut the vines off at the base of the tree, the tubers will provide substantial energy for repeated regrowth. Poison ivy, on the other hand, doesn't have tubers, so once you

Old stands of catbrier (*Smilax* spp.) are tough to remove because their woody rhizomes seem to spread for miles, forming a solid crosshatching pattern, and their large tubers sometimes grow under roots of trees. But removing the tubers and the rhizomes is the only way to get rid of it without herbicide. Cutting it off at soil level is ineffective.

pull it up or hit it with an herbicide application during its spring growth season, you are likely to get rid of it with minimal regrowth.

Vines growing to the tops of mature trees is a natural phenomenon and the resulting wall of vegetation created in this way provides good habitat value, but in cases where there is an invasive vine or where the vining growth looks too overgrown or unkempt for your urban/suburban landscape, you may choose to remove at least some of the vines. To remove them, start by cutting them off at ground level and pulling down as much of the vine as possible, especially if it is bearing fruit. Don't put too much stress on the trees or your back, because after the vines have been cut from the roots, the vines in the trees will die off. After cutting off the vines, see if you can dig out the roots or tubers without too much disruption of the soil. As mentioned above, some vine roots are easier to remove than others, so if you cannot remove all the roots, wait for them to sprout and either cut off the new growth and dig out as much of the roots as possible or carefully apply herbicide. You don't want to spray the whole area at the base of the trees, because you might end up harming the trees and other desirable vegetation. It may take several removal or herbicide sessions to actually kill the vine.

If vines have deformed a young tree, carefully remove all the vines from the tree, dig up as many roots as possible without disrupting the tree's roots, and then see if you can urge the tree into a more upright position—some staking may be necessary for the first few months until the tree stands tall by itself. Do not leave the stakes in place for more than a few months. If some of the vines' roots were left in the ground, pull out the new growth or treat with herbicide as soon as possible.

If the vines are crawling across the landscape, the best strategy for starting removal is to pull up as much as possible. It is likely that new rooting has occurred in many places. Depending on your reason for removing ground-covering vines, your next step will vary. If it's an invasive, you'll then go after the new sprouts by more pulling or by applying herbicide several times until you can get rid of it. If it's a native vine that is just too wild looking for your landscape, maybe there is a way to restrict it to a smaller area so it can become an attractive ground cover. You don't want it to crawl up your newly planted natives, so keep it controlled in those areas.

Often various vine species grow together in a mass, which will make maintenance more difficult if you wish to target one species but not others. In this case, it's best to first pull out as much of the targeted vine from the trees or shrubs as possible. Then see if it's possible to dig out the roots without disturbing the other vegetation. If not, careful herbicide treatments will be necessary so that you hit only the selected vine. It will probably take more than one treatment.

Solarization

If you have a sunny and well-defined area where you want to get rid of all the plants growing there, one option is a six-week solarization treatment during the hot summer months. First mow the area at the lowest setting, remove the excess plant material, and then irrigate. Cover the soil with clear plastic that is thick enough to last the six-week period. Bury the edges with enough soil and rocks that there is no airflow from outside and wind from an afternoon thunderstorm can't rip out the plastic. Note: black plastic does not work as well because it doesn't allow the sunlight in and it will not get as hot.

During solarization, the greenhouse effect produces enough heat in the top 6 inches of soil to kill the plants (including St. Augustine grass, *Stenotaphrum secundatum*), most of the seeds, and all the soil inhabitants from toads to nematodes. This process will also melt the components of a drip irrigation system, but other underground structures built with PVC or other hard materials should be fine.

As with any method of getting rid of weeds, there are pros and cons. Solarization uses no poisons and so is favored by organic growers, but it takes a lot longer than treatment with herbicide or physical removal. More collateral damage occurs to the soil and its inhabitants, and it is ineffective for deep-rooted plants with vigorous rhizomes or tubers. The populations of soil inhabitants will eventually recover from the treatment, so maybe this is one way to provide a clean start for a new native garden before new weed seeds have a chance to repopulate the area.

For more solarization information, see this article from Florida's extension service: edis.ifas.ufl.edu/in856

Removing Herbaceous Plants

While it may seem that herbaceous plants would be the easiest to remove, they are often the most difficult to deal with in the long term. We don't call them weeds without good reason.

Removing Perennials and Grasses That Spread
Via Rhizomes, Tubers, or Runners

Sometimes it's relatively easy to eliminate unwanted perennials where you can pull or dig up the plants, apply some mulch, and then a few weeks later come back for a second session to remove any survivors. More often than not, the process for rhizomatous plants is more complex than a simple pulling session or two. Perennials that spread via deep rhizomes or tubers are not only difficult to dig up, but each little piece left behind might produce a whole new plant. In addition, solarization or mulching rarely works well for these plants since their underground structures are deep and retain so much energy that they can grow through mulch no matter how thick, or they can sit and wait until after solarization is finished, then grow into the sterilized soil. Some of these troublesome plants are known invasives such as torpedo grass (*Panicum repens*), while others are aggressive natives such as Florida betony (*Stachys floridana*) and dollar weed (*Hydrocotyle umbellata*), and you may even have a problem with exuberant escapees from the garden such as mints (*Mentha* spp.).

For most situations, it's best to use physical methods to pull or dig most of these weeds first. Then when, not if, they sprout from the leftover roots, dig them again and maybe again before finally spraying the new growth with herbicide. This process maximizes the herbicide's effectiveness because you're applying it to new growth of a previously weakened plant. On the other hand, you may want to scrape the whole top layer of soil to rock layer or below the area where the seed bank is located. This remedy might be called for if your natural habitat is nutrient poor such as a sandhill or pine rockland.

If your target habitat is normally nutrient rich and you don't scrape away the soil, every time you disturb the soil you will be unearthing the seed bank, and you may end up with many more weeds than when you started. So when you do pull or dig up unwanted plants, lay down a thick layer of mulch to help suppress germination. If you will not be growing natives from seed in that newly cleared area, you can apply corn gluten or some other germination inhibitor in the area to reduce the germination of seeds. It will eventually turn into an organic nutrient. Pine-needle or wood-chip mulches also act as germination inhibitors. See more on mulch on page 64.

You may find that removing these aggressive plants will be the biggest challenge in your landscape-wide maintenance, but keeping after them will eventually lessen the problem, especially once your native plants fill in and mature and as your soil settles into an equilibrium under a natural native mulch.

Removing Herbaceous Plants with Abundant Seed Dispersal

As previously mentioned, unless you have scraped away the live soil layer, any time a disruption in the soil occurs that is not mulched right away, there will be nearly instant germination of the many seeds already in the soil. This stash of seeds just waiting for the opportunity to grow is called the seed bank. You can rob the seed bank by disturbing the soil, letting the seeds sprout and then killing the new seedlings with an herbicide, solarization, or a deep layer of arborist wood chips. On the other hand, maybe some of those newly germinated plants are desirable native plants that you'd actually want in your landscape and here they are volunteering, right where you might want them. Learn to recognize the seedling stage of the plants you want and the ones you don't want. The mix of seeds in your seed bank depends upon many conditions:

- soil type: acidic or alkaline, sandy or clay;
- recent history of the landscape (within the last ten years) (Was it forested, agricultural, or urban/suburban?); and
- nearby plant populations—likely the most important factor.

When you care for a landscape, you will learn soon enough which plants are the most prolific and how to deal with them. You may be able to reduce some seed production by mowing or removing the weeds before they set seed. That being said, many of the most prolific plants are also favored by pollinators. A good example of a pollinator host plant is beggar ticks (*Bidens alba*), a Florida native. If you wish to keep a small patch of these aggressive seeders in your butterfly garden, you'll probably want to keep them trimmed back to an acceptable size. You'll also need to suppress the seedlings outside their defined areas by eliminating places for them to sprout: keeping the soil undisturbed as much as possible, adding more mulch, and encouraging a cover of other plants that will shade out the new seedlings. You will need to learn what those seedlings look like; when they grow in inappropriate places, pull or poison them before they bloom. One interesting aside: those *Bidens* seedlings are edible; you can add them to a salad or a mess of cooked greens, but not if they've been sprayed. These plants can also be used for chicken or rabbit food.

Dealing with unwanted seedlings will be a major maintenance task, especially for the first few years after a native landscape is planted, unless you remove the seedlings' favored habitat: disturbed soil. Your strategies could include pulling weeds before they flower and set seed, spreading heavy mulch after planting and also after pulling weeds, and sowing seeds of easy-care plants in a dense pattern and at a time to give them a head start over the weeds. The replacement plants should be ones that sprout quickly, thrive in your landscape conditions, and provide the dense cover that keeps out the majority of weeds. Good choices for sunny areas are the tough ruderal or pioneer species that sprout quickly and can thrive in your landscape (see box on page 61). For most species, it's best to sow seeds in the fall so they can get a good start before winter, and then they'll be ready to take off in the spring. In tropical areas, unless you've scraped the topsoil away, open sowing doesn't usually work well because there is no dormant period.

Several species of sand spur (*Cenchrus* spp.) are native to Florida. They are pesky annual grasses with spiny seeds that may need special attention in dry sandy areas, especially where a lawn is mowed infrequently. They bloom and set seed early in the fall; you'll probably notice them when your foot gets stabbed. You'll learn to distinguish them from other grasses by their unique aboveground creeping habit. Since sand spur is an annual, the best thing is to don your leather gloves and hand-pull or cut away all the plants you can see. Cutting it doesn't disturb the soil, so there will be fewer new weeds. In a few weeks return to the area and pull any you may have missed. The next year, there will be fewer individuals and finally, your landscape will host other plants instead.

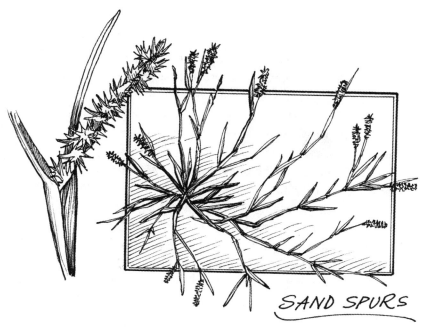

SAND SPURS

Sand spurs (*Cenchrus* spp.) are undesirable natives in yards where people walk. Since they are annuals, removing them before they drop their spiny fruits is the best way to discourage them, but it will take a couple of years to get rid of a well-established population.

Ruderal and Pioneer Species

Whether the soil is disturbed by your digging and pulling out weeds, or by natural disturbances such as uprooted trees, fire, and flood, the soil becomes available for pioneer or ruderal plants to grow. Pioneer species are the first ones to colonize a disturbed area, while ruderal or "of rubble" species thrive in altered landscapes. The first plants to grow on disturbed soil will vary depending on planting zone, soil type, moisture, the cause of the disturbance, and serendipitous propagules. These plants often have the capacity for wide and abundant dispersal of small seeds, or their seeds can lie dormant in the soil's seed bank for many years, or both, until a disturbance happens. Then they take off.

When the conditions are right, they'll germinate quickly, grow fast, and then flower profusely and set seed. Pioneer plants are able

continued

to accomplish this in poor or rich soil, on dry or moist sites, and on a wide range of soil types, but almost always in sunny areas. With disturbed soils, there is less competition for water and soil nutrients, often key for many fast-growing ruderal species. It's often said that Mother Nature hates a vacuum, and her ability to quickly colonize disturbed areas is proof of this.

In the normal scheme of nature, there will be a succession of different sets of plants. The pioneer species will be replaced over time by other more slow-growing plants that send down deeper roots or ones that spread via rhizomes. Previously forested areas, especially ones not too far from forest remnants, may become a meadow of sorts until the tree seedlings take hold. Once the trees gain some height and produce shade, the surrounding plants are eventually replaced with ones that are more shade tolerant. But if a site would normally be filled with herbaceous plants because of a limiting factor such as salt spray, the succession of plants may not include many trees or shrubs.

Sometimes ruderal sites, such as the gravel-covered areas near railroad tracks, may be too altered and too aggressively managed, keeping trees and shrubs at bay for normal succession to occur so the pioneer species may continue their reign much longer than normal. In your own landscape, remove rubble from growing areas and do what you can to restore the soil with composting and mulching to provide better conditions for your plants. That being said, some of our favorite wildflowers are ruderals that thrive in poor conditions.

Plants that you see growing untended in ditches and other waste places are ruderal. If they are native species, you may want to put them on your list of desirable plants that know how to survive under tough conditions. (Unless they are on your property, you should not dig plants from these areas, but acquire them from legitimate native nurseries. Roadsides and rights-of-way are public properties.) Some favorite ruderals are black-eyed Susans (*Rudbeckia* spp.), spotted beebalm (*Monarda punctata*), tickseeds (*Coreopsis* spp.), starrush white-top (*Rhynchospora colorata*), and goldenrods (*Solidago* spp.).

Once your native landscape fills in and matures, there will be fewer places for weeds to grow. This beginning phase of site preparation and initial weeding is an investment that will lead to much less maintenance in the future.

Weeding Strategies

Once you have begun the process of planting natives in your landscape, it will be necessary to deal with weeds for at least a few years. As discussed in this chapter and elsewhere, weed problems can be reduced in various ways, including mulching and complete removal of undesirable plants before planting, but weeds will still plant themselves in inappropriate places. Here are some weeding guidelines:

- Learn to identify seedlings that grow in your landscape. Some may be desirable native plants that can be left in place or transplanted to other sections of your landscape.
- Set weeding priorities so the most critical areas are weeded first. First weed around your newly planted natives so they have the best chance to thrive. Next weed along the edges and most visible areas of native beds where neatness counts. Then work the less visible areas to remove the most aggressive weeds and invasives, maybe leaving some native volunteers in place. After all, if Mother Nature planted them there, they'll probably do well.
- Try to accomplish most of your weeding before the wet season or warm weather when weeds grow faster.
- Pull prolific, seed-producing plants before they set seed.
- For plants that spread via rhizomes or produce tubers, remove as much of the root or tuber as possible because each piece can grow into a new plant.
- Do not add weeds bearing seeds, rhizomes, or tubers to your compost pile.
- Do a little weeding every time you're in the landscape. You might even be able to do some light weeding while talking on your cell phone. Of course, you'll need to concentrate on the weeds several times in each of the first few years after installing a native landscape, but this chore will lessen as your natives gain in size and the soil is not disturbed as much.

- After disturbing the soil by pulling weeds, apply mulch to cover the bare soil. Do this as soon as possible (at least within a day or two) for most effective weed suppression. Alternatively, cut off the annual weeds at the soil line so the soil is not disturbed.

Trimming Strategies for Herbaceous Plants

A number of desirable pollinator plants do tend to get rangy and flop over in high winds or hard rain, such as goldenrod (*Solidago* spp.), spotted beebalm (*Monarda punctata*), and snow squarestem (*Melanthera nivea*). In their natural meadow ecosystems, this is not a problem because they are usually surrounded by plants of similar heights and they hold each other upright. When these plants flop into paths, lawns, patios, or other human-use spaces in your landscape, they need to be trimmed back or transplanted to wilder areas. Or maybe you have room to move the paths or remove more lawn to accommodate the drooping or overhanging plants.

One method of handling such plants is to trim them back along human-use areas such as paths, patios, or lawns fairly early in their season, with the shortest trim near the path and gradually increasing in height until you reach an area of growth far enough from the path so its leaning will not be a problem. When you trim them early in the season, you will delay, but not prevent the blooming on those stalks. See chapter 7 for more on managing edges.

For plants that die back in the winter, leave the stalks as long as tolerable in your landscape. They may hold seed for winter birds or be used as overwintering shelter by beneficial insects. If you trim back any that look too sloppy near the edges of the natural areas and leave the rest, add them to a brush pile where the birds can still find the seeds and dormant insects can complete their life cycles.

Using Mulches in Site Preparation

Wide expanses of mulch should not be the goal in your native landscape, but using organic mulches, such as wood chips, sawdust, pine needles, straw, or bark nuggets, will suppress weeds, help hold in moisture, prevent the soil surface from crusting, help prevent erosion on level grades or gentle slopes, and provide a buffer to protect trees and other plants from mowing injuries. Because they are organic, they will eventually add humus to the soil. Mulching with organic materials in the landscape is sometimes called sheet composting: it is slow to decompose because there is not enough mass to raise the temperature. Choose a coarser mulch for the best staying power and for the best water penetration; coarse mulches around trees allow aeration of their roots. Fine mulches break down more quickly, but sometimes they form a crust that repels water. The maintenance of mulched areas will be reduced as your natives grow.

On the other hand, many organic mulches are flammable and may cause problems for homes surrounded by fire-dependent natural areas. In these cases, it is best to keep the mulch a safe distance from the house and other structures. Even in standard urban/suburban landscapes, you need to keep flammable mulches away from outdoor cooking areas. If your target habitat is nutrient poor, go easy on the mulches, because in this case you don't want too many extra nutrients. See appendix II for a list of pros and cons of various mulching materials.

Mulching works to suppress weeds in several ways:

- It creates a physical and light barrier if it is at least 2 or 3 inches deep. Weed seeds in the seed bank may be killed or remain dormant.
- Moisture and microbes (particularly the fungi) under the mulch will cause most small seeds to decompose as part of the sheet composting process.
- Microbes that work to decompose organic mulches absorb nitrogen from the surrounding soil for energy. This temporary nitrogen depletion suppresses weed seed germination and reduces new plant growth. Offset this nitrogen depletion as you mulch around newly planted trees and shrubs by adding a topdressing of compost all around the plants but outside their root-balls, before you lay on the mulch.

Mulching is recommended for most new native planting areas, but the idea is not to make the mulch the centerpiece of your landscape. It is only a tool to keep the weeds down until the plant groupings grow thicker and can take over the mulching duties with their shade and their own fallen leaves and twigs.

Best Mulching Practices

- Do not allow any type of mulch to touch the plants' stems or trunks. It's not uncommon to see a foot or more of mulch leaning against tree trunks—called volcano mulching. This is harmful to trees in several ways:

  1. Water is shed from the mulch away from the tree because of the steep angle.
  2. Rodents and other animals can burrow and nest in this much mulch and chew on the tree bark.
  3. Fungi and bacteria harbored in the mulch can rot out the base of the tree, making it prone to falling.
  4. Some species of trees and shrubs will form new, adventitious roots within a thick mulch layer, reducing plant stability and drought resistance. In droughts the mulch will dry out first, and trees with roots in the mulch can be strained.

- Layered mulching can be used to keep down weeds in an established bed or to start a new bed or other nonlawn area. First

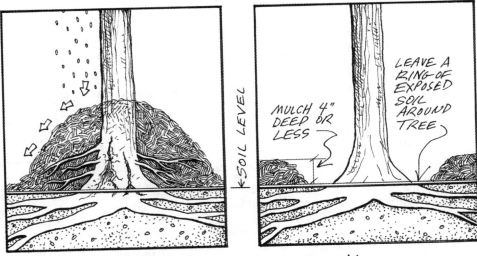

"VOLCANO" MULCHING and PROPER MULCHING

remove highly aggressive plants like torpedo grass, Mexican petunia, poison ivy, and catbrier from the area. Dig a trench along the edge of the area so the plants under the layers are not supported by those still in the open. Then tamp down the rest of the plants. Lay down a thick layer of mulch (4 or 5 inches) such as leaves, pine needles, or shredded tree trimmings. A layer of paper or cardboard is not recommended in a native landscape because of possible problems with fungi or molds festering under the paper and because it reduces the habitat value for wildlife that need access to the soil.

- Don't use organic mulch next to a waterway, pond, lake, or other wet area because it can wash into the water during heavy rainstorms, adding to the nutrient load in the water as it decomposes. In the buffer areas around waterways or wet spots, arrange the plants in such a way that their shade reduces weeds.

Maintaining Mulched Beds

These beds can be set up and cared for in several ways; the method you use will depend on your goal for the area. Restoring most types of native habitat works best if your mulch looks like one that Mother Nature would use in that region. Shredded leaves and wood trimmings laid directly on the soil may be the best choice—simply let the leaf droppings and dead wood stay on the ground. This mulch rots into the soil and needs reapplication until your trees and shrubs are large enough to create enough of their own leaf drop.

In an area with many plantings including bulbs, spring ephemerals, and other perennials, apply no more than a 2-inch layer of mulch—it will hamper weeds from below to some degree. New weeds will continue to sow themselves on the top of the mulch unless you've used sawdust. A light raking of the top layer uproots the small weeds and helps to rejuvenate the look. If you find that the mulch is less than an inch thick, add another inch of new mulch as you rake.

If you are sowing wildflower seed in an area, rake the mulch to spread it out and expose the soil. Plant your seed at the ideal time for your desired plants and maybe they'll get a head start on the weeds. More on growing seeds in chapter 6.

5

Selecting, Planting, and Caring for Natives

While natives have adapted to your climate, the conditions in urban/suburban environments often override the natural climatic conditions with heat islands, nighttime lighting, and barriers such as buildings or fences. Select natives that are flexible enough to adapt to your conditions. As you add native plant groupings over the years, your yard may become more like local native ecosystems, but it will take time for this transformation.

Trees

Trees are the bones of your landscape. If you are purchasing trees, they may be the most expensive items on a per plant basis. The time you spend in choosing, planting, and caring for new trees is a long-term investment; if done correctly, it will increase the value of your property. First, as discussed in chapter 1, be sure the trees you select are bred from local stock to give them the best chance of thriving.

You may wish to plant your primary, canopy-producing trees two or three years before you plant the smaller understory trees and shrubs. This gives the trees a chance to establish themselves, to begin to fill out, and to cast some shade.

Choosing Trees

The old gardeners' tale about buying the biggest trees you can afford for a head start on your landscape is usually bad advice. When it comes to the probability of survival and the time needed to acclimate, a large tree needs much more time to adapt to a new site and a much longer regimen of extra irrigation than a small one. Your money and effort will be better spent on smaller, less expensive specimens that will adjust quickly to their new locations, require less initial maintenance, and begin their vigorous growing cycles much sooner. It's likely that a 1-inch-caliper sapling will catch up in size to its much more expensive counterpart with a 4-inch caliper within five years. (Caliper for saplings is the diameter of the trunk at 6 inches above the root-ball.)

Another old gardeners' tale is to choose trees that are bushy or branching. As a result of this bad advice, many growers and nurseries top the saplings so they produce branches too early in their life cycles. The reality is that saplings of many tree species do not branch naturally for several years. Tree experts tell us that, for most species, the best specimens for strength and wind resistance have one main trunk; in addition, single-trunked trees require less pruning and ongoing maintenance. So when you see trees for sale, look for ones that have not been topped or trimmed back. Single-trunked specimens (also known as whips) may look puny compared to those forced to branch out, but that sturdier form will fare better in Florida's tropical storms.

Consider the ongoing maintenance of a tree species, because some trees are messier than others with abundant fruit, continuous dropping of leathery or spiny leaves, or the breaking off of many small branches. If a tree is to be planted near human-use areas, choose a species with "neater" habits. Reserve the messy ones for the wilder areas where their droppings do not matter and will become mulch. Include neatness as a factor in researching your trees.

Once you get to the nursery, choose specimens with good leaf color, new growth, and general vibrancy; if the plants are dormant when you buy them, look for good bud formation. When choosing several trees of the same species for an area, select specimens that vary in size and shape for a naturalized landscape. In addition, when choosing a variety of tree species for an area, choose at most only two or three species of complementary sizes and textures. Your landscape is not an arboretum, so don't plant one of everything.

After you narrow your tree selection by form and size, consider the

This magnolia seen at a big box store has been topped, and many side branches have grown to make it bushy. If you can find unpruned specimens, they will have a better one-trunked form for good wind resistance and reduced need for future pruning. The owner of this tree will have to choose a main leader from one of the top braches and will probably end up with a crooked and weakened trunk.

pots and roots. Look for the root flare—the spot at the bottom of the tree trunk where the roots begin to grow out. The root flare should be above the soil line; if it's not, the tree has probably been repotted too deeply at least once, or maybe it's been grown from a cutting that does not form a root flare at all. If the pots are old or cracked with roots growing through the drainage holes, the grower hasn't kept up with the trees' growth and the trees will be pot-bound. This doesn't mean you shouldn't purchase them, but since you'll have more work to do when you plant them and there will be a longer adjustment period, maybe you can negotiate a better price.

If there are lots of weeds in the pot, this means the grower has not spent the time to care for each specimen and the plant has had to share its meager resources. On the other hand, if the pot looks brand new and the soil also looks new, the tree has probably been potted up recently and may still have circling roots and a very small root-ball, but you can't tell from its outward appearance. You'll find out only when you rinse away the soil upon planting. Also, avoid plants that are over-fertilized in their pots. You can usually see the little colored balls of slow release fertilizer in the soil. You'll know if a plant is overfertilized usually by its poorly developed roots combined with numerous stems and leaves. These plants usually take longer to adapt to inground sites, especially in nutrient-poor soil.

Developing a good relationship with your local native nursery is invaluable, because the knowledgeable personnel can help you pick the best specimens for your needs. That said, don't let anyone talk you into another choice just to make a sale. You should have already created a list of acceptable trees for your project, and if that alternative tree is not on your list, don't purchase it until you do some research to see if it would work within your plan. It's a good idea to bring plant reference books when shopping for plants so you can make educated decisions on-site. Don't be hurried or rushed, because time and effort taken in choosing the best trees will pay off in the long run with the right trees for your landscape.

Planting Trees

The timing of tree planting depends on where you are and the type of tree. In tropical areas, it's usually best to plant at the beginning of the normal rainy period. Farther north, early fall is a good time to plant deciduous trees, when they are not trying to put out new growth or produce new leaves, plus September and October are part of Florida's wet season. Later in the fall and into winter also works well when the trees are dormant. You will need to irrigate more during those normally dry months—both when you first plant the tree and then again as its leaves begin to emerge.

Most trees available for home landscaping are in containers, but you may also find some bare-rooted or balled and burlapped specimens. (Balled and burlapped (B&B) trees or shrubs have been field grown; when dug up, their root-balls are wrapped in burlap or other fabric.)

Palms Are Different

Since palms don't produce real wood with annual rings, they are not considered a true tree botanically. Of course, they act as trees in the landscape, but the guidelines for purchasing and planting palms are different.

- Palms don't have a root flare, but they do have a root initiation zone.
- Upon transplanting, many palms, including Florida's state tree, the cabbage palm (*Sabal palmetto*), regenerate all new roots. Root-pruning is ineffective since they will grow all new roots anyway.
- Palm roots don't increase in diameter and therefore don't crack sidewalks, foundations, or other hardscape features.
- Since palms don't produce wood and don't increase in girth, if a palm trunk gets gouged, the palm cannot heal itself. Most palms will survive these injuries, but why invite trouble?

To plant a palm, whether it's container or field grown, find the rooting zone and make sure that this is at or just below soil level. Create a swale around the base of the trunk to keep irrigation water from draining away. Irrigate palms over and above general landscape irrigation: every day for the first month, tapering off to once a week for several months after that. For sandy sites, even more irrigation may be necessary. After this initial phase, irrigate during droughts for two or three years.

Unlike true trees, the time it takes a palm to establish and put out new growth does not relate directly to its size. As a matter of fact, juvenile palms (less than 10 years old) that have not yet established their trunks do not transplant well from the field because they have not established their root initiation zones and cannot grow new roots. It takes nearly a year for a palm to produce all new roots; during that time, it should be staked firmly so it doesn't fall down.

In the case of palms, you might wish to spend the money for larger trees since they take so long to start growing no matter what size they are. When you purchase field-grown palms, they are likely to have had most of their fronds removed, but at no other time is this necessary or desirable. Trim only completely dead fronds that are drooping well below horizontal, even if there is a hurricane threatening your area. You may also wish to trim away seeds or seedpods to reduce the potential mess. The trimmer should not use spikes to climb the tree.

Reference: Florida Extension Service article, "Transplanting Palms in the Landscape." edis.ifas.ufl.edu/ep001

For container-grown or balled and burlapped specimens, handle the trees by their root-balls, not by their trunks. For bare-rooted or balled and burlapped trees, keep the roots moist at all times until planting. If you need to store trees for more than a day or two, it's important to prop them up in an upright position so the trees don't have to struggle to bend upward toward the light or against gravity only to bend back again when they are finally planted.

Before you remove the tree from its pot or wrap, set it where you want to dig the hole to check for placement. Prop it up if necessary, and then stand back to view it from all angles—look up as well to make sure it's not under wires or too many overhanging branches; of course you will have previously checked for underground infrastructure. Go inside and also view it from windows to make sure that your new tree will not block a prized view. Remember to visualize its mature size. Only after all this checking will you be ready to plant.

Rinse the Soil from the Roots

There are a number of reasons to rinse away all the soil from the roots as you remove the tree from its pot or wrap. (For container-grown plants, you may have to soak the root-ball in a bucket of water to loosen the soil.)

- If a tree has been in the pot for a year or more, the soil will have no nutrients left for the tree and may harbor unwanted plants or pests.
- Rinsing away the soil will reveal the root flare (where the first

main roots are attached) and any coiling roots. You cannot necessarily tell by looking at the outside of the root-ball because the tree may have been potted up several times with the root flare below the soil line, and roots may have traveled out into the new soil so the root-ball might look fine from the outside. (Note: a tree grown from a cutting will not have a root flare, so approximate the location by its first roots.)

- In natural areas you won't be introducing alien soil or weeds and pests into the ecosystem.
- The tree will adjust faster to its new environment.

Although some people advocate leaving the burlap wrap in place when planting the tree, today's burlap may be synthetic and it will not

Step One: Rinse all the soil from the roots to
expose the circling roots and the root flare.

Step Two: The planting hole should be firm in the center so the root flare is above soil level and wide enough so the circling roots can be stretched out in all directions radiating from the trunk.

Step Three: Mud in the whole area around the roots, and build a watering saucer so supplemental irrigation water stays in place. This 1-inch caliper tree will require daily irrigation with 3 gallons of water for three weeks and several times a week for another month or until new growth is evident. Further irrigation will be needed during drought for the next year.

rot away—forming a barrier against new root formation. Even though circling roots are not usually a problem with field grown trees, carefully rinsing away the soil before spreading out the roots will result in faster acclimatization and more drought resistance. Unwanted plants in the root-ball may be in the form of seeds or pieces of rhizomes. These weeds may be a larger problem in field-grown trees than among container-grown trees where conditions are more controlled.

Dig a hole the same depth as the rinsed-off root-ball and at least twice as wide—wider is better, but may not be easy if you're planting in a rock substrate. The root flare at the base of the trunk should be just above the soil line. Be sure that the bottom of the planting hole provides a solid footing so the tree won't sink once it's in place. As you place the root-ball into the hole, stretch out the roots as far as possible and in as many directions as you can—this is why you want a wide hole. If the roots are coiling or hopelessly entangled, some breakage or cutting will be necessary. While this will stress the plant right now, coiling roots will be fatal for the tree years later as it slowly chokes itself.

Fill the hole with water as you gently shovel the soil back into the hole—this is called mudding in. No amendments to the soil are recommended. Scientific studies have shown that compost, fertilizer, or other soil enhancing materials added to the planting hole discourage the roots from spreading as quickly into surrounding soil. On the other hand, for small trees or shrubs planted in contained space, where the roots can't spread too far from the planting site, you could amend the whole area with compost if needed.

After the hole has been filled in, press the soil gently in place to remove the air spaces. Then create a shallow saucer equal to the size of the root-ball or planting hole by building a berm of soil two or three inches high. Lay two to three inches of mulch over the saucer area and beyond, but not up against the trunk.

If the tree is wobbly and could be knocked over by a gust of wind, staking may be necessary until the roots grow into the surrounding soil. Make sure that no stakes enter the root-ball and that no wires or ropes abrade the trunk. You may wish to use wide flexible bands of rubber or cloth to hold the tree. Except for palms, stake in such a way that the trunk can bend some in the wind so the tree can build strength in its trunk. When the tree starts to add new growth, it's time to remove the stakes.

Don't prune the tree at planting time, except for broken branches. Auxin, a type of hormone produced in the terminal buds, suppresses growth of side buds, and more importantly for transplants, it stimulates root growth. Pruning a newly planted tree removes this natural auxin, which could have helped in root regeneration. In addition, the tree is under stress at this time and will need every bit of energy manufactured by photosynthesis in its leaves. This means that a damaged root system will have to support a full set of leaves, so extra irrigation is *the* key to long-term success. Save the shaping of the tree until the following fall and then prune only 20 percent of it, at most, to begin its shaping, including cutting away suckers, promoting proper branching, and encouraging a true header. The guidelines for shaping will vary depending on species, and it may take three years or more to complete the initial shaping. After this stage some regular pruning might be necessary, but it should be much less frequent.

Unless there has been an inch or more of rain within the last three days, your new tree will need watering daily for several weeks or longer with a gradual tapering to three times a week for a couple of months. After this initial period irrigate for two years or more during dry spells to allow the roots time to fully develop. Larger trees require longer irrigation periods—establishment takes approximately three to five months per inch of trunk caliper. Do not depend on an area-wide sprinkler system for this extra watering; this irrigation is over and above a normal watering cycle or light rainfall. A good rain gauge is an important tool for making sure you're providing enough irrigation. If you've planted a tree in a site that is wet or damp all the time, this extra irrigation may not be needed.

Each time you irrigate, it's best to water with three gallons per inch of trunk caliper. For example, use six gallons for a 2-inch caliper tree. Apply slowly, so all water soaks into the saucer area you constructed around the root-ball. You may wish to use watering bags (horseshoe-shaped bags that lie on the ground around the newly planted tree or bags that attach to the trunk of the tree) or install a temporary drip system to provide the extra irrigation for your newly planted trees. This way they will receive a slow-drip of a measured amount of water at each watering. A higher volume of water does not reduce the need for irrigation frequency because the extra water will sink out of reach of the roots, especially in sandy soils.

A month or so after planting, unless you are working in a nutrient-poor ecosystem, rake the mulch aside and apply an inch or so of compost on the soil surface in a wide circle from just outside the root-ball out two feet or to the drip line of your tree, whichever is greater. Don't dig it in, but gently irrigate the compost with rain barrel water to initiate the composting action on the underlying soil. If you don't have access to rain barrels, let your municipal water stand for two days before using or skip this step, because you don't want the chlorine to kill the compost microbes. Cover the compost with a fresh layer of mulch to keep it moist for a few days. Repeat this composting just before the next period of growth, but not during a severe drought.

Some gardeners also like to include slow-release organic fertilizer with the compost, but use it only if your soil is lacking in nutrients. In addition to its organic nutrients, the compost provides life to the soil, including worms, fungi, bacteria, and other critters. The soil underneath will then become more like compost with a loose texture and higher water retention. Your tree's roots will be enticed to grow out into this conditioned soil. When the roots grow outward, the tree will become more tolerant of wind and drought.

Several reasons can be given for using compost and/or organic slow-release fertilizer instead of a synthetic fertilizer such as 10-10-10 around your new trees:

- If the plant absorbs a heavy load of nitrogen, it may grow too fast and produce a flush of growth that may be hard for it to sustain with normal watering. This weakens the wood, making it more susceptible to wind damage or attack from disease or pests.
- Synthetic fertilizer is bad for the soil's ecosystem and many of the microbes will be adversely affected.
- In most Florida soils, phosphorus (the middle number in the 10-10-10) is rarely needed and often the cause of water pollution when it runs off your property.

Locally made compost offers a much safer alternative and can be reapplied throughout the year as needed, plus if you make it yourself, there is no cost except for your labor.

Transplanting Trees

If a sapling would be better suited for a different spot in your land-scape, you'll have a better chance of success if you follow these trans-planting guidelines:

- Transplant trees that are no larger than 2-inch caliper.
- It's best to transplant deciduous trees early in the fall so the roots will have time to develop before the spring growth spurt; as mentioned above, September and October are part of our wet season months. In South Florida the best time for trans-planting is usually at the beginning of the wet season.
- Root-prune the tree a month or two before transplanting. Use a sharp shovel to cut a circle around the tree—sink the shovel into the soil right up to the top of the blade. The circle should be about 18 to 24 inches out from the trunk. Keep in mind that this will be the size of the root-ball. Root-pruning cuts the surface roots, encouraging the tree to adjust to the loss while still in place and to develop more roots close to the trunk.
- Irrigate the tree deeply the day before the transplant.
- Dig the planting hole before digging up the tree. Remove any deep-rooted weeds in the area.
- Proceed with planting and ongoing care the same as with any other tree, as described above.

Transplanting gives you more flexibility in your landscape and can be a significant source of native trees that you know are adapted to your area. You should not transplant or harvest plants from public or private property, including roadsides, without permission.

Ongoing Tree Care

Encourage desirable young trees in your landscape, whether you planted them or not, with semiannual composting outside their root-balls and extra irrigation during droughts, by removing vines from the branches, and by keeping the area around the trunk relatively free of weeds and vines.

Some trees have good growth habits and need very little in the way of pruning, but some trees may need some guidance to ensure the best form, especially if they were cut back by growers or nurseries to encourage early branching. For the first year or two after you've planted a tree, you should do very little pruning to allow it to fully establish itself. After that you may need to choose a main leader for the strongest, most wind resistant form. To accomplish this, prune back any potential co-leaders by about one-third. Cut them back to a side shoot growing in the direction that seems appropriate, but do not cut back the main trunk yet. Depending on how the co-leaders grow in the next year or two after pruning, you may decide to train them as main branches or to cut them back again. If you will be pruning them again, the first year you'll cut them back by half and the next year back to the trunk, but be sure to leave the collar tissue at the base of the branch. This pruning will not be necessary if the tree already has one main trunk as discussed above.

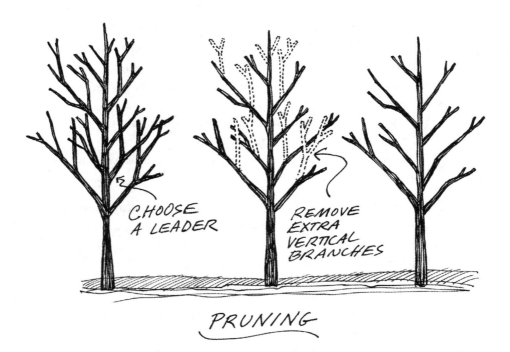

CHOOSE A LEADER

REMOVE EXTRA VERTICAL BRANCHES

PRUNING

To produce the strongest tree form, some tree species need guidance in the form of pruning, but don't begin pruning until two years after planting, when the tree is well established.

Another pruning task that may be needed for some types of trees is to encourage some main limbs—the ones that will remain on the tree permanently. Ideally, the main limbs on a large tree would be positioned 2 or 3 feet apart along the main trunk and emanating from all sides of the tree. Again, you accomplish this by reducing the length of branches between the chosen main branches, eventually removing them. Many tree species such as conifers may grow this way naturally and should be left alone, but others need some guidance and planning for the overall shape of the tree when small to prevent bigger problems in the future.

In your native landscape you will be striving for diversity, so in a case where a more desirable or rarer tree is growing too close to a common tree or under its branches, you may decide to prune back the branches of the common tree to make room for the more desirable tree. In a natural ecosystem, it's survival of the fittest, but you are free to select favorites to encourage in your landscape. In addition, in a natural ecosystem, if an extreme drought occurs, some of the trees can be adversely affected and maybe even die from water shortages. In your landscape, if you don't want your trees to die, plan for some type of temporary drip irrigation or other means of getting water to your trees.

Propagating trees

Self-Seeding Trees

Some trees such as oaks (*Quercus* spp.) and maples (*Acer* spp.) are so efficient at reseeding that you'll have as many of them as you could possibly want. Actually, they are likely to become weeds and their removal will become a maintenance chore in an urban/suburban landscape. In a wild area, these tree seedlings would languish under the dark shade of the canopy until a tree falls. Then the puny saplings will suddenly put on significant growth to take advantage of this newly opened, sunny spot. If you have a bunch of tree seedlings or young saplings growing in the wrong spot, you can easily transplant them at this stage.

If you're transplanting seedlings, you can dig them out at any time during the year. You may want to put them in pots for six months to a year until you can see some new growth. After this phase, you can either pot them up to let them gain more size, or if they are big enough at this point, plant them in the landscape where needed. The reason for planting them in pots first is to keep them where you can keep an eye on them so you'll see right away when they need irrigation, and you also get to choose the ones that do the best. If you transplant them directly, you may end up with some struggling and nearly invisible seedlings that might be mistakenly pulled during landscape maintenance.

Asexual Propagation

Several methods are available for cloning trees to increase your population more quickly: cuttings, air layering, and harvesting of root suckers. See chapter 6 for propagation techniques.

Shrubs

The line between shrubs and trees is a little hazy, but generally shrubs have multiple canes (stems) and are less than fifteen feet tall, while trees have a single trunk and are taller than 15 feet. Certainly, there are many exceptions with some trees having multiple trunks and some shrubs having just one. Trees and shrubs may in fact have more similarities (such as long life and woody tissue) than differences.

While an individual shrub is usually less expensive than a tree, many native landscapes contain three to five times more shrubs than trees on a per plant basis. Shrubs of various sizes and textures will provide interest and add to habitat value. As with trees, select only two or three species of shrubs for an area to create natural-looking groupings that allow for the mature size of the shrubs. Because you will allow space for their full growth, the shrubs will look too far apart at first. Fill in the spaces between newly planted shrubs with bunching grasses or showy wildflowers, or both.

The sequence of planting trees and shrubs should account for the trees' mature sizes that will eventually provide a canopy for that area in the landscape. If the shrubs and understory trees that you wish to plant do best in the shade, you may want to wait two or three years before planting them to give your trees a chance to grow to provide the needed shade. Groupings of shrubs should be far enough from trees to create a visual separation and also to prevent competition between roots of the trees and shrubs as they become established. Of course, as your landscape plants mature together, there will be much overlapping and intermingling of roots; at the same time, the trees and shrubs will be providing most of their own mulch. Both the mat of surface roots and the self-mulching help reduce needed maintenance and weeding. As native gardeners, this is what we strive for, but the key word here is "reduce." In your maturing urban/suburban landscape you will still need to pull up weeds (maybe mostly tree seedlings at this point) and remove vines that crawl up your trees and over your shrubs on an annual or biannual basis. This is another reason for leaving spaces between your trees and shrubs—to provide good access for these chores.

Selecting Shrubs

Most shrubs develop a multiple cane (stem) form, but many of the plants for sale will have only one cane. A pot with multiple canes may actually be three separate plants that might have been started as cuttings—you'll find out when you rinse away all the soil. If they are indeed separate plants, plant them separately with enough space for

Plant for the mature plant size. A beautyberry shrub (*Callicarpa americana*) is a good example—it may be a 12-inch stick when you plant it, but it will grow to 12 feet across in some locations.

PLAN AHEAD

their adult size within a grouping. Do your research so you know what the adult forms of your selected shrub species look like and how large they will grow.

Choose plants with good leaf color, new growth, and general vibrancy. Bushier is not necessarily indicative of a superior shrub, but shrubs are generally more forgiving than trees of being trimmed back. Look at the condition of the pot and whether roots are growing through the drainage holes or circling in the pot. Use the same guidelines for choosing potted trees to choose the best shrubs.

Planting Shrubs

In most native landscape designs, you'll want to plant an odd number of shrubs in groupings that allow for their adult sizes. In order to avoid the "one of everything" look, most of your groupings will probably be all the same species. The next grouping could be the same shrub again or a different species. If you're building a hedgerow, you'll want to keep the look as natural as possible. See chapter 9 for more on hedgerows.

Use the tree guidelines for planting shrubs, but generally, the extra irrigation schedule for shrubs will be shorter than for trees because of their smaller size and better rooting capability. The smaller the shrub (or tree), the faster it will become established in your landscape.

Transplanting Shrubs

In general, shrubs are easier to transplant than trees because of their ability to generate new roots, but an overgrown foundation shrub may require as much care as a good-sized sapling. As with trees, it's best to root-prune them at least a few weeks ahead of the transplant date. The best time to transplant shrubs in your area will be similar to the best time for trees. Treat a transplant like any other shrub you are planting.

Ongoing Care for Shrubs

Much as with trees, encourage desirable shrubs, especially the younger specimens, by laying on compost just outside their root-balls, by watering them (in addition to general landscape irrigation) during dry weather, and by keeping the areas around their root-balls free of aggressive weeds and vines.

To create a low-maintenance native landscape, plant shrubs to ac-

A year after it was planted, this bluestem palmetto (*Sabal minor*) received a topdressing of compost, enhancing soil fertility and texture out and away from the root-ball to entice new root formation. Never add amendments, even compost, to the planting hole.

commodate their mature size with the goal of not having to shear or shape the shrubs on a regular basis. In cases where you do wish to thin a shrub, remove an awkward cane, or cut it back to better fit an area, do not shear the tips of the canes, but cut the canes individually back to a branch or a bud and maybe even back to the ground. You can also use shovel pruning to remove sections of a shrub if necessary. See chapter 6 for more on shovel pruning.

If a shrub has been previously sheared, you may be able to "unshear" it. In random areas around all sides of the shrub, reach in with your gloved hand past the sheared edge toward the center of the shrub, grab a handful of branches, and then cut them off just below your hand. These newly-cut branches will need further trimming back to the next branches, a main cane, or the ground. For a shrub with diameter of five feet, create ten to fifteen holes in the smooth surface of the shrub. This way light will reach into the interior of the shrub and cause a change in the branching pattern. Repeat this exercise in different sections of the shrub each season; after a few years, your shrub will have a more natural shape that will be easier to maintain.

Propagating Shrubs

Seeds and Seedlings

Only a few shrubs are prolific self-seeders such as salt bush (*Baccharis halimifolia*) and firebush (*Hamelia patens*); most shrubs produce too few seedlings to become weeds. Learn to recognize the shrub seedlings so you know what you have. If a desirable shrub seedling has started in an inconvenient spot, transplant it to a pot or to a new spot in your landscape. Either way, it will need some extra watering and careful weeding until it becomes established. Using seedlings as new stock ensures genetic diversity, while the various asexual propagation techniques do not.

Asexual Propagation

Clones of shrubs can be produced in several ways: cuttings, shovel pruning, layering, and air layering. More details on these in chapter 6.

Vines

Use woody vines with caution in urban/suburban landscapes, even if native, because if left untended, most of them will try to climb over and choke out your new trees and shrubs. A woody vine twisted around the trunk of a young tree can prevent the trunk from expanding in future years. On the other hand, many native vines grow easily, have showy flowers, serve as larval food for butterflies, and provide nectar for hummingbirds and butterflies, plus they may produce berries to feed the birds from late summer throughout the fall. In urban/suburban landscapes, vines may be most appropriate covering fences, pergolas, trellises, or arbors where you can confine them to some extent and keep them out of reach of the rest of your landscape. In areas where you'd like to create some fast screening, a homemade trellis of

A trellis with vines and bunching grasses can fill in an area while you're waiting for planted natives to fill their allotted spaces.

bamboo stalks tied together will fill up in no time. Some vines tend to crawl over the ground, so they can serve as ground covers. So before you choose a vine, be sure you know what to expect and that you know what role it will play in your landscape.

Planting Vines

Vines are usually sold in pots and are easy to plant. While it's best to plant them at the same depth as they were in the pot, there will be no root flare and no worries about strangling roots. If your soil is lousy, you may wish to amend the whole bed with compost where you are planting the vine. Adding compost is especially important if the vine will be climbing and this will be its only contact with the soil. Irrigate well until the vine becomes established.

Ongoing Care of Vines

In urban/suburban landscapes, it's usually best to trim back exuberant vines growing in highly visible areas on a fence, trellis, or pergola on an annual basis after their blooming cycle is over. Some vines produce an abundance of seedlings, while others may send up shoots. You could just pull them up like weeds, but why not transplant them? Put them in a pot to hold until they become established and then plant them in a new spot. In wilder sections of your landscape, the vines might not need annual attention, but do watch out for tree strangling activity and strip the vines away before they do permanent damage to your trees.

A climbing vine with roots only at its base may need extra irrigation during a prolonged dry spell, but crawling vines normally root in many places and are generally more drought tolerant because of this.

Propagating Vines

Most vines root readily, and adventitious roots form whenever a stem touches the soil. If you have a climber that you'd like to clone by cuttings, use active growing stems for your cuttings and treat them like any other cutting. Another option is to tease a few stems out of the climbing mass to use for layering in a pot or pots.

Herbaceous Perennials

The life spans of perennials can range from a couple of years to decades. Herbaceous perennials have no woody tissue by definition and many of them die back in the winter; in South Florida, some of these plants may not die back each year and can become woody, but this is not the same as wood with annual rings. Many low-maintenance native landscapes contain a large number of these fast-growing plants because they don't need to be replanted each year, plus they offer color and attract pollinators—blooming times range from a few weeks to a whole season. They can be a permanent part of a landscape plan or used to fill in empty spaces while trees and shrubs mature.

Herbaceous perennials come in many different sizes, forms, and textures. For simplicity, this book includes graminoids (grasses and grasslike plants), forbs (broad-leaved flowering plants), and ferns in this group. The arrangement of these plants may be the defining look in your landscape with your trees and shrubs serving as a backdrop.

Some native perennials require rich soil and shade, while others grow best in well-drained soil and full sun. Some grow neatly on their own, while others can become rangy and may lean over other plants toward the end of the summer. Learn as much as you can about the plants you want from books, websites, and seminars, and by getting out in gardens and parks. Even with all your studying, managing the perennials will be an on-site learning experience. General or theoretical knowledge may or may not apply to your landscape.

Planting Perennials

While seeds for perennials are available and the least expensive way to fill in your landscape, it will take longer to get adult plants. Be sure to purchase seeds bred from local stock—but even then, some native plants are not easy to grow using seeds. See chapter 6 for details on working with seeds.

Many people building native landscapes in urban/suburban areas start with potted plants. Larger potted plants give you the best head start on getting to a size that makes a significant impact in the landscape, but smaller plants may be in better shape. You need to make a judgment depending on your budget, your needs, and the available specimens. If you're using these plants to fill empty spaces between newly planted trees and shrubs, you may want the larger specimens.

Look for plants with the best color and fullness. If roots are growing through the drainage holes, you'll have more work to do to, but at least you know where you stand. Small plants in big pots may have just been transplanted, so proceed with care. Purchase enough to fill your drift area, keeping in mind that a crowded pot may hold a dozen or more plants. Another option for large quantities is to buy plants in liners instead of potted plants. Liners are trays that hold 50–80 sprouts—an inexpensive alternative to larger plants in containers.

Prepare the planting area by getting rid of weeds, especially making sure there are no deep-rooted weeds that would spoil your perennial

One container of tickseed (*Coreopsis* sp.) can include 10 or more individual plants. For the best results, separate them and plant them individually in a drift in your garden or meadow area.

bed. Normally in a native garden, you plant irregularly shaped drifts for the most natural placement. Some natives are relatively understated in their showiness, so the groupings can make a stronger statement in your landscape. As with your trees and shrubs, make sure you'll have access to your perennials to care for them. Plan for a narrow, mulched walkway between the perennials and the shrubs or other backdrop for these plants. This way the path will be hidden to some degree, but test it to make sure space is adequate for you to bend over to get close to the plants.

Soil preparation (after getting rid of the weeds) depends on your plants and the condition of the soil. If your soil is nutrient poor (e.g., sugar sand) it may a good idea to amend the whole bed with a layer of compost—an inch layer is probably enough to be effective. Once things are planted you won't have such good access to the soil again. On the other hand, you can limit the enrichment to only the areas near plants so the rest of the area will be less attractive to weeds. Of course some of those volunteers might be desirable natives, and some ruderal species will thrive in sand. As with most landscaping decisions, there is no one right answer.

Water the plants heavily the day before planting or at least soak them in a bucket a few hours before planting to allow them to become fully turgid. It's best to remove the plants from their pots by sticking your fingers through the drainage holes and pushing the root ball out from the bottom, or by cutting away the pot if it's too root-bound— don't pull it out by the top of the plant.

Your next step depends on the state of your plant and its normal habitat. It's usually best to rinse or shake away the soil (or soilless mixture) before planting. While you don't have to worry about coiling roots, the plants can adjust more quickly with direct access to the native soil. If a perennial is root-bound in the pot and made up of many individual plants or growing nodes, you may want to rinse all the soil away so you can pry the plants apart. Depending on the size of the clump and the type of plant, there are a couple of ways to accomplish this:

- If it's a fairly large plant mass, stick two garden forks into the center of the mass back to back and then pry them apart. This will help to retain the roots that go with each growth nodule.
- If the plant mass is fairly small (one-gallon pot or less) pry the plants apart using two handheld claws, or hold the root-ball in place by pinning it to the ground with a garden fork and then prying the smaller plant nodes from the mass.
- Use a high-pressure nozzle on a hose to squirt the soil away and use the water stream like a knife.
- If the plant is just too entangled to pry apart, cut the root-ball with a straight-bladed shovel into two or four pieces. The advantage to this method is that it's quick, but the disadvantage is that those sections of plant mass are still overcrowded and under stress. These pieces may grow for a while in your landscape, but they are unlikely to be as successful as the separated plant nodes.

Prepare the planting holes so the plants sit at the same level they sat in their pots. Spread the roots out and work soil back into the planting holes so the roots splay out as far as possible. Flood the planting holes and press the soil into place so there are no large air spaces. Build a watering saucer with a ring of soil around the plants so all the water from irrigation or rainfall soaks into the soil. This is especially important if the soil in the surrounding area is sandy and dry.

Unless more than half an inch of rain falls, water your new perennials every day for a week or until they stop wilting during the day. This holds true even if the plant is normally drought tolerant, but not for cacti and bulbs—water them sparingly after the original planting so they don't rot. Add a light covering of pine-needle mulch to the drift area where your perennials are planted to keep down weed growth and keep in moisture.

With perennials, it's not as important to allow for adult growth as it is for trees and shrubs because they can be easily dug up when they become overcrowded; they will create a better environment together, with fewer places for weeds to grow. On the other hand, if you do leave enough space for their adult sizes, you may be saving yourself some ongoing maintenance down the road.

Caring for Perennials

For the first few months after planting perennials, keep the area weeded, and be sure to remulch and irrigate after pulling the weeds. Once your plants start showing new growth, they've begun to acclimatize to their new space, but they will still be vulnerable to being taken over by weeds or wilting during periods of hot or dry weather, so keep an eye on them. After they're established, it's a good idea to weed, add compost, and remulch perennials on an annual or semiannual basis, especially in highly visible locations. For groupings that are not so visible or are in established areas with fewer weeds, you may be able to tend them less frequently.

At the end of the growing season, some tall or rangy herbaceous perennials such as spotted beebalm (*Monarda punctata*) and snow squarestem (*Melanthera nivea*) might look messy and may lean over as they begin the process of dying back to the ground, but those stems also provide seed for birds and places for butterflies, insects, and other critters to spend the winter. Hopefully you knew about this tendency before you planted them in your landscape, so you placed them in

Add stalks trimmed from perennials to your brush pile so overwintering bugs have a chance to complete their life cycles and songbirds can find seeds during the winter.

areas where some untidiness is acceptable. If you do feel the need to trim these plants back to the ground before spring, add the trimmings to a brush pile so you don't kill the critters hiding in the stems and so the birds can still find the seeds.

You can manage ranginess in the spring when stems start growing. Before they get too tall, cut back the stems near the front of the bed severely and then trim back the successive stems so each rank is a little taller. The trimming will delay their blooming cycle, but they'll have a much neater appearance later in the season. To offset the effects of the delayed flowering, leave some plants in other places totally untrimmed so the pollinators can find their nectar sources at the right time of the season.

Should You Deadhead in a Native Landscape?

There is no single correct answer to this question. If those flowering plants are in a visible spot in your landscape, deadheading will make them look neater and most plants will bloom again to fulfill their seasonal agenda of setting seed. Humans and pollinators enjoy the extra flowering cycle, but maybe the seed-eating birds needed that seed for their young or maybe the extra flowering took a toll on the plants. On the other hand, if you're looking for a lower-maintenance yard, dead-heading is another chore when you could just let the plants and all their allies follow their natural cycles. If you're collecting seeds from your landscape, the rule of thumb is to leave at least half the seed heads undisturbed, but if these plants are sowing so many of their seeds that they've become weeds, then collect as much as you can to save on weeding chores the next season. More on collecting seeds in chapter 6.

After several years, some clumping perennials tend to die out from the center, with new sprouts located around the edges. For some plants this is a natural progression, but it may be time to dig it out. This way you can inspect the roots to see if they are healthy—they should be firm and spread widely in the soil. If the roots look good, divide the clump into smaller pieces, fill the hole with compost, and then plant one of the pieces back in the same hole. You may wish to plant the other pieces in pots until they are established before placing them in the landscape.

If the roots are mushy or stunted, that dead spot in the center of your clump is probably a symptom of a greater problem of too much moisture: attacks by root predators, or infestation by a fungal or bacterial disease. Dig it all out and remove it from that location entirely. If there are parts worth saving, rinse away all the soil to flush out soil-borne organisms, and then put the pieces in pots with fresh soil or compost away from the garden. When they start to grow again, place them in new locations. Plant something entirely different in or near the original spot to thwart those pests, whatever they were, like crop rotation in a vegetable garden.

Propagating Perennials

While some herbaceous perennials live for many years, others may last only a few years even if well cared for. When you collect seed, take cuttings, and make divisions, you ensure that you'll have new plants to replace those that die out. A native landscape is never set in stone; it keeps changing. If a sun-loving plant used to thrive in an area, increasing shade might cause it to languish. Be aware of these changes and plant your new perennials in the most appropriate places.

Some perennials bunch and need occasional dividing to keep from self-crowding such as gamma grasses (*Tripsacum* spp.) and swamp sun-flower (*Helianthus angustifolium*), but others send out runners or rhizomes and create new plants at a safe distance so they rarely become overcrowded, such as most goldenrods (*Solidago* spp.) and passion vines (*Passiflora* spp.). New plants formed along the rhizomes are called offsets; these may be transplanted as they are, but you may also wish to pot the offsets to give them a good start before being placed in the landscape.

Annuals

Annuals have a quick life cycle: germinate, grow, flower, and set seed all in a single year. Some annuals may actually live longer than a year in South Florida or when winter is mild, but don't plan for their persistence over the long run. Since their life cycles are so short, it is more important to plant only locally produced seed.

In a low-maintenance landscape, annuals can beautifully fill empty spaces between your widely planted new native trees and shrubs, and each year they'll pop up in new configurations as they reseed themselves. As the trees and shrubs mature and begin to cast more shade, the annuals will begin to die out in the shadier spots. Eventually a mature native landscape can outgrow some of its annuals, except in meadows and other mostly sunny treeless areas, which are by design maintained this way.

Planting annuals

Sowing Seeds

Because of their quick life cycles, most annuals have good seed germination rates, but see the next chapter for more details on seeding. Once they sprout they grow quickly—they have no time to waste. You may even end up with more than one blooming cycle in one year, especially in South Florida. Once you have annuals in your landscape, they'll probably reseed and maintain their populations for years as long as the conditions are favorable. If you want to increase the genetic diversity, you may wish to sow some new native seed into the mix every other year or so. For large seeded areas, see chapter 8 for suggestions on creating and managing meadows.

Starting with Seedlings

Buying seedlings of annuals can give you a head start and allow you to more carefully control their initial placement and spacing. Choose seedlings with good leaf color and healthy-looking roots. If a few seedlings are growing in one pot, carefully separate them and plant singly for the most coverage. If the plants are pot-bound, soak the pot in water and then carefully remove the plants and the root mass by squeezing the pot, pushing the root mass up from the drainage holes, or cutting the pot away. Do not pull on stems or leaves to remove the plants. Seedlings of annuals that are already blooming in the pot are probably not a good choice because as far as the plant is concerned, it has already completed its life cycle and the rigors of transplanting might kill it.

Plant seedlings in appropriate spots in irregularly shaped drifts of one species together for the best statement in the landscape. Weed the planting areas and amend with compost if needed as you plant the seedlings. Water liberally and then apply a thin layer of mulch—only 1 or 2 inches. Irrigate every day for several days, then gradually taper off. It shouldn't take very long for annuals to adjust to your landscape.

Ongoing Care of Annuals

Once annuals are established they won't need much attention from you unless there is a severe drought. You can do some deadheading to extend the blooming cycle, but as discussed for perennials (above), in a natural landscape, it's probably not necessary for most situations. However, since annuals don't last forever, gathering seed is one way you can give the population of an annual some help in perpetuating itself. Remember, a thick layer of mulch will inhibit the growth of new seeds—both weeds and desirable plants.

Propagating Annuals

Collecting seeds is the most often used method of perpetuating annual populations. Most people don't bother taking cuttings of annuals, but it can make sense if you get an early enough start in the season or have a sheltered place where you can hold cuttings through the winter for an early spring planting.

6

Propagation Techniques

If you already have some natives but would like more, you might be able to gather seeds, take cuttings, or divide bunching plants to create more plants. While asexual reproduction (by cuttings and divisions) does not create genetic diversity the way seeds do, it's still an important tool to fill your landscape with native plants inexpensively.

Seeds

Some natives, especially annuals, are abundant reseeders and sprout in the blink of an eye, while others are more recalcitrant. It's important that your seeds are bred from local stock, especially for the fussier plants. In Florida, a good place to start is the Florida Wildflowers Growers Cooperative (www.floridawildflowers.com).

Seed Details

After the sexual union of male and female flower parts, a seed is borne singly or in large groups in some type of fruit or structure. Seeds vary greatly in size, but the seeds of most angiosperm (flowering plants) consist of three parts:

1. Seed coat: protects the contents from drying out and from disease. To some extent it may prevent the seed from being eaten, or if eaten, that it will survive the digestive process intact.
2. Endosperm: the stored food that provides the initial energy for sprouting until the first leaves emerge that can start providing new energy for the new plant through the magical process of

photosynthesis. Some plants, such as those in the bean family, store their energy in fleshy cotyledons (seed leaves) instead of endosperm.

3. Embryo: The immature plant. It consists of one or two cotyledons (if one, it's a monocotyledon or monocot; if two, it's a dicotyledon or dicot); the radicle, which will become the primary root; the hypocotyl, which will become the stem below the cotyledon(s); the epicotyl, which will become the stem above the cotyledon(s); and the plumule, which will become the first true leaves.

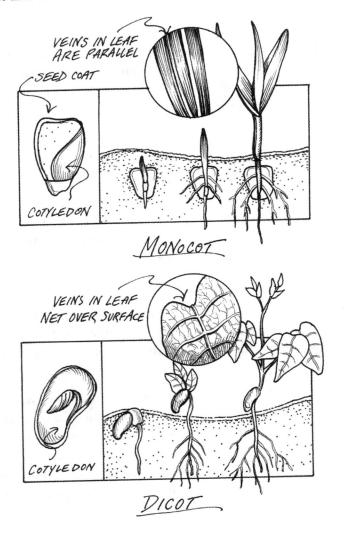

After a seed is formed, some type of dormancy or delay in germination normally occurs until certain conditions are met. Seeds of some plants won't break dormancy until something happens to the seed coat such as heating in a fire or being eaten by a bird. Some seeds may need to be chilled or exposed to light. The dormancy period controls the timing of seed germination to give it the best chance of success by growing when other plants are not, by waiting until there is enough rain, or by waiting until there is enough light.

As gardeners, we know the aggressive reseeders and probably consider many of them to be weeds. If you're making the effort to collect seeds from your landscape, you're most likely collecting from the plants with low seed volume or low germination rates. When you try to grow the more reluctant natives from seed, you'll need to learn about their special requirements to start the process. For instance, saw palmetto (*Serenoa repens*) seeds have a low germination rate and an average time until germination of six months, but if you scarify the seed (nick or abrade the seed coat) or soak it for a day or two before planting, you might increase the germination rate and decrease the waiting time. After germination, you will still have a long-term project because it will take at least three years for a seedling to become established. Do your research before you start collecting seeds to grow. You may decide that it's worth the money to skip this step and purchase established plants to move your native landscaping along at a faster pace. Once you have palmettos and have neighborhood birds eating the seeds, there will be plenty of seedlings in your landscape.

Collecting Seeds

Do not collect seeds, fruits, or plants from public property, including roadsides and parks, or private property without permission. Make sure you know what you are collecting. Take photos of the site and close-ups of the flowers and seed heads for further reference if a question arises later. Carefully document the location and coordinate that with the collected seed and note the conditions. When you're taking the photos, include the site ID and date in at least one of the photos and use that name as a label for the seeds.

Locate sites with a healthy population of your target plant and work to be there at the peak of ripening. Within each area of collection, choose parent plants in varying habitats and ones that are on the opposite sides of the population. Choose the best-looking plants and don't pick seed heads that are touching the ground. Check to make sure the seeds are ripe. It's easy to see if wind-dispersed seeds are ripe—they will be ready to fly away. Grass seed is generally hard when ripe. Seeds borne in fleshy fruits are hidden, but the fruit often turns color when ripe. It may take several visits, because some native plants produce seeds that ripen unevenly on each infructescence or seed head, while others ripen all at once. Make sure there are seeds in the seed heads—the flowers may not have been pollinated, or birds may have eaten the seeds. Collect from no more than half of the population—even on your own property—to save some seeds for birds and insects and for natural distribution.

There are several methods of collecting seeds:

Cutting: Gather all the stems from one or two plants and then lop off the heads into a bag or a container. This is a good method for grasses and other herbaceous plants.

Stripping: Use when the seeds are ready to fall off. Pull along the seed head or stem with your gloved hand to dislodge seeds into a bag or container held beneath.

Hand picking: If the seed is fleshy and within reach, picking works well for causing the least injury to the plant.

Shaking or Beating: For seeds that are out of reach, lay a tarp under the shrub or tree, and then shake or tap the canes or trunks to dislodge the seeds.

Don't mix the seeds of different species, unless you're going to sow the seeds as a mixture directly into your meadow or other mixed-species populations within a few days. If you'll be drying the seeds, bring enough bags or containers into the field to accommodate all the different species you'll be collecting and enough markers or tags to identify the source plants. Be sure the containers and bags are washed and thoroughly dry before using.

Hard seeds such as grass seeds are somewhat tolerant of heat out in the field, but keep fleshy seeds in a cool, shady place while you're out collecting and spread them out to dry as soon as possible so they don't rot.

Drying Seeds for Storage

To ensure optimal quality when storing seeds, it is important to dry them well. You can dry seeds in a paper grocery bag by storing in a cool, dry area. Stir or shake the bag every couple of days so the seeds don't clump. For larger quantities, spread the seeds in a thin layer on a tarp or screen and cover with a screen to keep them from blowing away or from being eaten by birds. Put them in a sunny spot during the day, but not if the temperature is greater than 90 degrees. Bring them inside during cool or moist nights. Be aware that some seedpods explode upon drying as a dispersal method.

After the seeds are dry, remove the other plant parts like stems and flower heads—the chaff. If you have a sieve that will allow seeds through, that may be just the thing, but you can accomplish the task by turning the seed harvest over and over—it's sort of like scrambling eggs. If you have a huge quantity of seeds, you can turn it with a pitch-fork. If the seeds are still not entirely dry or released from the flower heads, continue drying for a few more days and repeat.

Once processed, store the seeds in a cool dry location. If the seeds require stratification (cold treatment), as many temperate plants do, you can accomplish this by simulating a winter soil habitat. Store those seeds with damp medium such as coconut coir or sphagnum moss in a refrigerator (in an opaque container) for a few weeks, move them to a cool place for a week, and then back into the refrigerator for a few more weeks. Time this treatment so that after the second cooling session it will be the perfect time to plant them in the spring.

Sowing Seeds

You can either plant seeds in a controlled environment such as flats or starter pots to give them the best chance for survival or plant them directly in the garden or meadow to provide a more naturalized arrangement. Research whether your seeds germinate quickly or slowly—this way you can determine your timing strategy for the best success.

Whichever strategies you choose, it's important to learn what the seedlings look like so you can distinguish them from other plants. Also as you tend your landscape, you can be on the lookout for desirable seedlings growing wild. You'll eventually learn to recognize the seedlings, but this reference from the Florida Wildflower Foundation will shorten your learning curve for some of Florida's favorite natives: www.flawildflowers.org/resources/pdfs/pdf10/SeedlingImageProject_ Report-Ver2007-96DPI_Images.pdf.

Sowing into the Landscape

Sowing seeds directly into your landscape requires thorough site preparation and good timing; otherwise, the percentage of seeds that germinate and successfully grow to maturity will be quite low. The recommended sowing dates vary by species, the site exposure or other site-specific conditions, and your planting zone and regional climate. In general, you'll sow spring bloomers in the fall and fall bloomers in the spring. Germination rates are generally highest when the air temperatures range from 65 to 90 °F (18–32 °C). See chapter 8 for specifics on site preparation, planting methods, and ongoing care for wildflower meadows.

When sowing seeds in an area smaller than a meadow, such as a bed around some existing natives, kill the weeds by using solarization, smothering them under a deep mulch, or carefully pulling the weeds to minimize disturbing the soil. Use the two-finger method for pulling weeds from a mulched area—press two fingers down on either side of the weed and pull out slowly. Your fingers hold down the mulch or soil crust. Do not use a pre-emergence herbicide such as corn gluten right before sowing your seeds.

- For small seeds: If the species of the seed prefers poor soil, mix the seed with sand, sow thinly on the exposed surface, and then cover with a light dusting of compost. If the species prefers richer soil, lay a quarter inch of compost on the exposed soil, mix the seed with sand, sow thinly, and then dust the area with more compost. For either the poor or rich soil bed, tamp the surface with your hands or feet so the seeds make good contact with the soil, then add a thin pine-needle mulch. You should still be able to see the soil through the mulch. (The pine needles help keep the seeds and soil in place, plus they remind you where the seeded area is located.) Irrigate thoroughly with a fine spray.

The two-finger method of pulling weeds in a mulched area reduces the amount of disturbed soil. Remulch the area to keep out even more weeds.

- For large seeds: Cover the exposed soil with a quarter-inch layer of sand or compost, depending on the needs of the plant species. Create planting holes the right depth for that species and at the recommended distance apart, then put two seeds in each hole. For instance, if you are planting sunflower seeds (*Helianthus* spp.), the holes should be a quarter-inch deep and 10 to 24 inches apart depending on species. Don't plant them in rows like a vegetable garden, but in naturalistic groupings, but still at the recommended distance apart. Pat the surface so the seeds make good contact with the soil, then add a thin pine-needle mulch. Irrigate thoroughly with a fine spray.

Once the seeds germinate, do not let them dry out. This is the critical stage of development. When you do irrigate, use a fine spray or a watering can with fine holes so you don't knock over or injure the seedlings. It's important to water thoroughly so the water soaks into the soil and doesn't just wet the surface—about a quarter of an inch each time. (A 3-gallon watering can will irrigate 2 square yards—3 by 6 feet—to a depth of one-quarter inch.) You want the roots to grow deep into the soil for the best drought tolerance. Once the seedlings grow a set or two of true leaves, start to cut back on the frequency of irrigation, but still water deeply. If you end up with two seeds of the large seeds sprouting from one hole, wait for a few weeks, choose the best one, and then cut the other one off at the ground level or dig up both, separate them, and replant an appropriate distance apart. If you end up with a mass of the tiny seedlings all in one place, either choose the best ones and cut off the rest or dig up the mass and replant them at reasonable distances.

When your seedlings have grown to 6 inches or so, carefully pull the weeds around them, lay in some compost if they need rich soil, and then mulch around them with pine needles, straw, or wood chips. You'll want to baby these plants for a few months during dry periods,

Hire a Nursery to Grow Your Seeds

For better results and less work, you might be able to make a deal with your local native plant nursery to grow the seeds for you. Nursery growers are experts and generally turn out a fine product. The grower will want to see your photos to observe the conditions and confirm the species identification.

The seeds are the least expensive portion of producing a seedling for sale, so expect to pay for these seedlings. If your seeds were collected from plants that are not typically sold in the native plant trade, there may be a good reason why they're not commonly sold. These species may not do well in nursery conditions, or maybe they're too fussy to succeed outside their native environment. So there are not going to be any guarantees. On the other hand your collected seeds may be quite successful and you will have expanded that grower's regular offerings, which would increase the diversity in the area's native landscapes.

but they should soon assimilate into the same lower-care regimen as the rest of your native landscape. This initial care is the investment to produce healthy plants.

Sowing Seeds in a Controlled Environment

When you control the environment for seedling production, you can eliminate many of the dangers found out in the wild jungle of your yard. It usually takes from two to six months to produce a seedling that's ready to plant, depending on the plant species, the time of year the seeds are sown, and whether there is a cold requirement.

In order to avoid problems with soilborne diseases, be sure to pre-wash used pots and flats, rinse them with a weak bleach solution or wipe down with alcohol, and then dry them thoroughly before adding the growing media. Use a sterile media such as coconut coir (a more sustainable and nonacidic substitute for peat moss), vermiculite, or perlite. These sterile media also contain few nutrients, so you'll need to lightly fertilize with a fish or seaweed emulsion or a compost extract. Another option is to create a mixture of one or more of the sterile media with good, finished compost—fifty-fifty is a practical ratio. You'll still use a sterile media for the top inch to reduce airborne mold or fungus infestations. This way the roots of your plants will have access to the nutrients in the compost and be encouraged to grow deeper.

There are several strategies for starting seeds in pots or flats, but whichever method you choose, keep the seedlings close at hand so you can see when they begin to wilt or need other attention. Follow the directions for each seed type regarding whether to presoak and how deep to plant, and make sure that seeds come into good contact with the soil.

The following are two different methods for starting seeds:

1. Plant several seeds in each little pot. When they sprout, save only the two or three best seedlings in the pot, and cut the rest off at the soil line. Continue to grow them in the pots until they are ready to set out in the garden, or separate and pot them up in larger pots as they grow.
2. Sow the seeds thickly into a flat filled with one of the sterile media and keep it damp. The seedlings will be crowded.

After one or two of their first real leaves appear, transplant the seedlings into the starter pots, where they'll have more room to grow. Depending on size and how well they take to transplanting, you could plant them singly or in groups of two or three in each pot. This is a delicate transplant because the seedlings are so small. Handle each one as little as possible and don't squeeze the stem—use the tough cotyledons (seed leaves) or root mass as a handle, or if they're too small to pick up with your fingers, use an old kitchen fork or tweezers. Even though this method adds an extra step, the advantage is that you've eliminated the germination issue because you're dealing only with seeds that have sprouted and have the best growth. This is probably the best way to deal with seeds with low germination rates or ones you've stored for more than a year.

Keep the planted seeds warm and provide good light. Outside light is best, so put them out in the morning sunlight, but if you can, move them into the shade for the afternoon so they don't dry out as quickly. Cover the flat or pots with screening; this provides shade, mitigates heavy rains, and also prevents birds or squirrels from raiding your seeds or uprooting your seedlings. It's best to keep these elevated rather than on the ground to discourage ants.

If you're working inside, set them under and close to white fluorescent bulbs turned on for twelve to sixteen hours a day. If the seedlings become spindly, they need more light. Good air circulation helps prevent fungal problems. Set up a small fan to blow across your seedlings for an hour or two each day. This airflow also helps to build strong stems.

You can water by placing your containers in a pan of water for twenty minutes once a day; don't let your seedling pots or flats sit in water all day. You can also use a soft mist to water from the top. Some people use both methods to ensure good moisture. Be sure to test your watering to make sure the water soaks into the soil. You want to train the roots to grow down, not come to the surface.

A week after they sprout, fertilize the seedlings weekly with diluted compost extract or a gentle organic fertilizer such as highly diluted

Using Containers

When planting in pots or containers, whether for a short-term project like nurturing a seedling until it's large enough to plant or for a more long-term container garden, it's important to provide good drainage for the best growing environment for your plants. Here are some guidelines to provide good drainage:

• A pot needs drainage holes, but you don't want the soil to leak out. You can use a handful of pine needles or leaves in the bottom of the pot to cover the holes. You can also use a circle of weed-barrier cloth or screening cut larger than the diameter of the bottom of the pot. If the weed barrier cloth continues up the sides of the container for a few inches or more, it can deter ants from nesting in the pots.

• Do not use gravel or potshards in the bottom of pots. Despite what we've been told, gravel actually impedes drainage. Water molecules are attracted to each other, as you've seen when it beads up on a waxy leaf, so water will super-saturate the fine soil medium before separating from the rest of the water to jump the gaps in the gravel. Gravel reduces the amount of soil in the pot, which also increases plant stress.

• A tall pot provides better drainage than a short one—important for a long-term planting.

• The soil mixture should contain a lot of compost to keep it loose—at least half by volume. While this may seem counterproductive since compost has good water retention properties, it's important that the soil not cake or harden as it dries out.

• If you intend to grow plants in a container for two months or longer, use compost as a topdressing once a month to rejuvenate soil microbes.

• To keep soil microbes alive, use rain barrel water to irrigate containers or let municipal water sit for a day or two to allow the chlorine to dissipate to some degree. Don't use softened water, which contains salts that are harmful to plants, also avoid fertilizers that are not slow release (granular fertilizer is essentially a salt).

fish or seaweed emulsion. Once they have one or two sets of true leaves, start hardening them off by setting them outside in the vicinity where they will be planted and start to taper off their watering. This way their stems will build up strength and they will acclimate to the sun exposure.

Storing Unused Seeds

If you treat leftover seeds right, you can use them for the next few years to augment populations or start new native areas. Seeds are living organisms in a dormant state; while some seeds may survive for years, others are more fragile. To maintain dormancy, keep seeds in a cool, dark location with low humidity—an opaque container in the refrigerator works well.

Once you are ready to sow saved seeds, you can test their viability by soaking them in water for a few hours. The ones that are still living usually sink to the bottom, while the dead ones will float on the surface. Some people carry the germination test further by actually germinating a batch of test seeds in moistened paper towels. This way you can estimate your likely germination rate and adjust how many seeds to plant. If only half the seeds germinate in the paper towel, then you know to plant twice as many seeds in your pots or out in the field. You'll also gain knowledge about which plants have long-lasting seed. Be sure to take good notes in your garden log.

Asexual Propagation

When you force a cutting to grow roots or divide a bunching plant to produce a new plant, it will be identical to its parent. This type of propagation is often done with plants that possess a certain characteristic such as silvery leaves that may not be true to seed, or with plants that have low or slow seed germination. If you're trying to produce a large number of new plants, it's best to use cuttings or divisions from several individuals to create as much genetic diversity in your landscape as possible. If a tree or shrub is dioecious, with separate male and female specimens, be sure to collect cuttings from both genders or your landscape will be unbalanced. Maples (*Acer* spp.) and hollies (*Ilex* spp.) are examples of dioecious trees.

Propagating with Cuttings

When you use a stem to create a new plant, you need to convince the stem tissue to grow roots. Roots that form on stem tissue are called adventitious roots. Some plants root readily and may even have the beginnings of adventitious roots formed at every node to quickly take advantage of contact with soil. Some plants, including many trees, are more difficult to root and will need the help of a rooting hormone to send a signal to that part of the stem that it is now a root-bearing tissue. A cutting will not develop a root flare like a seed-grown tree. Warning: Some tree cuttings may never develop a full root system, making them somewhat more susceptible to wind damage.

The terminal bud of a stem contains hormones (auxins) that suppress the side shoots from sprouting and also encourage root growth. You've probably noticed the result of this hormone when you cut off a shoot: one or two new shoots will quickly grow from the next nodes that were just buds before. Since those same hormones also help with rooting, your cuttings will be more successful if each one includes a terminal bud.

The other factor to make your cutting percentages higher is to incorporate more than one node or bud in the soil. The nodes are growing areas that contain meristem tissue or undifferentiated cells that would normally become leaves or branches, but those cells can also become roots. These are literally stem cells.

Some plants root readily in water, but water roots have a different structure. When you plant a stem with water roots in the soil, those roots will rot away and the stem must generate all new roots that work in soil. So prerooting in water may actually slow down the process of developing "real" roots and is not usually recommended for woody plants. On the other hand, temporarily holding your stems in water will keep them turgid until you have a chance to process them properly.

General Procedures for Cuttings

Cuttings should generally consist of the current or past season's growth. Avoid stems with flowers or flower buds; if that's not possible, remove them when preparing cuttings. You want the stem to use its energy for

Types of Cuttings

Herbaceous Cuttings

Herbaceous cuttings for a native landscape are typically taken from nonwoody perennials early in the season when they are growing rapidly. Most landscape managers don't bother with cuttings from annuals, but sometimes it makes sense when you need plants quickly to fill in a space. Many herbaceous plants root readily, but some do not.

Softwood Cuttings

Cuttings taken from woody plants early in the growing season will be soft and bendable. This succulent new growth is just beginning to harden (mature) and will have a gradation of leaf size (oldest leaves are large and mature; newest leaves are still small). These soft shoots have a higher probability of rooting than woodier cuttings, but they dry out quickly, so keep them cool and damp.

Semihardwood Cuttings

Partially mature wood of the current season's growth is taken after its flush of growth in the spring. The wood won't bend much and all the leaves are mature. You may have success with semihardwood cuttings for broad-leaved evergreens and some conifers, but deciduous trees and shrubs generally don't do as well.

Hardwood Cuttings

Cuttings taken from dormant, mature stems in late fall or winter with no obvious signs of active growth other than leaf buds are hardwood cuttings. The wood is firm and does not bend easily. Hardwood cuttings are used most often for deciduous shrubs, but you may have some luck with evergreen woody plants.

producing new roots rather than flowers. The stock or parent plant should be young, vigorous, disease-free, and not wilted. Cuttings from lateral shoots often root better than cuttings from terminal shoots, and it's also better for the parent plant. It's unlikely that all your cuttings will survive, so cut twice as many as you need—maybe more if you know the plant is a reluctant rooter.

If possible, harvest cuttings early in the morning, before plants begin their daytime transpiration when they lose water. Keep the cuttings cool and moist in a cold box or refrigerator until the next step.

The terminal parts of the stem are best, but many people have had success dividing a long stem into several cuttings—the ones without a terminal bud will look ugly at first, but you can select a new header as it grows. Use this technique for species that are easier to root, because the shoots without a terminal bud will be missing the natural hormones or auxins that aid in rooting.

Cuttings are generally 5 to 12 inches long, with tree cuttings being on the longer end of the range. Harvest the cuttings with a sharp blade or sharpened garden shears wiped down with alcohol to prevent the spread of fungal or bacterial diseases. Also make sure your gloves are clean. When you harvest cuttings, choose the best examples of the trees or shrubs in the area. Don't take cuttings from plants that look diseased—the last thing you need is for all your cuttings to become infected by disease or infested by pests. After you remove your cutting, take the time to correctly prune the stem on the parent plant back to the next side branch or bud.

When you get back to your work area, carefully prune the leaves from the lower one-third to one-half of the cutting—you do not want to injure the bud or node tissue by carelessly stripping off the leaves. This is the portion of the shoot that will be in the rooting medium; you want the buds or nodes to be in good shape so the meristem tissue can spend its energy on forming new roots, not on healing wounds. Various commercial hormone powders are available, but you can also make a willow tea for a more natural solution. (See box on page 112.)

To prevent possible contamination of the entire supply of rooting hormone, put some in a separate container where you will treat the cuttings. If it's a powder, dip the end of each cutting into the hormone powder until it's coated on all sides, then tap the cuttings to remove excess hormone powder. Make a hole in the sterile rooting medium, carefully place the cutting in the hole so the powder doesn't scrape off, and then press the medium firmly around the shoot so it stands upright. Don't put the leftover hormone back in the original container, but you could sprinkle it on the soil surface.

The rooting medium should be sterile, low in fertility, and well drained to provide sufficient aeration. It should also retain enough moisture so the cuttings don't dry out. Materials commonly used are coarse sand alone, or a mixture of coconut coir, perlite (or vermiculite), and coarse sand in equal volumes.

Most people use nursery flats or liner trays for cuttings because they are easier to cover for a large number of cuttings, but pots may work better for longer cuttings. Insert the cuttings one-third to one-half their

Making and Using Willow Tea

Willows (*Salix* spp.) root so readily that if you just stick a branch in the ground, it is likely to grow. You can extract the natural willow hormone (indolebutyric acid, a specific type of auxin) and use it to aid in the rooting of cuttings. Harvest the young wood that still has green bark—early in the year is best. Cut the shoots into 1-inch pieces, bruise or mash the twigs to extract more of the hormone, place them in a mason jar until half full, fill the jar with boiling water, and then let it sit uncovered overnight. Use your willow water within a few days and refrigerate when not using.

There are two ways to use this on your cuttings:

1. Pour 2 or 3 inches of willow water into smaller jars, put your cuttings in the water like a bouquet, and then let them soak up the water for several hours or overnight before placing them in the rooting medium. It's best not to mix species in these small jars because they could react differently.
2. Arrange the cuttings in the moist rooting medium so they stand up. Use willow water for the first two or three irrigation sessions.

length into the medium. Make sure the cuttings are right side up—if you included the terminal bud, this will be easy to determine. Be sure to allow room for the leaves so they are not blocked from the light. Irrigate after inserting all the cuttings and then cover them with plastic and place in indirect light. Keep the medium moist until the cuttings have rooted—the plastic cover helps, but lifting the cover and misting them on a regular basis keeps the air circulating. Some people place the flats out in the morning sun to keep the cuttings from turning pale, but if you're rooting dormant stock during the winter, skip this step.

Rooting time varies with the type of cutting, the species being rooted, and environmental conditions. Broadleaf plants usually root faster than conifers. If your cuttings are started in late fall or early winter, they may be left in the rooting medium until spring. Transfer your newly rooted cuttings to pots or into a shaded holding bed so you can

Pinching the flowers off these dune sunflower (*Helianthus debilis*) cuttings will direct their energy into creating more roots.

continue to baby them and let them gain more strength. While this step adds a few months to the process, those larger plants with stronger roots will have a much better chance of survival. The larger plants will also have more impact in your landscape; if they are visible, they are less likely to be walked on or pulled up with the weeds. Of course, you will have weeded the area before you plant them and put down good mulch around them, but rampant weeds can move in quickly.

Layering

Layering is a variation on rooting from cuttings, but the stem is not separated from the parent plant until roots are formed. Simple and compound layering involve branches coming in contact with the soil, while air layering is done without soil contact. For hard-to-root species, layering may be the best alternative because the shoot is not removed from the parent plant until after the roots have formed. Layering has two main advantages over cuttings:

1. Once the branch is in contact with the soil or rooting medium, you do not need to closely monitor it—plastic tents and misting are not necessary, although keeping the soil moist, if it's really dry, will help speed the process.
2. The branch continues to be supported by the parent plant, so even if it takes a long time to generate roots, it's not at risk of dying. With cuttings, when you separate the twig from the parent plant, it's a race to see whether roots form before the twig dies.

Soil Layering

Use soil layering where branches of the tree or shrub can be bent down to the ground or to a pot. You can bury a stem in several places to produce several new plants. Be sure to keep track of the branch's direction away from the parent plant. The root end should be on the side toward the parent plant, while the stem or top of the plant should be on the side toward the branch tip. This is called compound layering.

Air Layering

Air layering is a bit tricky and more time-consuming than using cuttings. Use it for hard-to-root woody plants lacking branches that could

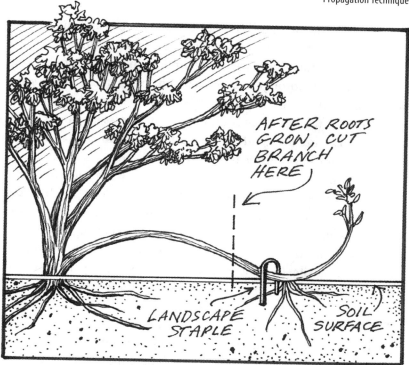

SOIL LAYERING

For hard-to-root trees or shrubs, you can force a branch to root by touching it to the soil. Since it's still attached to the parent plant, it has a better chance of survival even if it takes a long time to form new roots. When you make a cutting, it needs to produce roots quickly before it dies. In this case the branch will not die since it's still attached to the mother plant. After you trim off the new rooted plant, be sure to prune the branch stub back to the parent plant.

make contact with the soil. It's best to make air layers in the spring on shoots produced during the previous season, or in midsummer on mature shoots from the current season's growth. Choose stems that are pencil sized about 10 to 24 inches from the terminal bud. Find a node or bud on the branch and locate your air layering below the node. If there is bark, use a sharp knife to peel off about a 2-inch-wide circle all around the stem just below the node. If there is no bark, make a two inch-long slice at a shallow angle toward the terminal bud and hold the gap open by inserting a twig or piece of toothpick. Slice open the bottom end of a clear plastic sandwich bag and slide it over the branch to below the wound. Sprinkle rooting hormone powder on the exposed cambium layer (or paint it with willow water), wrap with a handful of thoroughly dampened sphagnum moss, and slide the plastic bag up the twig so the bottom is below the wound, the moss in inside, and the top of the bag is above the wound. Use long twist ties or duct tape to secure both ends of the plastic bag so no moss is hanging out and no air can get inside the package.

The clear plastic allows you to see when roots are formed, but some people also cover it with aluminum foil so it doesn't get too hot. Depending on species and time of year, it could take five to ten weeks before enough roots have formed to support the cutting. When you are satisfied with the root mass, cut off the twig below the bottom of the air layering site. Complete the pruning job so the parent plant is not left with ugly stubs. Treat the same as any other cutting.

Division

One of the most important methods for propagating plants is crown division. Herbaceous plants such as bunching grasses are good candidates. The rule of thumb: Plants that bloom in spring and early summer should be divided in late summer or fall, and those that bloom in summer and fall should be divided in early spring before new growth begins.

For a crown division, locate the outer edges of the root ball by carefully digging a shallow trench on the outer perimeter of the foliage to locate which direction the roots are growing and how big the root system really is in comparison to the plant. Use one or two garden forks, rather than a shovel, to pry and lift a large intact root ball from the site. The garden forks do less damage to the roots that spread out from the crown. Rinse the soil from the root-ball to reveal the structure of the roots. For the best results choose individual growing nodes or eyes from the outer edges of the clump and separate them out with their roots to make new plant starts. The eyes will be more obvious in the spring when they are getting ready to sprout. You can leave several together if a larger clump is desired. For your best chance of success in dividing large old crowns, discard the older center portions and replant the young, more vigorous shoots that have developed around the edges of the clump.

If the crown is so tightly packed that pulling out single shoots is too difficult to do by hand, you can split the clump up with a shovel or machete. These gross divisions do make smaller plant colonies, but each one is still overcrowded, so cut a large crown into six or more pieces and cut away older parts.

You could replant the divisions directly back into the landscape or plant them in holding pots until they start to grow. Treat like any other transplant.

Shovel-Pruning Shrubs

Quite a number of native shrubs produce many canes as they mature. If you have a well-established shrub or shrub thicket with lots of canes that may be getting too large for its space, you can shovel-prune some of those extra suckers and plant them elsewhere. This really isn't the

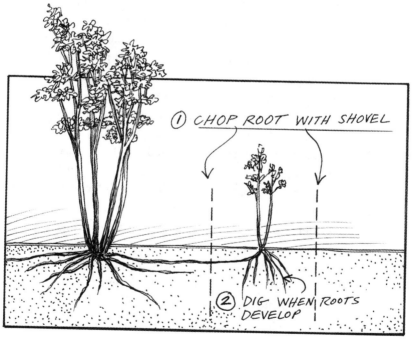

① CHOP ROOT WITH SHOVEL

② DIG WHEN ROOTS DEVELOP

SHOVEL PRUNING

You can reduce the size of a tree or shrub thicket with shovel pruning. A month or more before transplanting a root sprout, chop its roots with a shovel all around the sprout. This gives the sprout time to produce its own roots before the transplant.

same as dividing an herbaceous perennial because you will be leaving the majority of the shrub in place.

First, choose one or two outlying canes—the farther from the parent plant, the better. If possible, several weeks before transplanting, root-prune around the canes.

Irrigate the whole plant thoroughly the day before the shovel pruning, or wait until just after a half-inch or more of rain has fallen. Dig along the line of your root pruning, but this time dig a little deeper than the shovel depth and begin to pry out the canes from the soil. After that, find the underground stem that attaches them to the parent plant and cut it cleanly with a lopper as close to the parent plant as reasonable. Using a lopper instead of a shovel to cut the underground root protects the parent plant from undue downward force and possible root damage. You'll want as much of the underground stem as possible because it is root tissue that will help the newly separated cane generate new roots and better adjust to its new space.

After digging out the canes, take care of the parent plant. Fill the hole with water, add soil, making sure to tamp it in place to fill the air pockets, and then mulch the soil. Depending on the distance, the parent plant may need some extra irrigation too.

If there is a good root mass under the removed shoot, you can plant it directly in the landscape and treat it the same as any transplant, but with an extended irrigation schedule. If there are not a lot of roots, plant it in a pot or holding area and keep it moist. It won't need rooting hormones because it already has root-generating tissue. When your shoot shows new growth, scale back the constant moisture to harden it off for a month or two before planting it in your landscape.

When you remove part of a shrub, the shape of the offshoot is likely to be skewed in one direction, and it probably won't begin to look good until it puts out new canes or branches. For shrubs, when the new plant has acclimated itself to its new location and the new canes are large enough, you may wish to trim back the original cane to a compatible size. Even though this process may take a couple of years, shovel-pruning may be the quickest way to generate a full-grown shrub that's derived from your own stock.

Tree Root Suckers

If a tree produces a root sucker at least a few feet away from the parent tree, you may be able to transplant it. Gently dig around the surface root from the parent plant to check its size. If the root is an inch or less in diameter, your chances of success are pretty good and pruning away such a small root will not harm the parent tree. Use a lopper to cut the surface root four to eight inches on either side of the sucker's upright stem. If possible leave the sucker in place for several weeks after the cut has been made. This is a special form of root pruning. If the tree root is several inches thick, the sucker will probably not be transplantable, but if the sucker is from a desirable tree, you may be able to use it as a cutting.

If you're lucky, there will be a nice root mass under the sucker growing into the soil. Dig out as much of this root mass as you can, plant the sucker in your landscape, and then treat it like any other transplanted tree. If there is little or no root mass under the sucker, plant it in a holding area or large pot in the shade and keep it moist at all times, take extra care of it, and see if it will generate roots. You do not need rooting hormone because the sucker already has its root tissue—the attached surface root. When the sucker starts to produce new growth, it has probably developed some roots. When this happens, taper off the constant moisture routine to harden it to the real world; after a few additional weeks of extra care, it will be ready to plant in the landscape.

If trees and shrubs are producing suckers are in a wilder portion of your native landscaping, you may want to just allow them to grow into a thicket. Isn't one of your goals to produce a native ecosystem that will reduce your maintenance work? If so, let them grow.

7

Minding Your Edges

Unless you're restoring an actual wildland, the edges of the native plant habitat will interface with lawns, paths, patios, sidewalks, and other human spaces. Often a tidy edge along an area planted with natives will keep it looking more like a planned landscape than a weedy mess in the eyes of the neighbors. Your landscape may have a number of edges, or ecotones, and each type will have a different maintenance scheme.

This chapter covers the maintenance of these edges, but keep in mind that one of the most important goals in your task of minimizing landscape maintenance chores is to reduce the total number of edge-feet, a linear measure of the edges between two different ecosystems in your landscape. As discussed in chapters 2 and 9, it's usually best to plant your natives in compatible groupings that emulate what Mother Nature would do in your region. Several good arguments can be made for this arrangement, but the most significant for this chapter is that groupings have fewer edge-feet to maintain than an equal number of singly planted specimens.

Edges of Lawns

Some people who strive for a more native landscape will get rid of their turfgrass lawn in one dramatic removal, but others reduce their lawn areas a little at a time until finally left with only patches of lawn as needed for use as outdoor venues; the lawns that are left can be more sustainably managed, without using poisons. See chapter 8 for more details on "freedom lawns."

Ecotones

Have you ever noticed that at the edge of a forest, a thick tangle of vegetation extends from the ground to the canopy in the tops of the trees, consisting of low-hanging branches, vines, understory trees, shrubs, and various herbaceous plants all clamoring for maximum light? But when you break through that wall of vegetation, into the darker forest, it's suddenly easy to walk. That transition between two ecosystems is an example of an ecotone, and the ecotone between forest and open landscape is one of the most dramatic. Normally, an ecotone is host to a wider variety of plant and animal species than either of the neighboring ecosystems, and it often plays an important role in providing good wildlife habitat.

As you reduce the size of your lawn, you'll want to create gentle curves at the edges to provide a boundary that's easy to mow and maintain. This way a mower can make one sweep of the edge and without having to go back and forth around a sharp corner or leaving clumps of uncut grass that will need to be trimmed later. It's a good idea to create obvious edges for hired mowers or groundskeepers who may mistake a native ground cover for a weed that needs to be mowed along with the grass.

Avoid vertical hardscape features next to lawns. For instance, if you have raised beds, an elevated patio, or the foundation of a building that abuts the lawn, build a buffer area at the same elevation as the lawn so the mower can cut the grass at the edge along with all the rest. This reduces the maintenance because you won't need to use a string trimmer to cut the grass next to those vertical walls. If the space next to that vertical wall is a high-traffic area, consider creating a path covered with a thick layer of mulch such as wood chips, or you could install stone or concrete pavers a little above soil level so the mower's wheels can roll on the pavers.

If the edge of the lawn is mulched with wood chips, it's best to keep it tamped down so loose chips don't get sucked up into the lawn mower.

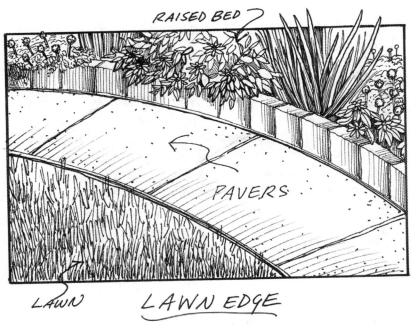

RAISED BED

PAVERS

LAWN   LAWN EDGE

Avoid vertical edges next to a mowed area. Pavers provide a clean edge without the need for extra trimming.

You can maintain a relatively clean lawn edge with an annual spade cut. Some people find it's easier to maintain a clean edge by using an edging strip. There are several types, but for the lowest maintenance, use only those that are almost flush with the lawn so the lawn mower can roll over them to trim the edge of the turf. The following are some strategies for managing the edges of lawns.

Spade-Cut Edges

Using a flat spade with a straight cutting edge, dig a narrow trench between the lawn and the planting areas and toss the soil into the planting area. This trench keeps the turf out of the planting bed and the weeds out of the lawn, but before you dig away too much of the soil, make sure the lawn mower wheels won't get stuck in the trench. It's a good idea to fill in the trench with clean wood chips or accommodate the mower wheels on the bed side of the trench. Over time, both the turfgrass and the plants in the beds will grow toward the edge and begin to cover it over.

An annual trip around the edges of a lawn is an opportunity to reduce the size of the lawn and increase the size of the native areas. Fall is a good time to do this because you can then use fallen leaves to mulch the edges of the beds.

Ongoing maintenance will include a yearly trip around the edge, or if you're lucky, every other year. On subsequent trips around the edge, first clear away the old wood chips by raking them into the adjacent bed, pull the encroaching weeds and creeping turfgrass, and then refresh the trench. If you keep the spade's cutting blade sharp, it will make your job easier. Each edging trip is also an opportunity to remove more lawn to make more room for the natives growing in adjacent beds or to create significant new extensions to the natural landscaping.

Edges with a Strip Barrier

When you place a physical barrier between the lawn and the bed, it blocks underground roots (rhizomes) and surface runners (stolons) from both sides. Normally, the top of the barrier is just above the soil surface but well below the lawn mower blades. Strip barriers can be plastic or metal. Plastic is less expensive, more pliable, and easier to install. Metal edging comes in steel or aluminum and lasts longer but is less pliable. Also, sharp metal edges can sometimes become a cutting hazard.

After a few years, the strip barrier may sink out of sight as the lawn builds up on one side and the garden bed on the other. At this point you'll need to pull it out and reinstall it at the new proper height, and again, maybe this is also a perfect opportunity to give the plants in the bed more room by removing more of the lawn.

Using Landscape Timbers or Logs

Logs and timbers provide a rustic edging, but to avoid the vertical maintenance problem, create a mulched mowing strip on the lawn side. If you have trees taken down as part of your initial plan, use the trunks as edging. After some years, depending on the original size, they will need to be replaced after they decompose. Logs will further benefit the yard as they provide habitat to wildlife as they rot, so even if you don't wish to use them as edging, lay them on the ground back in a wooded area or as borders for a woodland path.

Edging with Masonry

Masonry edging includes concrete, brick, or stone and is probably the longest lasting, but it is more expensive. Stone and brick are attractive and may coordinate well with existing hardscape used in the landscaping or the exterior of your home. It's best to lay it flat at just above lawn level so it's easy to mow over. Concrete pavers are less expensive and come in a wide selection of shapes and styles—some interlock to provide a more stable edge.

These pavers are durable and will last for many years, but they are not maintenance-free. Ongoing maintenance includes pulling weeds and grass from the cracks between pavers. If your soil is sandy and loose or if the turf of the lawn and the mulch in the garden beds build up, you will need to reset the blocks every few years.

An additional method for using concrete is to dig out an edging trench with a flat-bladed shovel, as described above, and then fill it with a concrete mixture. The poured concrete becomes a solid barrier between the lawn and the garden, and the top forms a flat area for the lawn mower wheels. Purchase a premixed concrete product, mix with water in a tub (if you add small pebbles to the mixture, it will go further), and then shovel it into your predug trench. If you'd like to have the concrete extend above the soil and turf level by an inch or so, you'll need to find a way to contain the amorphous mixture until it sets. The advantages of this method are that it's relatively inexpensive, it will fit your landscape no matter how it's configured, and there are no cracks for roots or runners to wiggle through. The big disadvantage is that you won't be able to rearrange the bed or the lawn without removing it with a pickaxe. In effect your landscape will be carved in stone.

Whatever method you choose to edge the lawn, sooner or later the grass will grow into the nonlawn areas, and the meadow or other natural area plants may overgrow the edge of the turf. These edges will need to be trimmed and weeded—the frequency depends on the plants on the other side of the ecotone, your tolerance for plant creep, the season, and the situation in your landscape. Of course, as the natives grow to overhang the edge of the lawn, you will probably want to move the lawn back instead of trimming the native plants. In many cases the edges of lawns create the most visible maintenance chore, so spend some time thinking about how to lessen your workload.

One other item to think about as you remove the outermost edges of the lawn is that sprinkler heads formerly at the edge of the lawn will now be in the midst of more natural areas. Even though you may be reducing the use of your irrigation system as part of your transformation to a more native landscape, you may still want it to function. Replace the mowable, in-ground pop-up sprinkler heads with rotating heads

Conservation Areas

If your property abuts an open area, whether a park owned by the community, county, or state, or a conservation area owned by the local water management district, use native plants growing in that conservation land as a guideline for your own landscape. You cannot edit that land by mowing, cleaning out fallen wood, pruning back woody plants, removing vines, or planting anything on that land without specific permission to do so. The best strategy is to embrace that open land as good habitat and try to expand that feeling into your property. But if you'd like a neater border or a barrier to deer or other large animals, you can plant a native hedgerow on your side of the property line to screen out the wildness.

This sprinkler head has been raised on a pipe extension from its original configuration of flush with the lawn. The sprayer is higher than the ferns in this wooded edge bed, but now a volunteer magnolia, a sweet gum, and some oaks are growing too close and will have to be removed or transplanted.

installed on a riser (pipe extension) to give them some height so the spray is effective. Your maintenance will be to keep the vegetation in front of the head relatively short and to remove trees that sprout too close to the head.

Edges of Wooded Areas

Few ecotones are as dramatic as the one between an established forest and a meadow or lawn. If you're fortunate enough to have a wooded area on your property already, you may want to modify this edge to reduce the maintenance needed to keep the jungle from taking over the space you've reserved for human activities. Your initial treatment will vary depending on several factors:

- distance from buildings, driveways, or high-use areas;
- presence of invasive plants—many invasives are vines and understory trees or shrubs;
- direction the edge is facing—a north-facing edge will be shady all the time, while a south- or west-facing edge will be sunny and growth will be more rambunctious;
- the ecosystem next to the trees—in an urban/suburban landscape, it's likely to be a lawn;
- presence of strangling vines, even if they are natives;
- species of canopy trees, understory trees, and shrubs.

If the edge of a wooded area, which includes many tall trees with large overhanging branches, is within 20 or 30 feet of your house, it's probably best to work with an arborist to trim back overhanging branches or even remove some of the closest trees if they are endangering the structure. For fire-prone areas near wildlands, a 30-foot cleared green space is recommended as a minimum.

The edge of a paved driveway may provide a solid barrier, but overhanging branches and tree suckers will need trimming to prevent damage to vehicles. When you're deciding which trees to retain in your landscape, keep in mind that growing tree roots (except for palms) may also crack or dislodge the driveway's pavement. Installing a transition area of low-growing shrubs and ground covers can help alleviate these problems.

If the wooded area is full of invasive plants, these should be first to go, before any pruning of edge trees or planting of natives takes place. Invasives are opportunists, and the ecotone at the edge of a wooded area often provides the opening they need to get a foothold in your landscape. They could be vines, trees, shrubs, or herbaceous plants, so be sure you know what you have before you proceed.

You'll need to make decisions on which trees to trim back and which to encourage. For the large trees, you'll work with an arborist as discussed above, but for the smaller trees in the understory, either saplings of full-size trees or true understory species, you can probably handle the trimming yourself. When making the decisions about what

The edge of a wooded area will have a network of surface roots that need to be accommodated. Here, the edge of a lawn is pulled away from these roots, because in the contest for water, the tree roots will always win.

to keep and what to trim back or remove, as discussed in chapter 2, you should encourage the more desirable trees and shrubs by pruning back the more common trees or their branches to make room for the less common species. If space allows, leave the trimmings of noninvasive plants in a brush pile in the wooded area.

In urban/suburban landscapes, it's often the lawn that abuts the trees. This is not conducive to a healthy lawn, and it's not good for the trees, either. Most tree roots are just under the surface, and in a battle for water and nutrients, the trees will win. On the other hand, lawn-care practices can expose these surface roots, making them vulnerable to damage. It's best to remove at least 10 feet of the turf from the forest edge and replace it with ground covers or low-growing shrubs nearest the new lawn edge and tall shrubs near the trees. If the edge faces north and is shady all the time, maybe plant a spreading fern such as netted chain fern (*Woodwardia areolata*) and some shade-tolerant shrubs like gallberry (*Ilex glabra*) and beautyberry (*Callicarpa americana*). If the edge faces south or southwest and is sunny most of the time, plant some powderpuff (*Mimosa strigillosa*) as a ground cover with some coontie (*Zamia integrifolia*) as a low shrub with maybe some of the native blueberries (*Vaccinium* spp.) as a taller shrub. Be sure to mulch and create a good edge of the lawn for easy mowing, as discussed above.

If the forest's edge has been in place and untended for a number of years, it's likely that a curtain of vines and low-hanging branches have completely covered the edge. This wall of vegetation is important habitat for birds and other wildlife, so unless the vines are invasive, leave as many of them in place as possible. If the jungle look is too wild

If you just cut off a tree or shrub in the edging area, it will grow back with more vigor each time, so it's probably worth the extra effort to dig it out to reduce future trimmings. This tree was cut back several times and developed a swollen root as a result.

for you or your neighbors, you could open up the edge of the forest in the most visible or high-use areas and leave the rest of the vegetation intact. If the vines have totally covered the trees right up to the canopy, removing them will not be easy and will most likely need to be done in several stages. See chapter 4 for suggestions on removing vines.

In most cases, after the initial treatment, ongoing maintenance will consist of a combination of pruning and weeding in the low-growing edge plantings. If you have small trees growing in this area, it may seem easiest to just chop them off with pruners or a lopper. In the long run, though, if you leave the roots in place, those little trees will grow back with a vengeance because of their established root systems. You

Edge Feathering

Often recommended for large landowners where land used for growing crops or grazing animals abuts a wooded tract, edge feathering increases habitat diversity to encourage pollinators and other wildlife. This process removes the straight or even semi-straight lines along the forest and replaces them with a broad undulating edges weaving in and out with pockets of dense thickets offset by more open meadow areas. Many wildlife species depend on dense shrubby areas for cover and the higher diversity of plants for food. In effect, maintaining the edge feathering slows the natural succession toward a climax forest of tall trees with little understory.

If your suburban development was carved into a forested area, many of the lawns around the houses probably abruptly merge to mature trees in the remnant forest. If there is room in your landscape, feather the edge to create a transition zone of shrubs, vines, and herbaceous vegetation between the wooded area and the rest of the landscape. In addition, this type of transition area may greatly reduce the need for pruning and other ongoing maintenance in the long run. Even if your property is small, you can construct wildlife habitat somewhere on your lot. To be of the most value for wildlife, this area should not include much human use and by all means keep out the cats and dogs, especially the cats.

may find it's worth the time and effort to dig out the roots to reduce your future maintenance chores.

If you plan for this, maybe once every three years will suffice. In many cases the trip around the edges of the lawn will need to be performed on a more regular basis depending on the situation. You could divide the job into three equal parts, so you're tackling only one-third of the edge maintenance over the course of a few weeks. If you hire outside help to accomplish this job, having it all done at once will be the most efficient and the least expensive.

Eventually your newly planted groves or wooded areas will also become more dramatic as the trees and shrubs fill in. Your landscape plan to accommodate the adult sizes of the trees and shrubs and the building of planned transition zones filled with low-growing shrubs, ground covers, or other perennials should minimize ongoing maintenance compared to an abrupt forest edge.

Fences

Fences can complicate a low-maintenance landscaping scheme, especially if they abut a lawn. You can use a number of strategies to lower the ongoing maintenance chores along fences, but first you need to figure out the role the fence is to play—privacy, keeping animals in or out, or just providing a backdrop to your landscape. If you have a large property, you may even want to create a fencerow 20 feet wide, with or without an actual fence, with a combination of trees, shrubs and grasses to prevent erosion and create good habitat. See chapter 9 for more details on how to accomplish this. Just a reminder here if you live in a fire-prone area: fences made of, or covered with, flammable material (including plants) should not attach to buildings—they can act as a fuse or wick that provides fuel and leads the fire right to your house.

Fences without Climbing or Tall Vegetation

To keep a fence cleared of weeds and vines, the most common maintenance methods are to use a string trimmer every time the lawn is mowed or to spray herbicide along the fence line one or two times each year. Neither of these methods is especially efficient from a maintenance point of view, and the dead area along the base of the fence as a result of herbicide use is unattractive and damaging to the ecosystem. If you need to keep the fence clear for some reason, an alternative is to install interlocking pavers under the fence so a mower can ride on the pavers to mow right up to the edge without extra machinery or herbicides. A thick layer of mulch could also work to lessen the weeds, but it would still need to be refreshed on a regular basis. One thing to be aware of is that some of the plants that grow next to a fence are desirable berry-producing shrubs and trees—they will have been planted with a dollop of fertilizer by birds perching on the fence. You may want to transplant these wildlife-supporting plants to roomier locations.

Maybe a better way to handle a fence line is to plant or encourage bunching grasses such as hairawn muhly grass (*Muhlenbergia capillaris*) along the base that can crowd out most of the weeds. If you also apply a pre-emergence herbicide such as corn gluten as well as mulch, the need for weeding between those grasses will be lessened, but not eliminated.

Fences Next to Gardens or Native Areas

Since fences often demarcate the edges of properties, it's common that they serve as a backdrop for gardens—native or otherwise. If the garden or native area is more than a couple of feet wide, then it's probably a good idea to build in a path next to the fence to provide easy access to both the fence and the back side of the garden. Use mulch or pavers to line the path to reduce the weeds. You can trim back vines that may be growing on the fence or tend to other fence maintenance chores such as washing, staining, or painting.

If the fence is open at the bottom, extend the path mulch or pavers under the fence so anyone maintaining the other side also has a clean line. If the other side of the fence is a right-of-way, there may be rules that dictate what is allowed on that side of the fence, so be aware of regulations before you start a project like planting grasses or vines to cover the fence.

Fences with Climbing Vegetation

Many native gardeners allow and/or plant vines to grow and sprawl on and over their fences. A mixture of vine species works best for good habitat values and a year-round supply of nectar for butterflies, hummingbirds, and other pollinators. A variety of vines will also be attractive to you.

Most people find that trimming the vines back before the spring growth works best to keep them looking fairly neat. Of course, you wouldn't trim the native yellow jessamine (*Gelsemium sempervirens*) in the winter, because that's its blooming period. You'll need to find a time that works for your situation. Some vines like the native passionflower (*Passiflora incarnata*), will die back each year (except in frost-free zones) and you never know where they will pop up in the spring—maybe many yards away from the original planting spot. If they sprout in an inconvenient spot, dig them up as soon as you see them and plant them where you need to see more butterflies—passionflower is the larval food for both gulf fritillaries, Julias, and zebra longwings, so you can never have too many.

In most cases the vines will stay on the fence and continue to grow over each other, but they may also start climbing nearby vegetation, especially trees. You can remove the errant vines, but maybe they provide extra privacy or cover. Native vines such as catbrier (*Smilax* spp.) and poison ivy (*Toxicodendron radicans*) may volunteer in your mix; if these are unwelcome in your fence flora, they will need to be removed—the sooner you get to them, the better. Hand pulling and digging is probably the best way to avoid damaging the other plants, but you may also decide to tease these interlopers out of the tangle of vines, lay them on the ground or a tarp, and paint them with herbicide. This is why you need to monitor the vegetation annually, so you can weed out the offending vines quickly. On the other hand, both poison ivy and catbrier provide berries for birds and they tend to look good through most of the year, so maybe you can keep some in out-of-the-way sections of the fence. More on fencerows in chapter 9.

Edges of Wet Areas

Whether your wet area is a shoreline or a seasonal pond, maintaining a buffer zone of natural vegetation on the landward side of the water is an effective way of protecting water quality, coastal habitat, and shoreline stability. These buffer gardens or natural areas next to a shoreline can protect the waterway from nutrient runoff, blowing trash, and organic waste such as leaves and lawn clippings. Remove as much turfgrass from the waterfront area as possible for your situation. The plants you choose for this area should be low-care and mostly native woody plants and perennials suited for the level of moisture and salinity. As usual, observe what grows naturally in areas similar to your site. If existing vegetation (other than turfgrass or invasives) is doing well, let it stay. Any buffer is good, but 30 feet or more is recommended for the best treatment along a coastal shoreline; a more modest buffer can work well for a pond.

Build pathways to upland areas adjacent to the shoreline to provide access for turtles and amphibians. It's best not to mulch areas near the water's edge because you don't want any mulch to wash into the water—it becomes yet another nutrient overload.

For easy mowing, build a good clean edge if the upland side of the buffer interfaces with a lawn, but if the next habitat is a meadow or a wooded area, a more amorphous edge is best. See more on gardening around moist spots in chapter 10.

8

Managing Freedom Lawns, Lawn Replacements, and Meadows

Our country has been in love with lawns as a status symbol since the middle of the last century, but back in the 1950s the sizes of suburban lawns were controlled because they were mowed with hand mowers. Now our civilization has "advanced" the lawn-care culture so that millions of acres of monocultural turfgrass lawns are mowed, trimmed, and edged weekly with power tools, over-irrigated, and then treated with herbicides, insecticides, fungicides, weed and feed, and too much fertilizer. Many people hire contractors to manage all this acreage, so lawns have become an expensive and toxic carpet.

As a result of this assault on the environment, we have polluted our rivers so that many turn green each summer. We have overused our dwindling water supplies. Pest bugs and weeds have become resistant to our poisons. We are contributing to air and noise pollution. And even after all that, when the lawns fail, homeowners, communities, and municipalities pay top dollar to resod the whole lawn and start the cycle all over again. Finally, some people are beginning to understand the expense, unsustainability, and futility of this type of lawn-care regimen.

Sustainable Lawns

So how can you climb off the high-maintenance lawn-care regimen and still have some lawn left for the kids or as a carpet for outside rooms? Stop all the amendments and all the poisons, but continue to mow. Since the soil ecosystem is likely to have been ruined by the harsh high-maintenance regimen, apply compost or other organic slow-release amendments only once a year at the beginning of the turfgrass growing season. In Florida, apply it in the spring just as the grass is beginning to grow for the season and well before the summer wet season, which starts in June—never in the fall when it's going into dormancy for the winter. Build better edges, as described in chapter 7, for easier mowing and to reduce the use of peripheral equipment. Reduce the irrigation frequency so you water deeply and only when needed. If half an inch of rain falls in a week, do not irrigate at all. The turfgrass will probably react by slowing down its growth, which also saves on mowing. Some initial bug attacks will probably occur, and some other plants will come in to fill in the spaces, but don't worry about them; just mow everything.

Remove the heavy leaf cover in the fall by raking or mowing. Stop mowing in the winter, because if you're not forcing the grass with winter grass seed and year-round stimulants, it will become dormant. If you reduce your lawn to just the needed areas, it may be small enough that a manual push reel mower can easily accomplish the mowing tasks—just like the old days, except that today's manual mowers work better than your grandfather's.

It will take at least a full year for the poison and synthetic nutrient residues to subside to the point that your lawn will begin hosting enough alternative plants to be as green as it was before. In the long run some of the turfgrass will survive, but because it will be mixed with a good variety of other plants, you won't be fighting Mother Nature's abhorrence of monocultures. Your maintenance regimen just became a lot less expensive—if it's green, mow it. Plus, you will be doing your part to prevent pollution and water shortages.

**"Freedom lawns"—free from synthetic fertilizers
and free from all types of pesticides.**

Replacing Lawn

You can remove unneeded lawn all at once or chunk by chunk. Replacing lawn should be addressed as part of your overall landscape plan. Several lawn alternatives should be considered, including any combination of low-growing ground covers, meadows, ponds, or—the obvious choice since you're reading this book—native plant areas that mimic the habitat that might have existed in your location 500 years ago.

Lawn Substitutes

If you need something that resembles a lawn but may not need to withstand high foot traffic, there are some ground covers that may work for your situation. The best lawn substitute ground covers are native evergreen species that grow so thickly that they keep out the weeds, but you'll probably find that the plants that meet these criteria will also need to be edged regularly to keep them from spreading across your whole landscape. You may decide to use a few different ground covers so you have some that work well in the hot sun and others for shady or damp spots in your yard.

The best initial maintenance for low-growing ground covers (less than 5 inches tall) is a combination of semiannual mowing (at the highest setting on the mower) and hand-weeding. After a few years, when the ground covers become thick enough to outcompete the tall weeds, you'll only need to mow once in late winter to discourage the weeds and tree seedlings. Some examples of low-growing ground covers are powderpuff (*Mimosa strigillosa*), turkey tangle fogfruit (*Phyla nodiflora*), blue-eyed grass (*Sisyrinchium angustifolium*), railroad vine (*Ipomoea pes-caprae* subsp. *brasiliensis*), dune sunflower (*Helianthus debilis*), and Carolina jessamine (*Gelsemium sempervirens*), but the jessamine tends to climb anything vertical in the area.

For plants that are somewhat taller, say 6 to 18 inches, the mowing regimen will not work well. You can use a combination of hand-weeding and a weed-whacker or string trimmer held high enough to avoid damaging the plants you're trying to encourage. (You don't set the height of a string trimmer or weed whacker, you simply hold it higher.) Again, you'll need to go through the area more often in the first few years during the establishment phase, but later you may find that one editing session in late winter is adequate to keep out the trees and keep the area looking neat enough. Some natives that fall into this category are coontie (*Zamia integrifolia*), gopher apple (*Licania michauxii*), shiny blueberry (*Vaccinium myrsinites*), Adam's needle (*Yucca filamentosa*), and various bunching grasses. While these plants are a great substitute or replacement for turfgrass in lawns, using them is more like creating a meadow or a shrub layer than a lawn substitute. You'll need to create some pathways in and around this area for easy access, because these larger plants don't usually tolerate foot traffic.

For more information on sustainable lawn care and ideas for lawn replacements, see the website of the Lawn Reform Coalition (www.lawnreform.org).

Meadows

A natural meadow is a perpetual grassland ecosystem maintained by environmental factors that restrict the growth of woody plants. For instance, coastal meadows are maintained by salt spray and saline water, while desert meadows are perpetuated by low precipitation. Prairies are maintained by periods of severe drought, grazing, and wildfires. If you want a meadow on your urban/suburban property, you will need to implement an ongoing strategy to keep out the shrubs and trees, which would normally take over and turn it into a forest. In effect, *you* will be the limiting factor to prevent the woody plant growth.

You can build a meadow in a number of ways, and there are different types of meadows. You may have seen the beautiful flowers on the meadow mix seed packages or a meadow-in-a-can offered for sale with the implied promise that your yard will look like the picture with very little work. This is misleading because your meadow may look a little like the photo for one year, but then it will fade unless you kill existing vegetation and replant those seeds every year.

You might like the idea of a grassy meadow with grass stalks waving in the breeze or bending under the weight of seed-eating birds. A mixed meadow with both grasses (graminoids) and wildflowers (forbs) may work best to attract both pollinators and birds, and because the grasses usually hold the soil better, provide winter texture, reduce places for weeds to grow, and support the wildflowers.

Choose a sunny spot for whatever type of meadow you envision and consider what it will look like to the neighbors. If neatness counts in your neighborhood, first create a civilized-looking edge in the most visible areas by planting a border of showy bunching grasses or

Using a hand-powered weed whacker or string trimmer keeps tall weeds out of a meadow area. Tree saplings will probably need to be pulled or dug to keep them at bay. You become the controlling factor in stopping the ecosystem succession that would lead to a forest.

low-growing shrubs, or both. To be most effective, spend the money and time to establish plants that are large enough to be immediately obvious as your meadow border. Also, plan ahead for paths through the meadow and maybe a bench or two so you can enjoy the beauty up close. The pathways could just be mowed trails that will change each year, or they could be more permanent, with a deep mulch cover or stepping-stones. Keeping the pathways open will increase your meadow maintenance chores, but the pathways will also give better access to the area for weeding, watering, and other routine chores. Plus, paths will increase your enjoyment and add to the planned look.

Before you start building a meadow, remove all the invasive plants and determine what else you have growing in the area. Some of the existing plants could be desirable meadow species that you'll wish to

Providing paths and planned spaces for humans makes a meadow appear more civilized. Who would mistake this beautiful space for a bunch of weeds?

encourage because they've obviously adapted to the conditions of your property. The plants that are in place may also indicate whether the area is frequently moist. If you find soft rushes (*Juncus* spp.) growing in a lawn area, you know that this area is damp. If you are unsure of the plants, bring in an expert for guidance or take samples to your extension agent. Finding out what is growing on your property is another good reason for hiring a landscape architect or native plant consultant at the beginning of your planning phase.

A number of methods are available for creating a meadow in an urban/suburban landscape, but no matter how you begin, it will take several years for it to become a relatively stable ecosystem, with yearly eradication of trees and shrubs. It will change character over time, and you may want to reintroduce desirable plants as they die out.

Create a Meadow by Killing the Vegetation

You can start a meadow from scratch by killing all the vegetation before planting a mixture of selected plants and/or wildflower seeds.

There are several ways to accomplish this—each with its own pros and cons. Whichever method you choose, you'll have a more or less clean slate so your seeds or plants will have a good chance for survival.

Using Herbicides

This method is often used to prepare large meadow areas, and you see it used for highway wildflower meadows. As discussed in chapter 4, always follow the directions on the herbicide label to the letter. When you remove the dead vegetation, don't add it to your compost pile. Irrigate regularly for a couple of weeks to induce weed seeds embedded in the soil to sprout. Spray or rake away the newly emerged weeds. Wait three weeks before sowing your seeds until most of the herbicide is changed into harmless substances. Time the process of plant removal so that when you're done with all the steps, it will be the best time for planting your seeds.

Tilling or Scraping Away the Soil

Tilling might be appropriate for large areas where the soil is highly compacted or completely overrun with weeds. In most cases, using a rototiller, plow, or disk will bring forth a bloom of seed-bank weeds. If you till, you'll need to deal with the new weeds using some other method such as a preemergent herbicide like corn gluten, weed flaming, or a general herbicide. After tilling, smooth the soil surface to provide an even plane, so your wildflower seeds can make good contact with the soil. On the other hand, those seeds in the seed bank are sure to create a spectrum of well-adapted plants for your area.

Scraping away the top foot or two of the living soil is one way to avoid the seed bank problem. This method is best for areas where the soil is naturally poor in nutrients and is often used for restoring areas that are overrun with invasive plants.

Burning the Weeds

There are a few general methods for scorching weeds. An overall burn similar to a wildfire would probably be illegal in residential areas, but if it is allowed, it must be supervised by a professional and only with permission—you certainly don't want to be the cause of a destructive wildfire if it escapes. These burns emulate natural wildfires and will kill much of the undergrowth and sterilize the top layer of soil, but they don't kill the fire-resistant plants and may cause some fire-dependent seeds to germinate.

A general burn is usually impractical for most urban/suburban landscapes, but there are other ways to use heat to kill weeds. For large tracts of land, propane weed flamers can be hauled behind a tractor. For smaller sites or for touch-up weeding, portable propane flamers can be strapped on and carried into a meadow. For safety's sake, do only green treatments—just after a heavy rainfall or thorough irrigation. Don't flame on dry, windy days. The point is not to set the weeds on fire, but only to heat them enough to destroy cell walls—a 5-second exposure to the flame is usually enough. Another way to use heat is to pour boiling water on a weed—this will cook the plant tissues of the weed and any roots in the vicinity. Boiling water will also sterilize the soil and kill all the seeds. Obviously boiling water is practical only for small areas and for spot weeding.

Solarization

This heat-related method to kill weeds and seeds in the area where you wish to build a meadow works best during the hotter summer months. See discussion in chapter 4 on page 57.

Thick Mulch

A 6- to 8-inch layer of organic mulch such as arborist wood chips will suffocate most surface plants and kill weed seeds in the top layer of soil, but it will not do much to discourage plants with deep rhizomes or tubers such as catbrier (*Smilax* spp.), Florida betony (*Stachys floridana*), or torpedo grass (*Panicum repens*). To prepare for mulching, scalp the area with the lawn mower—set at its lowest level. Leave mulch in place for six weeks or more, and then clear mulch from that area. Dig out the resistant weeds (including their tubers), and then plant your meadow, whether you sow seeds or install plants. Many meadow plants do best with poor soil, so use the removed mulch somewhere else in your landscape. See chapter 4 for more discussion of mulches.

Manually Pulling Weeds

Hand-pulling is one way to selectively edit out the weeds while leaving desirable native meadow plants in place. This method would be a challenge for a large area unless you have an army of volunteers, but maybe you can tackle only small portions of the meadow at a time. You should try to minimize the soil disturbance when pulling weeds, so new weed seeds are not turned up in the process. Do not leave the weeds in the area, even though you've pulled them up and they'll probably die—they might shed seeds or even start growing again. It's best not to add weeds with seeds or noxious weeds to your compost pile. After pulling weeds, you may wish to add some preemergent herbicide such as corn gluten and wait a month or more before sowing seeds.

Start a Meadow from an Existing Lawn

A meadow can be started from an existing lawn using 2 different strategies—simply by stopping the mowing or by scalping it with a low mowing and planting seeds and plants. The method you choose will depend on the condition of the lawn and its recent care. Either way, since you have not killed the plants in place, these meadows will have a relatively high grass population to start, so you may wish to pull out the grass in some selected areas to start a denser population of some other type of plants. Each year you could start another new area with either the same plant or some different ones—obviously, this will depend on your situation and the ongoing condition of the meadow.

Stop Mowing

This strategy can work for a lawn in any shape—thick and lush or thin and straggly. At first the growth will be fairly uniform, but within a few months different types of plants will show themselves, especially if you've used sustainable lawn care without herbicides for a year or more. Once the mowing regimen stops, more plants will find their way into the former lawn. In a neighborhood where tidiness matters, this is probably not the best way to get started unless you've created a neat-looking border that hides most of the would-be meadow. While a

A neat border of bunching grasses or shrubs at the edge
of a meadow area can make it seem more civilized.

stop-mowing-the-lawn meadow will look weedy at first, it is definitely
the easiest way to start.

Scalp the Lawn

If the lawn is thin, you can start a meadow by mowing the lawn at the
lowest level on the mower. Rake up all the clippings and make sure to
loosen the soil as you rake. Time the mowing for the ideal time to sow
seed in the fall, which is also when grass will go into winter dormancy.

Planning and Planting the Meadow

Wildflower meadows are complex ecosystems consisting of annuals,
biennials, and perennials in sunny locales. In addition, a ratio between
graminoids (grasses and other grasslike plants) and forbs (broad-leaved
herbaceous flowering plants) should be considered. In a natural environment, a meadow may consist mostly of graminoids with only 20

Dealing with Weed Regulations

Before you stop mowing your lawn or begin planting a meadow, make sure you know the local regulations of your community or town or other municipality. While we have the "Florida Friendly Law" here in this state, it is open to interpretation. What you see as a native meadow full of native plants, someone else may see as a bunch of weeds. Find out what you need to do to comply, because the last thing you want is for the county to send in a contractor with a brush-hog to get rid of the "eyesore."

If weed regulations are in place, maybe they can be changed, or maybe if you can register your property as official habitat or get it certified in some other way, your property can be exempted. See chapter 11 for more discussion on giving presentations to help educate people about native yards.

percent or less coverage by forbs. In your urban/suburban meadow, you may wish to include a higher ratio of forbs for the beauty of their flowers and their habitat value—50–60 percent may be a good place to start.

If you weigh the ratio of your plant species toward perennials, your meadow's growth patterns will be stable at first, but sooner or later, other plants will introduce themselves in new and interesting patterns. Be sure to include a variety of species so that something is flowering throughout the growing season, and in Florida that means year-round. The various blooming cycles will be attractive to you, to your neighbors, and to pollinators.

Before you plant anything, inventory the site and its microhabitats, such as wet, low-lying areas, shadier areas, or dry open fields and determine the species best suited to each area. Not all the plants or seeds you install will survive in the long run—only species that are best adapted to the site will be the ones that thrive after the first few years. The graminoids-to-forbs ratio will sort itself out unless you add or subtract plants—edit the meadow.

Choose species native to your area and bred from local stock. In many places the local plants and seedlings are easier to find than seed for your local area, but it is worth the trouble. If you are creating a native wildflower meadow on public or community land, you may qualify for a grant to help with the expenses. In Florida, one place to apply is the Florida Wildflower Foundation (flawildflowers.org).

A Seed-Started Meadow

Sowing seeds is the most common method for planting meadows— particularly for large areas. The recommended planting rates vary from 4 to 12 pounds of seeds per acre, so if you have a tenth of an acre (4356 square feet or about 44 by 100 feet), you'll want to plant about 1 pound of seeds. If you want to plant four different species in more or less equal quantities, purchase one-quarter pound (4 ounces) of each species. Some seeds are lightweight; while others are heavier, so take this into account. The one overriding rule is that the seeds must make good contact with the soil. You may find that in the long term, you'll plant new seed in selected areas in your meadow every few years to maintain the desired mix of plants.

Ideally, native species should be planted following Mother Nature's schedule; for most meadow species, it's best to sow seeds in the fall because some of them need a chilling period (even in Florida) to break dormancy, while others have hard seed coats that need to be worn down before they can germinate. In addition, sowing seeds in the fall might give your newly planted species a head start over common weeds that might not begin growing until spring. That said, some fall-blooming species might do better with a springtime sowing, and in tropical Florida, sowing seed may not work well at all.

It's best to create your own mixture of native wildflower and grass seeds based on your location and the look you're aiming for rather than buying one premixed for the region. This way you can sow them separately, because the different sizes and weights of seeds makes it difficult to sow seeds evenly, and you can pick and choose where to concentrate one species more heavily than another. For instance, in low-lying or moist spots in the meadow you can sow only the species that will do well in that environment and skip that area for the species that do better in dry habitats.

Hand-broadcasting seeds is the simplest method, but you could also use an adjustable hand-carried or hand-pushed mechanical seeder. Mix the seeds with clean, fine sand in a ratio of four parts sand to one part seed in a bucket to ensure a more even coverage. Some seeds are so small and lightweight they might tend to blow away, but the sand will give them the heft they need to hit the targeted spots in your meadow. It's generally a good idea where wide and total coverage is desired to sow half the mixture while walking in one direction and the other half in a perpendicular direction—in a crosshatch pattern.

After seeding, as mentioned above, use some method to ensure that the seeds have good contact with the soil. You can tamp down the soil by walking on every square inch or by using some type of landscape roller. You can also rake the seeded areas with a flexible leaf rake or drag a piece of chain-link fence back and forth over the meadow area.

Cover the newly seeded area with a very light covering of straw (not hay, unless you want the hay seeds mixed in) or pine needles. You should still be able to see the soil beneath this thin mulch. The purpose is to keep seeds in place, reduce erosion, discourage birds, and retain some moisture. It's best to spread the mulch by hand to make sure it does not end up in clumps that might be too thick for the seeds to grow through after germination. If tamping the area is your strategy for ensuring good seed contact, then this spreading task and the tamping task can be combined.

For larger areas, particularly on slopes, hydroseeding can be used to keep the seed in place and reduce erosion. This requires special equipment that sprays a slurry of seeds, water, and hydromulch, normally made of wood fiber or paper. If you use this method, apply the seed and water mixture first and then the mulch slurry in a second sweep to ensure that the seeds make good contact with the soil and do not end up on top of the mulch where they could quickly dry out.

Unless a soaking rain of at least half an inch falls, you will need to find a way to irrigate your meadow on a regular basis for a month or more. In Florida, November through May is the dry season, so irrigation is important. Once the seeds germinate, they are vulnerable to drying out, but after they have developed some true leaves, you can slowly back off the frequency of irrigation so their roots move down into the soil.

It is useful to be able to identify the seedling stage of the species you planted, so you'll know whether the sprouting plants are the ones you want. While there is no substitute for experience, resources are available that provide pictures of the various commonly planted natives. Until you know, let it grow. You can pull out the weeds later, but it's important to pull them before they set seed.

A Plant-Started Meadow

For smaller meadows or for meadows-in-a-hurry, purchase native plants in flats, containers, or bare-root bunches. When you use plants from the nursery, it gives you a head start—you've eliminated the waiting period for germination. You have total control over the plant arrangement so the drifts of one species will be perfectly aligned with the next and all the plants will have enough space to grow. When you use plants, it's usually best to wait until late spring and plant just before the summer wet season to reduce the need for ongoing irrigation.

Follow the normal planting procedures as described in chapter 5, but be careful not to disturb the surrounding soil too much, and as you finish, pat the soil down. You don't want to stir up the weeds. If you are not going to also seed the area, apply a 2-inch layer of mulch around (but not touching) your plants to keep the moisture in and the weeds out. If you'll also be seeding the area, use a much thinner layer of either straw or pine needle mulch after you sow the seeds.

Be sure to irrigate thoroughly upon planting and regularly for several weeks unless there is a soaking rain. When you see new growth, you can cut back on the irrigation. If you plant in the fall, however, you may not see much growth until spring.

Combining Plants and Seeds for a Meadow

When you purchase container plants for slow-to-grow or difficult-to-germinate perennials, you help define the look of the meadow sooner. When you intend to combine seeding with installing potted plants, the question is, which do you do first? Of course, there are advantages to each method.

The entire area to the left of the mulched path and the path itself was a St. Augustine grass lawn. Eight years later, this beautiful pinxter azalea (*Rhododendron canescens*) and other native shrubs and trees have turned this space into a woodland.

A great purple hairstreak (*Atlides halesus*) nectaring on a snow squarestem (*Melanthera nivea*). Native plants provide good habitat for wildlife including food for adult and larval insects.

Early in the year, an infrequently mowed freedom lawn is covered in Canadian toadflax (*Linaria canadensis*), which could be called "mowed-flax" at this point. Later in the summer, this same lawn is filled with starrush white-top (*Rhynchospora colorata*). Of course, both species are there all the time, it's just that each one becomes obvious when blooming.

Hairawn muhly grass (*Muhlenbergia capillaris*) and coontie (*Zamia integrifolia*) have been widely planted in public landscapes as low-maintenance alternatives to traditional high-maintenance hedges and seasonally planted flowers. And who can argue with their beauty?

A bunch of blazing-stars (*Liatris* spp.) stand out from their backdrop of a mix of self-sown ferns.

A mixture of ferns provides a soft, low-maintenance edge along a north-facing wooded area.

A roadside meadow is filled with tickseed (*Coreopsis* spp.), Florida's state wildflower, in early May. Later in the season, the same meadow is filled with blanket flowers (*Gaillardia* spp.) and black-eyed Susans (*Rudbeckia* spp.). To keep this meadow going, it will need to be mowed once in the winter and reseeded at least every few years.

Atamasco lilies (*Zephyranthes atamasca*), blue-eyed grass (*Sisyrinchium angustifolium*), and meadow garlic (*Allium canadense*) inhabit a damp swale in a wild meadow.

Use powderpuff (*Mimosa strigillosa*) as a ground cover at the base of trees or around a grove. It's a legume, so it will grow in poor soils. As it grows into the mowed area, maybe you'll have less mowing to do.

Here an eastern redcedar (*Juniperus virginiana*) sprouted too close to this southern magnolia (*Magnolia grandiflora*). When trees plant themselves too close together, digging saplings can become a yearly maintenance chore. If you do this during the best planting season and are careful to get the majority of roots, these can be transplanted to other sites where there is more room. Wild seedlings offer good genetic diversity to your landscape.

Carefully choose the plants to save and those to remove in the edge areas. Here a wild-sown beautyberry (*Callicarpa americana*) is in a perfect place for the edge, but several oak saplings (*Quercus* spp.) are right next to it. After the oaks are dug, the beautyberry has more space to expand. This is where experience and education become useful—you need to be able to identify that beautyberry just by its vegetation.

A tree stump marks the outside corner of a shady area that will be transformed from an unmowed lawn to a meadow.

Eight years later the sweetgums (*Liquidambar styraciflua*) have grown and the two magnolias—on the left *M. grandiflora* and on the right *M. virginiana*—that were transplanted as small saplings from elsewhere in the landscape are almost 20 feet tall. Most of the bunching grasses, and all the rushes, goldenrods, asters, and ferns have grown on their own. Most of the maintenance has consisted of pulling out weeds, including tree saplings, and reworking the lawn edge. The stump at the corner has long since rotted away.

SOWING THE SEEDS FIRST

If you sow the seeds first, you have total access to the meadow area for raking, irrigation, and other initial care. If you install the plants within a few days after the sowing, well before the seeds have sprouted, then you'll have total access again to fill the areas with plants. The disadvantage is that you will have disturbed the newly planted seeds. In order to prevent some of the disturbance, mark out the areas where you intend to install the plants before you sow seeds. That way you can avoid that section of the meadow when spreading the seeds. You can also outline the planting area with some lime or mulch.

INSTALLING PLANTS FIRST

If you create drifts from container-grown plants in your meadow area first, you can water them in well and then smooth out the soil around them, all without worrying about previously planted seed. The seeding efforts may be somewhat more efficient since you can easily see where to avoid sowing seeds, or if you wish to sow a specific type of seed near your planted perennials, you'll know exactly where to sow them.

With the plants already in place, you'll be restricted in your methods of ensuring good seed contact with the soil. There will be no dragging of chain-link fence pieces over your new plants, and with the tamping and raking, you need to be careful not to rake outside the lines. If you've seeded in the planting area, tamping down will need to be done very carefully.

Ongoing Meadow Care

During the first year after planting, you'll need to cut the meadow at a 5- to 7-inch height two or three times during the growing season, to allow the perennials to get a better start; otherwise the fast-growing annuals will overwhelm them with their shade and exuberant growth. If your mower doesn't have a 5-inch setting, maybe you could use a string trimmer or a hand scythe for these initial cuts. To keep this task reasonable, you could cut one-fourth of the meadow at a time. For larger areas, you could rent a brush hog or pay a professional for a high mow. For the second year, one midseason mowing may be enough to keep the annuals and weeds in check. Don't skip this step or all your hard work to include a wide selection of plant species will be wasted.

For the long run, you'll schedule just a yearly mowing in late January or early February with the mower set at its highest possible setting. Again, you can also accomplish this manually with a weed-whacker or string trimmer for a higher cut that would be better for bunching grasses. This will keep the trees and shrubs from growing so the area can remain a meadow. If you wait too long between mowings, you'll

Editing the meadow. With an established meadow, you may wish to prune back the plants that tend to be too dominant early in the spring to give other species enough light and room to flourish.

need a brush hog to mow the area, or you can pull or dig out the trees and shrubs one at a time before mowing. You can leave most of the trimmings in place as mulch and to ensure that new seeds are planted in the area; if you are replanting the area with new seed, clear out the trimmings and rake the soil to provide a good substrate for your seeds. You can select what to leave in the meadow to reduce the reseeding of one species over another.

You'll probably wish to do some selective weeding to keep things from becoming too wild. For instance, removing most of the native dogfennel (*Eupatorium capillifolium*), a vigorous perennial that can grow to 12 feet tall, and most of the native beggarticks (*Bidens alba*), an aggressive annual or biennial that will take over the whole area, is probably a good investment of your time. An annual mowing doesn't discourage these aggressive plants, so if you leave them in place, they will compromise the nature of your meadow. On the other hand, both of them attract pollinators and provide food for butterfly larvae, so you may wish to leave a few in place in a back corner of the meadow.

Over the years, you'll find the mix of vegetation in your meadow will change. In order to keep a good mix of showy flowers that attract butterflies and pollinators, you could pull some plants and scratch up some rough spots in the soil in areas in the meadows and plant new wildflower seeds every couple of years. In meadows and in other natural landscapes, the plant species usually grow in drifts. Keep this in mind as you reseed or replant meadow areas so they look natural.

In severe droughts, natural meadows receive no irrigation; as a result, many of the forbs give way to the hardier grasses. In your meadow, you will probably want to irrigate deeply, but not frequently during severe droughts to preserve the diversity.

So let's fall out of love with those manicured lawns and plant more meadows.

9

Creating and Maintaining Groves,
Hedgerows, and Fencerows

Both groves and hedgerows are groupings of woody plants. A hedgerow is usually more linear in nature and normally used to define edges, while a grove is a more compact arrangement and more likely to contain full-sized trees. Fences and fencerows are also discussed here since they are often used in place of hedges.

Groves

A grove consists of trees, shrubs, and ground covers that grow together in their own small ecosystem. In a natural grove, the ecosystem is often contained by a physical difference such as a high or low water table. In an urban/suburban landscape, a grove should be situated in a well-defined area and more or less mimic an arrangement that you might find in a local native ecosystem.

Compared to singly planted trees, groves offer the following advantages:

- They provide better habitat value, especially shelter and nesting places for birds and other wildlife.
- They need less ongoing maintenance, because after establishment, this group of plants will shed their leaves to create their own mulch. This self-made mulch will not only keep down weeds but also become soil that is perfectly balanced for the plants that have produced it.

- They speed the growth of woody plants as they compete for space and light.
- They are more wind tolerant.
- They have fewer edge-feet, where groves interface with lawn, paths, patios, and the like, to maintain.

When arranging plants, pay attention to their texture and form. Texture generally relates to the size and shape of the leaf but also takes into account growth habit and twig arrangement. For example, the cabbage palm (*Sabal palmetto*), our state tree, has a coarse texture, while the southern magnolia (*Magnolia grandiflora*) has a medium texture, and willows (*Salix* spp.) have fine texture. Trees and shrubs have many different forms or growth patterns, but a newly planted tree or shrub may bear little resemblance to its mature form. A young beautyberry shrub (*Callicarpa americana*) may be a single vertical cane less than 12 inches tall, but in a few years, if planted in its ideal location, it could grow to 7 feet tall with arching branches that nearly touch the ground and a diameter of 12 or more feet. You'll need to accommodate that form in your planting plans.

It's a good idea to plant an odd number of trees far enough apart to allow for adult growth, but with some overlapping of their projected canopies and at varied distances apart for a natural-looking arrangement. Plant the understory shrubs or small trees within two or three years after the main trees so they can all grow up together and create their own mutually beneficial ecosystem. Meanwhile you could plant a meadow-like area with sun-loving bunching grasses, wildflowers, or ground covers to fill in the spaces.

Place your groves in strategic areas, so they will eventually provide screening, shade on the south or west side of your house, or a windbreak, but in a fire-prone area, make sure that the mature canopy will be at least 30 feet from buildings. Groves are more wind resistant than single trees because they present a more rounded profile to diffuse the wind. The area used for the grove could be a mound to give it greater height, or it could be a low spot or swale to act as a rain garden to soak up stormwater. See hedgerows on page 161 for more information about each scenario.

You can design a grove to be light and airy with a high canopy of deciduous trees and shrubs if you wish to maintain a view through it, which would mimic flatwoods, sandhill, and oak woodland habitats. Historically speaking, these are the most dominant habitats in Florida. On the other hand, your grove could be planted more densely with a thick canopy of dark evergreen trees and shrubs to block light, dust, sound, and sight. These forest-like groves provide more screening, better habitat and protection for some types of wildlife, and, given their dense nature, would be easier to maintain over the years than a light, airy grove.

Groves look better if they are not planted in a perfectly round shape—an oblong, kidney bean, or amoeba shape seems to work best. You can take advantage of the shade created by your grove by planning a space for a seating area or leaving room between two trees for a hammock.

When it becomes too shady to maintain the meadow or ground

HAMMOCK of TREE GROVE

Maybe you could plan a space for a hammock when planting your native grove, but you'll have to wait a few years for your trees to grow into the job.

cover layer you started, you could plant ferns or other shade-tolerant plants or install a mulch layer throughout the grove to keep down the weeds and act as a leaf layer. Once the trees gain enough size, their own leaf drop will act as mulch. A grove will need less and less maintenance as the plants mature. When you begin the process of developing a grove, it's the individual plants that capture your attention. As the grove matures and the canopy trees start casting significant shade and the understory fills in, you'll find yourself focusing on the whole grouping instead of the various individuals. In effect, you'll see the forest rather than the trees.

Your ongoing maintenance will be focused on the edges and on immediate removal of invasives, and every few years you'll probably wish to reduce some of the vines like grapes (*Vitis* spp.), catbriers (*Smilax* spp.), or poison ivy (*Toxicodendron radicans*) that may volunteer in the grove. Except for removal of invasives, the extent of this maintenance depends on the grove's purpose, visibility, and proximity to human uses.

Creating a Grove

Create an overall plan for your grove even if you will take a few years to finish planting it. Think about the layers in your newly emerging ecosystem—canopy, tall understory, low understory, and ground. Even though you'll be planting small saplings (3–7 feet tall) for the best survival and fastest establishment rate, they will grow up together at a faster rate and with a higher canopy than a single tree planted in the open.

When you select trees to plant, they can be all the same species or a few compatible, but complementary, species. For small groves with only three to five canopy trees, it might work best to use just one tree species. On the other hand, a variety of trees will be more interesting, with differences in textures, branching structures, leaf shapes, and rates of growth, but it's best to avoid too much chaos created by having one of everything. If you have several different tree species, maybe you could tie them together with several shrubs of the same species planted throughout. Again, look to Mother Nature to see how plants are grouped in nearby natural environments and try to emulate that. During the process of naturalizing your property, you should continue to find inspiration in parks and natural areas throughout the nativization of your landscape, but your need for inspiration might be highest during the process of designing and building groves. Be sure to plan for the various textures and forms so the grove is attractive, but work to find compatible combinations that Mother Nature would have put together and work to find species that are underrepresented in your neighborhood to increase diversity.

When you have purchased the trees, place them, still in pots, in their respective spots in your future grove and then use a tape measure to draw the outline of the mature canopy of each tree and then the whole grove so you can see the extent of it. Look at this outlined space with its trees from various angles outside and also from inside through the windows. Ask for other people's opinions because they might see something you missed. Envision the trees' mature sizes as you are doing this initial walk-around to make sure they won't hit a power line, the house, or underground infrastructure. Consider the room needed for their roots to spread out—normally you'd leave at least 8 feet between a full-sized tree and a sidewalk or curb and maybe more between trees and buildings. Unlike the roots of regular trees, palm roots won't damage hardscape structures, but it's still best to leave some room so their fronds don't scrape the sides or roof of the building. Planting a bunch of trees is an investment in the future, so don't rush through this planning and visualizing process.

Only after you've taken this time to reevaluate your choices in their spaces are you ready to start planting the trees. If you're lucky, you'll be starting with bare ground, but it's more likely in an urban/suburban property that you'll be replacing lawn. You could rent a sod cutter and rip it all out and mulch the exposed soil, or you could at this point just dig out enough of the lawn to accommodate the trees' planting holes with a foot or more margin outside the root-balls. This way you'll still need to mow between the trees, but with a space of 8 feet or more between them, you might be able to handle that chore fairly easily. Or, instead of leaving the lawn in place while you're waiting for the trees to establish themselves, you could remove the lawn and plant a wildflower meadow with mostly annuals or install a sun-loving ground cover like dune sunflower (*Helianthus debilis*) or powderpuff (*Mimosa strigillosa*) over the whole grove area around the trees. One advantage to the mimosa is that it's a legume, so it will grow well in poor soil and, over time, enrich it with its nitrogen-fixing bacteria. Be sure to leave pathways through the grove for initial tree irrigation and weeding.

Two or three years later when you are ready to plant the shrubs and understory trees, do the same thing you did with the trees: place the potted plants where you think you want them and do the same walk-around to make sure they will work well. Maybe even leave them in place for a few days. If you left the lawn in place, now is the time to remove the rest of it. The smaller trees and shrubs should not take as long as trees to become established, but still make sure you irrigate well and long enough so they are happy. Mulch well throughout the grove unless you still have meadow plants, ground covers, or bunching grasses already growing there. The meadow plants will begin to change as the shade deepens in the center of the grove. If you don't have meadow plants, wait until the shrubs have acclimated and are showing growth before you start planting the ground covers. When there is some shade under the trees, it's time to plant any shade-loving ground covers such as ferns around them.

The plants around the edges will play a large role in defining the character of your grove. If the shrubs have canes or fronds that arch almost to the ground, such as beautyberry (*Callicarpa americana*) or saw palmetto (*Serenoa repens*), your grove will have a more informal feel. If the edge plants have a more upright form, such as Spanish bayonet (*Yucca aloifolia*) or coontie (*Zamia integrifolia*), your grove might look more controlled. A native plant can present a formal or informal appearance—it's your choice.

Building a Grove around Lawn Trees

Lawn trees, those plopped in the middle of lawns, are quite common in urban/suburban landscapes, but they can be a good starting place for a grove, especially if they're native. If a lawn tree is in an appropriate spot for its mature size, is (or will be) in scale with the surroundings, and doing well despite being surrounded by turf, you can use it as the focal point of the new grove. Create your grove by surrounding it with other trees, shrubs, decorative grasses, and ground covers.

Before planting anything, remove turfgrass carefully so that you

This magnolia lawn tree is a maintenance nightmare with its continuously falling leaves, overpruned shrubs that are planted too close to it, and vertical edging in a tight circle around it. Use the leaf fall as a guideline for creating a grove of trees and shrubs around it so its leaves will create nice mulch for the grove and won't need to be removed.

don't disturb the tree's surface roots. This usually means pulling out the grass manually, so while you're pulling you should also locate the main roots. Mark them with temporary stakes so you can avoid them in the placement of your new plants. Do not put soil on top of the tree's roots even if it seems that the area is low compared to the rest of the landscape or that the surface roots are fully exposed. Place your plants between the large surface roots and spaced with room to grow but close enough to touch when they mature. Once you have finished planting a section of the grove, apply no more than a 2-inch layer of chunky mulch such as wood chips or bark nuggets, to keep the weeds down and retain moisture. The chunky texture gives the tree roots access to air.

The following are a couple of scenarios of groves created around lawn trees:

STARTING WITH A LITTLE GEM MAGNOLIA
IN THE CENTER OF A SMALL YARD

The little gem magnolia (*Magnolia grandiflora* 'Little Gem'), a commonly sold, slow-growing cultivar in Central and North Florida, will eventually grow to 35 or more feet with a spread of 12 feet. It's often used as a lawn tree, even though it drops its leathery leaves throughout the year, making a continual mess on all those lawns. Just think, when you include the magnolia in a grove, you won't have to pick up its leaves anymore. Magnolias enjoy a slightly acidic soil, so choose its grove plants with that in mind. Since this is a small yard, you will not plant any full-size trees, but fill in with understory trees, tall shrubs, low shrubs, and ground cover.

Use native ferns as a ground cover near the tree and powderpuff (*Mimosa strigillosa*) as a ground cover at the sunnier edges of the grove. Offset the tree's medium/coarse texture with two to five tall shrubs with fine texture such as Walter's viburnum (*Viburnum obovatum*) or sparkleberry (*Vaccinium arboreum*). You may also want some of the na-

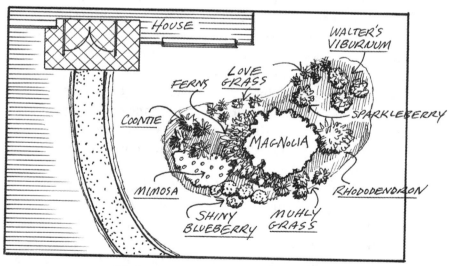

MAGNOLIA GROVE

Southern magnolias (*Magnolia grandiflora*) are often planted in the middle of lawns, but their continuous leaf drop is a maintenance nightmare. Build this grove around your magnolia and its leaves will provide a nice mulch instead.

tive azaleas in the mix (*Rhododendron* spp.). Place most of the shrubs as a group to one side of the tree—maybe diagonally away from the corner of the house on the opposite side from the driveway or entrance. At the outside of the grove plant groupings of bunching grasses such as hairawn muhly grass (*Muhlenbergia capillaris*) or love grass (*Eragrostis* spp.) and low shrubs such as shiny blueberry (*Vaccinium myrsinites*).

STARTING WITH TWO CRAPE MYRTLES IN A MEDIUM-SIZED YARD

Those tough, exotic crape myrtles (*Lagerstroemia indica*) are native to China and Korea. They are overplanted in the southeast, but if they are doing well in your yard, you might allow them to remain, at least temporarily. Say you have two planted about 20 feet apart and 15 feet from the front of the house. You will include both of them in one oblong grove with most of the new plants on the side away from the house and eventually when the new trees grow tall enough, you could remove the crape myrtles, so plan for places where they can fall when it's time to take them out.

The first thing to do with the crape myrtles in your yard is to stop the annual mutilation of hat-rack pruning. To work your way into a more natural growth pattern, in the fall or winter, prune back about half the sprouts that grew from the previous year's hat-racking, letting the strongest ones or best-placed ones stay. In the spring, remove any new sprouts so only the previous year's sprouts are left to grow; that fall, evaluate the remaining sprouts and choose the best ones to keep— these should amount to about two-thirds of the remaining branches. This way your crape myrtles will have a chance to grow into real trees and be more compatible with your native grove and your lower main-tenance regime.

Plant trees that may eventually replace the crape myrtles. There are so many good native choices, but while they are maturing, they should not conflict with the crape myrtles for space or texture. Make a skewed triangle with these trees so that one falls somewhere be-tween the existing trees, with the other two on the side away from the house. Skew the triangle away from the driveway and entry of the house. You could use winged elm (*Ulmus alata*), river birch (*Betula nigra*), redbud (*Cercis canadensis*), or cabbage palm (*Sabal palmetto*).

In the case of the river birch, you may wish to group three together (a few feet apart) and count as one tree.

For shrubs, you might want some coarse texture to contrast with the crape myrtle, such as oakleaf hydrangea (*Hydrangea quercifolia*) or maybe some evergreen hollies (*Ilex* spp.). Plant some tickseed (*Coreopsis* spp.) as a ground cover around the edges.

Ongoing Grove Care

A grove will eventually grow into a low-maintenance landscape feature, but it's not maintenance-free. Depending on the trees you've chosen, you may need to prune multiple leaders to select the best leader as the main trunk when the tree is still young. Some trees and shrubs send up many sprouts or suckers that may need some trimming as well to maintain a strong structure. In severe droughts you will need to water, but your biggest maintenance chore will be to keep the edge of the lawn from invading the grove and the ground covers out of the lawn, or you could continue to expand the grove as its plants spread out. Vines and weeds will find their way into your grove; it's easiest to pull them out sooner rather than later. Unlike for a lawn, though, the maintenance schedule for a grove is flexible; if you don't make your scheduled walk-through in the fall, it can wait until spring. The longer you have the grove, the easier it will be to maintain and the greater your enjoyment of all its benefits.

Hedgerows

Hedgerows have been used in Europe for centuries, especially in the British Isles, as property boundaries, as windbreaks, and to fence livestock in or out of fields. The linear measure of the hedgerows in Scotland alone is said to be longer than the circumference of Earth. Today there are grants for hedgerow restoration because so many have been lost to modern farming techniques. The European model of hedgerows is applicable here because of its low maintenance requirements. The plants are chosen so their mature sizes suit the hedge environment and therefore will not need constant trimming. A successful hedgerow will need pruning only every third year or less often.

This low-maintenance hedgerow includes oakleaf hydrangea (*Hydrangea quercifolia*), beautyberry (*Callicarpa americana*), and native azaleas (*Rhododendron* spp.).

A hedgerow is not the same as those unsustainable monocultures planted in straight rows and trimmed every few weeks to unnatural shapes. Hedgerows, made up of a variety of species, can serve similar purposes in the landscape, but with much less ongoing maintenance. Hedgerows provide privacy, moderate wind and dust, buffer sound, reduce the ambient temperature, and supply habitat for many types of wildlife, especially birds. You could think of hedgerows as elongated groves, and the suggestions for building and maintaining groves also apply here. You could use a hedgerow at the back of a long narrow lot or along the side of a wide lot to provide a screen. Obviously, a larger lot will be able to accommodate a larger and longer hedgerow than a small urban property. Since a hedgerow or fencerow is not normally found in the wild, you might find inspiration along roadside fenced areas.

Create a hedgerow by planting a mixture of shrubs and small trees so they form long, dense thickets. You can design your hedge to include trees or shrubs already growing in your planned hedge area. Choose plants that produce flowers and berries or seeds at different times during the year. Pay attention to the predicted growth patterns, foliage types, and other features so the plants complement each other visually. And of course, you'll choose plants that should do well in the environment of your property and also those that add to neighborhood diversity. Unlike planting a grove, you may want to plant all your hedgerow plants at once because the trees will not be the dominant feature here—the tall shrubs will be the stars.

In a naturalistic setting, you won't install woody plants in straight lines or in predictable checkerboard patterns, but the whole hedgerow could be arranged in a more or less linear pattern. While the end result could be rather dense, you should plant only a little closer together than the projected growth for each specimen within the row. You may want to create a double or triple row of plantings so each plant has its own space while creating the general effect of a dense thicket. The space available and the purpose of the hedgerow will guide your design and selection of plants. Be sure to leave room for access on both sides of the hedgerow—you don't want it to eat your neighbor's fence.

Building a Hedgerow on a Berm

You could boost the effectiveness of a hedgerow for screening by first creating a berm or low ridge of soil if you have room in your landscape and if such a berm would not cause drainage problems around buildings. A 2- to 3-foot berm will give hedge plants a head start in height and make a significant difference in the effectiveness of screening, especially in sound damping. The taller the berm, the wider it will need to be for slope stability. Note: having your hedge plants higher in the landscape also makes it more difficult to access the higher branches for pruning or other maintenance.

If you are importing soil to build the berm, try to match the soil type already in your landscape. If the berm soil is significantly richer than the surrounding soils, the roots of trees and shrubs are unlikely to move very far outside the berm, and their wind tolerance and drought tolerance might be compromised. In addition, berm soils high in organics (such as muck) will decompose over time, causing the ridge to shrink and flatten. If the soil is significantly sandier than the surrounding soil it will be more difficult to establish trees and shrubs adapted to your environment, but once the roots of the surviving trees reach the richer soil, those problems will lessen. For smaller shrubs and perennials, you'll need to choose species that do well in sandier soils because their roots may not reach the base soil.

Creating a natural-looking arrangement of plants growing up and over the berm is a little tricky, but grouping is usually the best. Establishing trees and shrubs on a berm will take longer than those planted at grade level because the moisture drains away. Be sure to create a good-sized irrigation saucer for each plant and keep up frequent irrigation for a longer period of time. Until hedge plants gain significant height, plant ground covers to hold the soil and increase habitat value.

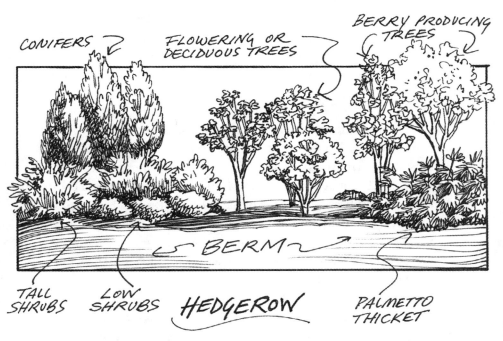

A hedgerow can be planted on a berm for added height or in a swale to serve as a rain garden. Hedgerows provide screening and habitat.

Building a Hedgerow in a Swale

Building a hedgerow in a swale in the landscape that accepts storm-water overflows would, in effect, turn it into a rain garden. In Florida, where we can receive several inches of rain in a day, it's important to have a large area where stormwater can sit until it soaks into the soil or is absorbed by plants. If that feature in your landscape can also provide privacy, buffering, and habitat, so much the better. The plants in a swale need to withstand both flooding and drought, because you don't want to have to water them during the dry season. See chapter 10 for more information on building rain gardens and a recommended plant list.

Fences in the Landscape

Fences are used in landscapes to mark boundaries, keep people or animals in or out of an area, or as decorative features. When fences are adorned with vining plants, they provide beauty and good habitat value in the landscape. Even without vining plants, fences serve as perching places for birds—and you know what happens when birds frequent an area? They poop. Berry-eating birds will deposit perfectly fertilized seeds at the base of the fence. This could be called the "fence effect," resulting in a higher population of seedlings of berry-producing plants along a fence or hedgerow. Eastern red-cedar (*Juniperus virginiana*), sassafras (*Sassafras albidum*), Virginia creeper (*Parthenocissus quinquefolia*), catbrier (*Smilax* spp.), and wax myrtle (*Morella cerifera*) are some of the more frequently found seedlings along fences and hedges.

As discussed in chapter 7, fences provide backdrops for landscapes and are sometimes the backbone of hedges. Sometimes the hedge is planned, but other times, it just happens when the area next to a fence is allowed to grow because it's not convenient to mow and because the birds plant their favorites in that long row. Either way, if you've inherited such a fencerow, there are ways to integrate it into your native landscape. Assuming you wish to leave the fence standing and you need privacy that may need to be higher than the fence, you can remove the traditional exotic hedge plants such as Asian privet

(*Ligustrum* spp.), weeping fig (*Ficus benjamina*), or even Australian-pine (*Casuarina* spp.). (You should know that Australian-pines are allelopathic and suppress growth of any type of plant within their drip line and beyond, and it may take a while to establish native plants where they have grown unless you replace at least some of the tainted soil.)

It's probably best to remove them all at one time and wait at least a few months to determine whether the former hedge plants come back. You could plant some tall herbaceous plants such as bunching grasses or vines along the fence to fill in the blank space while you wait. What you don't want is having old plants sprout up again in the middle of new hedgerow plants. Once they are gone, it's time to build a hedgerow with a variety of native shrubs that will fit the area. Yes, they will be along a fence, but that doesn't mean they need to be perfectly lined up. Vary the distances from the fence and between the various types of plants, but leave a pathway along the fence for maintenance access.

If you have a naturally or accidentally produced fencerow, your strategy will be different because it is likely that some desirable plants are growing along with the invasives or weed species or ones that are too large for the space. You'll probably have vines to deal with in an unplanned hedge, so remove the undesirable vines first and trim back the ones you wish to retain so they won't be so wild before you start managing the shrubs and trees—both wanted and unwanted. The next thing to do, once the trees and shrubs are uncovered, is to carefully prune back damaged, deformed, and out-of-place branches on all the shrubs and trees. During this pruning phase you'll have a chance to study all the hedge plants—there may be some invasives or desirable species you hadn't noticed at first glance.

The next phase will be removing all the invasives. Removing some plants while not disturbing others is not easy, especially if they're large and growing too close together. It's probably best to saw the offending plant as close to ground level as possible and then carefully paint the cambium layer (just inside the bark) with an herbicide. If you don't want to use herbicides, use an axe to make several vertical slashes into the trunk and dig out as much of it as possible without disturbing the roots. Later, when the sprouts grow from the stump, cut them off as soon as possible. There may even be sprouts growing from the herbicide-treated stumps. In either case, continue to remove the sprouts until the plant finally loses its vitality and dies.

Living Fences

A living fence is a specialized type of hedge in which the living plant material is woven into a fence. Build a living fence where you need a narrow, vertical wall. The weaving is done while the trees or sprouts are green and pliable; within a year after the weaving, those branches will become woody and hold their woven shapes.

You can build a living fence from pliable, fast-growing, and easily rootable branches such as willows (*Salix* spp.) or young saplings (whips) of trees or shrubs that readily produce water sprouts. Some other examples are arrowwood (*Viburnum dentatum*), red maple (*Acer rubrum*), Florida swampprivet (*Forestiera segregata*), and, for a prickly fence, hawthorn (*Crataegus* spp.). (The prickly hawthorns are the standard hedgerow plant in the British Isles; since they are allelopathic you'll have fewer problems with weeds or anything else growing in the vicinity—but of course, you'll use a native hawthorn, not the European species.) The cut branches or saplings should be 4 or 5 feet long with no, or very few, side branches. Insert both ends of each branch into the soil to make an arch at least 2 feet high; with a slight overlap continue the line

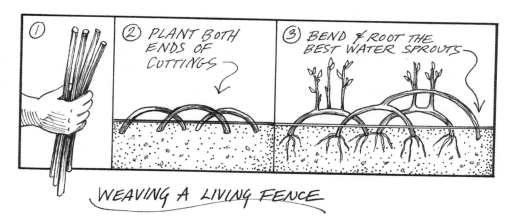

Use cuttings of easily rootable species such as willows (*Salix* spp.) to build a living fence. Over the first few years, bend and weave the water sprouts back into the fence until it's high and dense enough for your purposes.

with the next branch and the next. Mulch well and keep irrigated until there is growth and then gradually taper back the watering. When the branches are bent in this way they will send up vertical shoots (water sprouts) from the top of the arch. The next year, choose two or three well-placed best shoots on each of the original branches and cut back the others. While these shoots are still pliable, bend them into arches as well and weave the shoots together and tie in place with string, strips of cloth, or twist ties. Over a few years continue to select the best shoots growing from the tops of the arched branches and weave them together until the living fence is dense enough or tall enough for your needs.

A living fence in reality needs to be treated like a hedge, even if not a carefully pruned hedge; you will probably need to make a periodic trip along both sides of the fence to trim away errant shoots and sprouts, depending on the purpose of the fence and what is on the other side. If there is room for the height of full-grown trees along the fence, you can stop trimming and weaving the water sprouts and just let them grow up from there, but if you wish to restrict the height, then you will need to trim or fold back the top sprouts on a yearly basis.

You'll have the best success if you use a heavy mulch along your living fence to reduce weeds and keep the soil moist. In addition you could plant a dense ground cover at the base of the fence. While these tortured trees or shrubs will not enjoy a full life cycle, a living fence can last for many years; when the trees begin to die off, you can leave the fence in place. It may last for many more years depending on species and conditions. Vines will probably volunteer in and around your living fence; in an urban/suburban environment, it's probably best to keep them trimmed back while the fence plants are alive, but once they die, the vines could provide color, cover, and habitat just the same as they do for any other fence.

10

Landscaping in Moist Habitats

Wet areas in the landscape can be natural or man-made. A natural wet site could be the edge of a river or stream, a seasonal pond or shallow marsh, a swamp, a salt marsh, or the edge of a natural lake or pond. Sites that have been constructed include canals, artificial ponds, and those designed to capture stormwater runoff like retention ponds and rain gardens. Wetland and aquatic plants help stabilize shorelines, protect water quality, and provide important habitat for wading birds, fish, and aquatic invertebrates. Native waterfront plantings can provide color and texture that contrast with the rest of your landscape. Water is a necessary ingredient for building good wildlife habitat, and visits by birds, butterflies, frogs, dragonflies, and other wildlife will add further beauty to your property.

When you manage waterfront lands, you have a chance to improve the overall quality of Florida's waterways. Unfortunately people tend to think their own small actions won't make much difference, but when it comes to protecting our water, nothing could be further from the truth. Anything and everything you do to improve wet areas, especially the various shorelines, makes a real difference.

Before you do any planting in wet landscape areas, check with local authorities about regulations pertaining to your wetland or rules about handling the plants you wish to install or remove, including the invasives—some of our most noxious invasives thrive in wet areas. Also do a thorough evaluation of the stormwater outflows from your property toward a body of water or wetland and fix any possible erosion problems. If the drainage issues are complex on your property, it

Wet Site Terminology

The buffer or transition zone is the strip of land adjacent to waterways and other aquatic systems; it is the transition area between wet ecosystems and upland ecosystems. The ecosystem in this zone can be miles wide, such as a floodplain, or narrow, like a stream bank in an otherwise dry area. For streams and rivers, this area is called the riparian zone. The vegetation varies with the type of aquatic ecosystem and supplies significant regional habitat value for a wide variety of wildlife. When planning buffer zone plantings, be sure to account for the possibility of high water inundating lower upland areas closest to the shoreline at least occasionally.

The littoral zone is a type of ecotone that extends from the normal high-water mark at the shoreline out to a depth where the sunlight reaches the bottom of the water body. If there are tides,

THE WATER'S EDGE

Replacing lawn at the water's edge with an assortment of moisture-loving natives improves the quality of the water and provides habitat for many types of wildlife.

it will include the intertidal area between the high tide line and the low tide line. This zone can be miles wide, as in a salt marsh or mangrove swamp, or it can also be a narrow band if the shoreline is a steep slope at the edge of a canal or deep lake. The emergent and submerged plants in the littoral zone provide shelter, habitat, and food for a wide spectrum of wildlife from dragonflies and aquatic invertebrates to fish.

would be worth it to hire a landscape architect, civil engineer, or other professional to help design a drainage solution. For a severe problem, it's best to discuss your issues with several contractors to come up with the most suitable solution.

Choosing Plants for Wet Landscapes

You need to pay attention to the moisture preferences of plants no matter where you plant them, but this is particularly important in or near wetlands themselves. For instance, the cardinal flower (*Lobelia cardinalis*) is listed as a wetlands plant, so it could be a good choice for an area in your landscape that is almost always damp. On the other hand, its relative, the pineland lobelia (*L. homophylla*), is more drought tolerant and may be a better choice for an area that might dry out for part of the year. In addition, if there is any possibility of salt-water intrusion or salt spray, choose salt-tolerant species, especially the trees and shrubs because they are your long-term landscape investments.

Upland Landscaping Near Wet Sites

If your property fronts on a wetland or waterway, there is a good chance that at least part of your yard falls in the transition or buffer zone. While everyone lives in a watershed and we all should be careful with outflows from our landscapes, those who live near the water have a greater obligation to be good upland neighbors in our delicate water-based ecosystems. Here are a few ways to be proactive:

- Use sustainable lawn-care practices, with no pesticides and little or no fertilizer. If you must use fertilizer, apply only slow-release and organic amendments such as compost in early spring as the grass is beginning to grow, but well before the wet season. The conventional advice to apply fertilizers in the fall is wrong for Florida and other southern states because our southern grasses are going into dormancy at that time. Keep garden and grass clippings and leaves out of the water and out of the local storm-drain system. Leave the clippings on the yard or put them in the compost pile. Educate your yard service people so they understand that it is not acceptable to blow leaves, grass clippings, and other yard trash into the curbs, roads, storm drains, or water. Don't use mulch near shorelines because it can wash into the water. Yard debris increases the organic load in the water because as it decomposes, the populations of bacteria, fungi, and algae will increase, depleting oxygen levels in the water.

- Have the wetland water tested to find out about any problem with underground seepage from septic tanks or leaking sewer pipes. While buffer gardens and wild areas next to wet sites will filter out much of the visible aboveground outflow from nearby buildings, it's also important to be aware of what you can't see and to repair a leaky system.

- Keep nearby storm drains cleared of leaves, pine needles, sand, and other debris. While the county government should be clearing them out, the frequency of these small maintenance tasks has been greatly reduced with tight budgets. We can all make a difference by accomplishing these tasks ourselves and in a timely manner. Add the leaves and pine needles to your compost pile or use for mulch. Bring a trash bag, and collect litter that could also wash into waterways. Plus, if less litter is left along roadsides, then maybe people will be less likely to add more.

- Find ways to sequester the majority of the stormwater on your property. This is critically important because outflows of nutrient-laden water and eroded soil fill waterways with silt and nutrients. If your stormwater flows out to a community-wide storm system across paved driveways and roads, it will also pick up and deliver the poisons from vehicle drippage directly to nearby waterways. In some communities, some of this water can get into the sanitary sewer and result in overloading it; this overload can result in untreated sewage releases.

Controlling stormwater and erosion during Florida's five-month wet season (June through October) is not easy, because at least a few times during those months, we are likely to receive several inches of rain in a day. Even though most of the time you won't receive that much rain, you should still build in as much capacity as you can for rainwater in your landscape. That capacity can be used for capturing roof runoff in a series of rain barrels or a cistern, directing rainwater from impervious surfaces such as driveways to low areas, building rain gardens or bioswales where appropriate, building a seasonal pond to accept rainwater, or building large dry wells to absorb overflows.

Rain Gardens

Rain gardens or bioswales can be planted in natural or man-made low spots that are positioned to collect rainwater from roofs, driveways, or other impervious surfaces to reduce or eliminate stormwater runoff from your property. The rain garden plants will absorb much of the trapped water, while the rest will percolate into the soil and hopefully help refresh the aquifer below. Work to include large leafy plants in your rain garden because they will take up more water during the process of transpiration than smaller plants or those with small leaf area such as pines.

Locate a rain garden at least 10 feet away from buildings so the extra moisture has plenty of space to soak in without causing damage to foundations, but close enough so that collecting the rainwater is not too inconvenient. Also locate it away from your septic drainfield and at least 10 feet from large trees to avoid fighting with tree roots. On the other hand, those large trees will soak up a lot of water, so having them nearby could work well.

You will probably need to attach a flexible drainpipe from the downspout or maybe from the rain barrel overflows to reduce muddiness in traffic areas and prevent erosion. If you are collecting stormwater from a driveway or other impervious surface, you may need to install a French drain to soak up the water and then direct it to the top of the rain garden. Make sure the pipe slants downhill toward the rain garden. It's best to install a splash area made of rocks or a downspout splashguard where the water exits the drainpipe so it doesn't erode the soil there.

To avoid mosquitoes, the rain garden system should be designed to absorb most of the rainwater in three days most of the time, so mosquito larvae do not have the chance to mature. Heavy rains could quickly fill up your garden, so plan for overflows directed away from buildings. Create a dip in the berm on the low side of the rain garden so the overflows are directed either over the ground in a curving swale or into another drainpipe into a pond, a wooded area, a hedgerow built in a swale, or a large dry well.

When selecting plants for your rain gardens, choose those that are appropriate for your planting zone and can thrive with periods of both inundation and dryness, because they should be able to survive the dry season without special irrigation. You'll use mostly perennial and woody plants for long-term stability and for easier maintenance. Don't use chunky bark mulch because it will float away during major rainstorms.

For more information and details on rain gardens, French drains, and rain barrels, see *Sustainable Gardening for Florida* by Ginny Stibolt (University Press of Florida, 2009).

Dry Wells

If you are short on space, a dry well can be constructed to accept the overflows from rain gardens, rain barrels, or downspouts. The advantage of a dry well is that it won't be noticeable in the landscape when it's complete—you can install a lawn, herbaceous garden, or path on top of it. Before you go to all the work of digging out a sizable hole and getting the rocks and other materials needed for a dry well, dig a small-diameter test hole during the wet season to check for drainage. The test hole should be as deep as the intended dry well. Wait to see if it fills with water by itself when no rain is falling. If this happens, you have run into groundwater, and that spot will never work as a dry well. Fill up the hole and build another rain garden or a pond instead.

The size of the hole for the dry well depends on the volume of water

Rain Garden Plants Recommended for Florida and Most Southeastern States

This short list includes plants that can withstand flooding for several days and also dryness. Where only a genus name is listed, you can use any species of native plants in that genus. Where a species is specified, don't substitute other species. For instance, sweetbay magnolia tolerates frequent flooding, but some other magnolias do not.

Perennials

Black-eyed Susan (*Rudbeckia spp.*), Leavenworth's tickseed (*Coreopsis leavenworthii*), blue mistflower (*Conoclinium coelestinum*), ferns (*Osmunda regalis, Osmundastrum cinnamomeum, Woodwardia* spp., *Blechnum* spp., *Thelypteris* spp., *Acrostichum daneifolium*), irises (*Iris* spp.), goldenrods (*Euthamia* spp., *Solidago* spp.), narrowleaf blue-eyed grass (*Sisyrinchium angustifolium*), rain lilies (*Zephyranthes* spp.), rushes (*Juncus* spp.), most sedges (*Carex* spp., *Cyperus* spp., *Rhynchospora* spp., *Eleocharis* spp.), meadow garlic (*Allium canadense*), and grasses such as cordgrasses (*Spartina* spp.).

Woody Plants

Bald and pond cypress (*Taxodium* spp.), buttonbush (*Cephalanthus occidentalis*), dahoon holly (*Ilex cassine*), elderberry (*Sambucus nigra* subsp. *canadensis*), hackberry (*Celtis laevigata*), gallberry (*Ilex glabra*), sweetspire (*Itea virginica*), highbush blueberry (*Vaccinium corymbosum*), palms and palmettos (*Roystonea regia, Sabal minor, Sabal palmetto, Acoelorraphe wrightii*), red maple (*Acer rubrum*), sweetbay magnolia (*Magnolia virginiana*), anises (*Illicium* spp.), wax myrtles (*Morella* spp.), and some viburnums such as (*Viburnum obovatum*).

and the type of soil—clayey soil will require a larger hole because of slow drainage. Once the hole is dug, direct the drainpipe into its side, and then line it with landscape fabric or geotextile to keep soil out. If the dry well simply sits in a low area where water normally collects, then no drainpipe will be necessary because the water already flows there.

Calculating the Volume of Water

An inch of rain on 1000 square feet of impervious surface such as a roof or hard pavement will produce 600 gallons of water. Use this equation: gallons = 0.6 × (inches of rain) × (surface area in square feet). (The 0.6 is the approximate conversion factor to translate inches of rainfall to gallons—it's actually 0.62333, but 0.6 is close enough for landscaping purposes.) The angle of the impervious surface makes no difference.

For porous surfaces such as a mulched vegetated landscape or a lawn, runoff will be only about 10 to 15 percent of the volume for impervious surfaces. So an inch of rain on 1000 square feet of lawn may produce only about 60 gallons of runoff, but here, the increased slope of the lawn will produce a larger quantity. Many factors figure into degree of porosity, with soil type having the largest effect.

Once you have an estimate for the possible number of gallons in a heavier than normal rainfall, you can calculate the size of the hole. One gallon = 0.13 of a cubic foot; the reverse is that 1 cubic foot = 7.5 gallons, so 600 gallons of water will need a hole with a capacity of about 80 cubic feet or 4 × 4 × 5 feet, and that is without any gravel. If the area is sandy, that dry well will drain quickly, plus that 600 gallons will not be dumped into it all at once. These are rough calculations to give you a starting point for estimating the needed capacity.

The simplest configuration is to fill the hole to within 6 inches of soil level with washed gravel, fold the fabric over the top of the gravel, and then cover with soil, turfgrass, or mulch to bring it up to the soil level. (Note on gravel: Use large or medium-sized gravel, not crusher run gravel. Two-inch crusher-run gravel includes a variety of gravel sizes from 2 inches down to sand grain size. This will not offer the gaps you need to hold water.) A more effective design will create a larger void of some type to accommodate a larger volume of water. The void could be a large covered bucket or barrel with small holes drilled in it,

This dry well is about 4 feet in all three dimensions; extra water capacity has been added by use of porous drainage pipe covered with fabric socks.

Geotextile fabric was used on the bottom of the hole and then around the porous drainage pipes before clean gravel was added to the center of the pipes. After this, more fabric was laid on top to keep the soil out. Half of this dry well was covered with lawn and the other half was a mulched path.

surrounded by the washed gravel. The void could also be created with rings of fabric-covered perforated drainpipe laid into the hole one on top of the other. After you've created the void, make sure it's strong enough for people to walk on before you continue. The last thing you need is for someone to fall into the hole. Finally, fill in the rest of the lined hole with gravel, fold the fabric over the top and bring it up to grade with mulch or soil. In most cases, if it has enough capacity for the situation, no further maintenance will be needed for many years.

Buffer Zones

Buffer gardens built above the littoral zone next to the shoreline protects the waterway from nutrient runoff, erosion, and organic waste such as leaves and lawn clippings. Remove as much turfgrass from the waterfront area as possible for the situation. The plants you choose for this area should be low-care woody plants, graminoids, and other perennials suited for the specific zone and level of salinity. Observe what grows naturally in areas similar to your site. If existing vegetation, (other than turfgrass or invasive exotic plants) is doing well, let it stay. Any buffer is good, but a zone of 30 feet or more is recommended for the best treatment along the shoreline. If the lot slopes toward the water, a wider buffer is recommended; in this case it's a good idea to

Design buffer zones with swales that parallel the water's edge to reduce the direct drainage of stormwater.

install a swale and a ridge along the upper edge of the buffer to capture (or at least slow down) the rainwater on its way to the shoreline. If space allows, include another ridge and swale in the middle of the buffer parallel to the shore.

Plan for periodic high water in the buffer area closest to the water by choosing plants with deep roots and those most tolerant of occasional standing water. Most rain garden plants will work well in freshwater sites. Build access pathways parallel to the shoreline for maintenance. Make sure that turtles and amphibians have access to upland areas adjacent to the shoreline. You could mulch the upper section of the buffer to create clean edges for the lawn or pathways as long as the mulch can't possibly wash into the water. Don't use weed barrier cloth under the mulch—it reduces habitat value. Turtles need access to soil so they can lay their eggs, and toads need places where they can bury themselves during the day to keep cool in summer and to warm up during colder months.

While the buffer area can provide habitat for some wildlife, it can also be designed to keep out others. For instance, if there are geese or ducks in the area, a dense stand of sturdy, stiff bushes such as bluestem palmettos (*Sabal minor*), blackberries (*Rubus* spp.), hollies (*Ilex* spp.), or wax myrtles (*Morella cerifera*) might make your yard less suitable as goose habitat, but frogs, turtles, and other animals would still have access to and from the water. Thick buffer vegetation also prevents erosion and stabilizes the shoreline by absorbing wave energy, trapping sediments, and further slowing stormwater runoff. Even a small pond will be healthier and provide much better habitat value if it has a good buffer.

Ponds in Your Landscape

Ponds are desirable features in the landscape to provide a focus as well as wildlife habitat. They can range in size from small preformed tubs set in the ground to large groundwater or spring-fed bodies of water—the benefits vary depending on size and site. A well-designed pond and its local microclimate can provide good habitat for many years. Larger ponds can also serve as stormwater retention areas.

Whether a pond is naturally occurring, or added later as part of site development, consider how the pond will interface with general use of the yard. You may need to add a low fence, dense plantings, a berm, or a low wall to keep children safe as well as the pond plantings. That berm may also add extra flood control if the pond receives too much stormwater.

Natural Ponds

Naturally occurring ponds usually occupy the lowest points of a landscape and are wide and shallow, providing a large amount of littoral habitat. Sunlight penetration into the shallow water supports emergent plants and results in increased pond-life activity. Natural ponds less than 4 feet deep are often completely covered with plants, and the natural tendency is for ponds like this to fill with detritus, silt, and other organic matter, but this process (called eutrophication) is greatly accelerated if there is an artificial source of nutrients such as fertilizer runoff from neighboring lawns.

Before doing anything to a pond, evaluate it or have a professional do it. If there are invasive plants, have them removed. Depending on your situation and the local ordinances, you may need to obtain a permit or hire a professional for the invasive eradication. Ongoing pond maintenance will probably include periodic removal of some of the emergent and aquatic plants to maintain some open water. In addition to hand-removing the plants, you may also wish to dredge parts of the pond to a depth of 6 feet or more to discourage emergent plants in areas where you want open water pools and to provide better habitat for fish. A permit will likely be needed, and it helps to have the excavation done by someone with appropriate equipment since hand digging is hard work.

Ideally only about a third of the pond should be covered with vegetation. Other important steps to prolong the life of a pond are to reduce the amount of nutrients that flow into it and to remove excess organic matter like leaves, pine needles, and pond muck from the bottom. The best time to scoop out the bottom is at the end of the dry season, when the pond is at its lowest level and more of the bottom is exposed so you can see more of what you're doing, whether hand-digging a small pond or working with machinery to dredge out a larger pond. If your pond is small, don't stir it up too much or your fish will die. One alternative is to remove all the fish and keep them in a holding tank while you're working on the pond. After a good dredging and if the incoming nutrients are drastically reduced, the eutrophication process may be slowed enough so that your pond can provide years of pleasure without too much additional work.

The muck from a natural pond could be a great addition to your compost pile, but layer it in with brown or dry materials so your compost does not turn anaerobic. The muck from an urban pond with a questionable history should be treated separately, especially if there have been fish die-offs in the pond. Ask your local authorities for guidance on handling it. One option, if it's not too toxic, is to use it to make a mound or ridge in your landscape as part of your design—keep in mind that it will shrink as its organic material decays.

While excessive vegetation can cause problems for ponds and lakes, a moderate amount of underwater vegetation aerates the water as it photosynthesizes. Vegetation also offers good cover and food for aquatic animals.

Many communities install fountains in their ponds. While shooting water into the air certainly aerates the pond, a lot of water is lost through evaporation as it passes through the air. You may wish to add a solar-powered filtering system and gentle waterfall or bubbling system to clean and aerate the water more sustainably.

Lined or Artificial Ponds

If you'd like a new pond and your soil is sandy with no immediate groundwater to support the water level, you'll probably need to install a liner of some sort. One way to test the site is to dig a narrow hole 2 feet deep where you want to place the pond and fill it with water. If it drains within an hour, you'll need a liner. It might be a good idea to bring in a professional pond builder to help you evaluate the situation. Here are some guidelines for designing a belowground lined pond:

- Create as big and deep a pond as your space and budget allow. It's much easier to accomplish the digging, the laying of plastic or cement, and other work all at one time. Expanding it later is much more difficult than the initial work. Use a quality plastic liner (thickness of at least 45 mil), or use concrete for a more permanent pond without all the petrochemicals leaching into the water. If sizable trees (except for palms) are growing near the site, you may need to line the pond anyway, because sooner or later those roots will crack the cement.

- The pond should be at least 24 inches deep in the center, even for a relatively small pond, but deeper is better.
- Create a slightly sloping bottom so all the detritus sinks to one place making it easier to scoop out. You should scoop it out once a year so it doesn't build up. Don't skip this step. Incorporate this rich muck into your compost pile.
- Build a plant shelf approximately 1 to 2 feet below the water's surface around most of the pond to mimic the littoral zone along a natural waterfront. The shelf should be about a foot wide and sloped slightly toward the edge of the pond so your pots have plenty of room and will lean toward the wall as their plants get taller, instead of falling over into the water. Create some spots for containers away from the edge for rooted floating plants such as the American white water lily (*Nymphaea odorata*).
- Create a beach or flat area somewhere around the edge for turtle access and to provide a shallow area for birds and exposed mud for butterflies.
- If possible, use rainwater to fill the pond instead of municipal tap water. Inoculate the water with a bucket of water from a natural pond or lake to introduce beneficial microbes. If you do use tap water, let it sit for a few days to allow chlorine to dissipate. Should you ever refill your pond with treated tap water, never fill more than 20 percent of the water volume, or you may kill the fish and other wildlife in the pond.
- After the pond is filled, start installing pots of suitable emergent plants. Use dark green or black pots to reduce their visibility in the water, and cover the top of the soil in each pot with weed barrier cloth held in place by a layer of sand or gravel.

This way the soil won't move into the water and the pots will be less likely to shift with the extra weight.

- Allow the pond to settle with just the plants for a month or two before you add fish to the ecosystem. The water may turn green, but that's not unusual and it will eventually balance out. Meanwhile, frogs, dragonflies, and other beneficial wildlife will probably find your pond on their own.
- Expect herons and other fishing birds to visit your pond, so when you stock the fish, choose lots of small fish that are easily and economically replaced. Native fish, such as the eastern mosquitofish (*Gambusia holbrooki*), are a good choice.
- Consider a solar-powered pump to circulate water and drive a small, gentle waterfall feature. It will help aerate and filter the water without the installation of an external electrical system, plus the running water will attract birds.
- Depending on its size, a lined pond could receive some storm-water runoff, say from one downspout, but water retention is probably not the primary purpose of a small pond like this. Plan for the overflow in case of a heavy rain just as with any other water retention feature.

Seasonal Ponds

Because of Florida's typical wet and dry seasons, a common pond type found across much of our flatwoods habitats is the shallow "seasonal" pond—typically 2 to 5 feet deep and 100 or more feet across, though you can create one that is smaller to fit your landscape. Standing water recedes in the dry winter months, leaving a muddy pond floor that continues to provide moisture required by many amphibians, reptiles, birds, small mammals, and even small fish, including the mosquito-fish.

If you wish to construct a pond to replicate this important habitat, choose an appropriate area where it won't look out of place. Typically this will be a low spot in your landscape or an area in the buffer zone near shoreline property. The vegetation in this pond will most likely cover the whole area. It will be a damp meadow for part of the year and a shallow pond during the wet season. You'll probably find that the plants that do well in a rain garden such as rushes, native irises, and sedges will also thrive here. In fact, you could consider seasonal ponds to be a type of rain garden, and they do very well as stormwater retention features because of their shallow and broad, gently sloping profile. Seasonal ponds make good overflow areas to catch the excess water from bioswales, rain gardens, and rain barrels. When a pond fills up with water, add some eastern mosquitofish to keep the mosquito population in check.

Retention Ponds

A stormwater retention pond can be transformed from an eyesore into an attractive neighborhood asset with good habitat value. But before you take any action, you need to talk to the owner, such as an HOA or the county, as well as local officials to get permission to work on it, and you need to check on the state environmental resource permits that apply to surface-water treatment ponds. Also, find out if it is designed to be dredged or scraped out on a regular basis. If it is, you'll need to plan for access for heavy machinery on one or two sides of the pond. If you can arrange it, have the pond dredged or scraped before you begin any significant work; this way you'll start with a deeper body of water, and you'll know where and how the dredging takes place to plan for it in the future. Also talk to your water management district and local government for ideas about a reasonable plan for your pond. There may be neighborhood grants for projects like this.

Retention ponds are designed to collect stormwater from roads, parking lots, and neighborhood yards—sometimes their watersheds are surprisingly large. In any case, properties closest to a pond have the most to gain by its transformation. To be successful, any plan to improve the pond will need to include all the neighbors as well as the county or city's public works department.

The first phase of restoration could have as many as five separate initiatives:

1. To make sure that neighboring property owners or managers are not using the pond as a dumping place for yard waste or other trash. If trash is lying in and around the pond, hold a

"Clean Our Pond" workday. Enlist the aid of neighborhood school kids or youth groups—they may be looking for community service projects. This is a great time to publicize your pond project.

2. Remove exotic invasive plants from both the shoreline and the water area. Sometimes a simple pulling out or chopping down is not enough to wipe out these plants, so you may need to bring in a professional, especially where aquatic invasives such as hydrilla (*Hydrilla verticillata*) are growing. You may wish to get a permit to release sterilized Asian grass carp to keep the hydrilla or other waterweeds in check. Arrange their delivery so you're putting them in after most of the physical work is done. As discussed in chapter 3, the carp will live for several years and also eat native plants once the weeds are gone, so don't overstock.

3. Consider reducing some of the runoff from neighboring yards. Yes, this is a water retention feature and it may have a tightly engineered design, but many retention ponds hold more water than optimal. If so, and if you and your neighbors work to capture and retain stormwater on your properties first, the health of the pond will likely be improved.

4. If erosion has eaten away the soil from the sloping sides of the pond, try to figure out why. In some cases, the side slopes were designed to be as steep as allowed by law; in which case, the owner may be amenable to having at least some of the edges made less steep. In other cases, uncontrolled runoff may have flowed into the pond; here it would be desirable to find the source of the extra runoff that caused the erosion and work to slow it down. Each situation is different, and the best treatment depends on the slope, the soil type, and more. For instance, you might install a rain garden in a curving swale at the top of the slope to capture most of the runoff first. A couple of lengths of fiber-filled or compost-filled erosion logs staked into wide U-shapes and planted with sturdy plants could reduce further erosion. You'll need to monitor what happens during a storm to know for sure.

5. Reduce or eliminate fertilization in the vicinity of the pond.
   Too often, ponds receive such a large nutrient overload that
   they have a constant algae bloom, and this is not good for the
   long-term health of the pond's ecosystem. Install emergent
   plants, such as pickerelweed (*Pontederia cordata*), alligator
   flag (*Thalia geniculata*), arrowheads (*Sagittaria* spp.), rushes
   (*Juncus* spp.), and sedges (*Carex* spp., *Eleocharis* spp., *Rhynchospora* spp., *Scirpus* spp.) that will soak up the nutrients
   that still make it into the pond. Cattails (*Typha* spp.) and willows (*Salix* spp.) may already have planted themselves; you
   may wish to leave some of these natives in place to absorb
   the nutrients, because they are quite effective at doing so.
   You may eventually replace the cattails with less aggressive
   natives such as pickerelweed to reduce ongoing maintenance
   needs. Eventually you will be pulling out more of the cattails
   to contain them because they're aggressive, but at the beginning stages of restoring a pond, they serve a good purpose. If
   the pond's nutrients are drastically reduced, the cattails are
   less likely to spread as quickly. If the pond is deep, the retention time of water in the pond increases, and this extra time
   is extremely important for water quality improvement.

After you have removed all the trash and the invasive plants in
and around the pond and repaired eroding banks, you can start on
the second phase: planting attractive native waterfront perennials
and woody plants. Most deep ponds have littoral shelves that are designed to be planted. Plan to have at least one-third of the pond vegetated, similar to the buffer and littoral plantings described above.
During the first phase you should have determined the areas where
future dredging may occur. Don't use expensive woody plants in those
areas; install only herbaceous plants that are easily replaced, such
as rushes, grasses, and sedges. Commercial contractors can provide
cost-effective sources of pickerelweed and arrowheads that grow reliably and quickly, but do make sure they have a sustainable source for
these plants because some contractors harvest them (with permits)
from wild settings.

It will probably take several years to rehabilitate a neglected retention

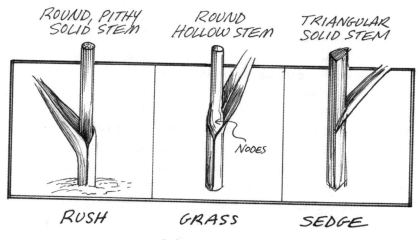

ROUND, PITHY SOLID STEM

ROUND HOLLOW STEM

TRIANGULAR SOLID STEM

NODES

RUSH   GRASS   SEDGE

Sedges have edges,
Rushes are round,
Grasses have nodes,
All the way to the ground.

pond, but as a water feature in the community, a rescued pond can offer a great habitat for native flora and fauna. It can also provide an attractive focal point in both residential neighborhoods and commercial parks. The community-wide effort and increased awareness of the pond may expand beyond the watershed of this particular pond. Be sure to take "before," "during," and "after" photographs of the pond and publicize what you've accomplished. Don't forget the educational value of the process of restoring an artificial system to a balanced and vital ecosystem. See the next chapter for more details on sharing your successes.

Mangroves

Mangroves do so much for Florida's shoreline, including cushioning storm damage, that they have their own regulations to govern their treatment—be sure you understand local and state regulations. In most regions, you will not be able to remove mangroves. Unless local government has added additional restrictions, the state has specific regulations that specify who can trim them and to what height. Do not violate these regulations. In some places, you cannot even pick up their propagules (the floating seedlings that drop from the parent plants) without special permits—even if you originally planted them.

In Florida there are three official mangrove species, each in a different plant family: red mangrove (*Rhizophora mangle*) in the Rhizophoraceae, black mangrove (*Avicennia germinans*) in the Avicenniaceae, and white mangrove (*Laguncularia racemosa*) in the Combretaceae. Buttonwood (*Conocarpus erectus*) is considered an unofficial mangrove because it's in the same family as the white mangrove and because it often grows in more upland habitats near mangrove communities. All can grow in either fresh or salt water, although they do not usually occur naturally in freshwater habitats.

The three true mangroves may not be closely related botanically, but they've all adapted to harsh saltwater environments. In both the red and black mangroves, the seeds germinate while still attached to the parent plant to form a propagule. Since this happens without a dormant stage or encasement in fruit, these mangroves are considered viviparous. The propagule contains the seedling and a floating container. The white mangroves are semiviviparous, with germination happening after the seed falls from the parent. When a propagule is dropped it will float away with the tides. The three species have different obligate floating periods to ensure dispersal—that of the red mangrove is 40 days, the black mangrove, 14 days, and the white mangrove, just 5 days. During this floating time, the seedling matures and photosynthesis takes place; once the propagule has absorbed enough water, it will become vertical and ready to sprout roots as soon as it touches bottom.

Black and red mangroves are hardier than the other species; their range extends from the Florida Keys into the northern regions on both peninsular coasts, although they can be killed back by extreme cold weather. Typically the red mangrove (the one with stilts for roots) grows farthest out in the water, followed by black, and then white as you move in from the open water. The buttonwood grows mostly on dry land, but it can withstand periodic flooding.

As a group, the mangroves provide habitat for many types of wildlife from birds to fish, absorb the wave action, and build new land as they hold onto sediment. If your property fronts on a bay, lagoon, or

Red mangroves (*Rhizophora mangle*) have been planted as a living shoreline along the Intracoastal Waterway in Palm Beach County as a public/private project to increase habitat and also to better protect the shoreline.

estuary in the southern half of Florida, consider mangroves in your waterfront plans. They will greatly increase the storm-worthiness of your coast and provide excellent habitat for birds, fish, crabs, and more. In North Florida, it may be more appropriate to consider mangroves as specimen plants, because historically it is the salt marshes that have provided the storm buffering.

For more on mangroves see the brochure on mangroves published by the Florida Department of Environmental Protection (www.manatee.ifas.ufl.edu/seagrant/pdfs/Mangrove_Trimming_Guidelines.pdf).

Managing a Seashore Landscape

A limited number of plants grow well on the beaches and sand dunes of either the Atlantic or Gulf Coast. It should be noted that these are not wetland habitats, but upland ones—they are discussed here because of their proximity to water. In order to stabilize the sand to some degree, use plants you observe in natural areas near your location that are tolerant of both salt spray and salt water. Even though this is not a wetland, per se, you may need some type of permit to modify sand dune areas.

Examples of species tolerant of salt spray are dune sunflower (*Helianthus debilis*) for the Atlantic Coast and west coast dune sunflower (*Helianthus debilis* subsp. *vestitus*) for the Gulf Coast, and also seaside goldenrod (*Solidago sempervirens*), spotted beebalm (*Monarda punctata*), sea grape (*Coccoloba uvifera*), and cabbage palm (*Sabal palmetto*). In addition to mangroves, other plants that are tolerant of saltwater intrusion include sea oats (*Uniola paniculata*), perennial glasswort (*Sarcocornia ambigua*), saltwort (*Batis maritima*), seacoast marshelder (*Iva imbricata*), smooth cordgrass (*Spartina alterniflora*), seapurslane (*Sesuvium portulacastrum*), and, for South Florida, bay cedar (*Suriana maritima*).

Plants that are salt tolerant may have a thick leaf cuticle or some type of mechanism to exude the absorbed salt. Most of these plants have extensive and aggressive root systems in order to survive in shifting sandy soils. Many benefit from being buried deep in the sand, even beyond the top of a pot. This prevents evaporation from the soil and, in some settings, may give them access to a lens of freshwater that floats on top of the salt water under larger barrier islands. While they are certainly drought tolerant, you will need to irrigate them liberally when you plant them until they become established. For herbaceous plants, water them every day for a couple of weeks unless there is a soaking rain, and after that, during dry periods for a couple of months. For trees and shrubs, irrigation requirements depend on the size of the plant; follow the guidelines listed in chapter 5.

Because all of Florida's coastal zones are vulnerable to tropical storms, your landscape plan should include stormwise landscaping principles. Planting groups or groves of wind-tolerant trees and shrubs on the windward side of buildings makes a big difference. Groves, as described in chapter 9, should be located far enough away that if a tree falls, it won't damage buildings, but close enough to disrupt wind currents. In day-to-day living, the grove buffers the breezes and removes some of the saltiness so the landscape behind it has some protection. With the reduced battering and less salt spray, you could plant some "normal" plants in your protected zone, but sooner or later a load of salt will be deposited. Use salt-tolerant woody plants in this second-tier landscape, because trees and shrubs are long-term investments and it's best not to have to replace them.

General Planting Instructions for Emergent and Submerged Plants

If you're purchasing a large number of emergent or submerged plants to restore a shoreline, you'll probably end up with bunches of small bare-root plants. Keep them moist and plant them as soon as possible. Dig holes that are 6 or more inches deep in the bottom of the lake or pond. If possible, plant when the site is dryer than normal so that there is time for them to become established before floating is a problem. Also planting in the winter works well because the plants are likely to be semidormant.

If the water is subject to wind, waves, and tides, drive a stake in the bottom for each little plant or small grouping and tie the plants to the stake. The stake will keep them in place and increase their visibility so people don't step on them. For woody species, plant singly at distances that allow for their adult size, but still use the stake for support and visibility. As a rule of thumb, plant woody plants in areas that will dry out occasionally.

Wetland Maintenance

Initial maintenance for the first few weeks of the restored or revegetated area includes checking for and replanting plants that have become up-rooted and are just hanging onto their stakes, then weeding at least twice a year to control the regrowth of exotic species and to pull out trash. Regular weeding will be needed for the first year or two, gradually reducing the frequency as the desirable plants become dominant. In salty environments, the weeds will be much less of a problem. This initial care allows expansion of the desirable native species.

After the first two or three years, when the plants have established themselves and if the nuisance species aren't too thick, weeding sessions can be reduced to once every other year. If you still have a sizable influx of undesirables, you'll find that it's easier to control the exotic species if you remove them before they grow too much, so an annual check will still be needed. Eventually, your natives will make it harder for the exotics to invade and your job of maintenance will become easier, except for pulling out the collected trash.

A well-managed wet area in your landscape will add interest and important habitat.

11

Beyond Your Yard

The native habitat you build in your yard will be worth more to wild-life if your neighbors also plant natives on their properties and if the community associations, local schools, churches, and town itself also work to reduce lawns and plant more natives. This community-wide effort will provide good flyways and corridors where wildlife can find refuge, birds can find shelter and nesting sites, and butterflies can find nectar and larval food sources. In addition, as more nearby properties eradicate invasives, fewer will be available to be carried back onto your property and neighboring wildlands. As far as controlling invasives goes, everyone's maintenance will become a little easier. There are various ways to participate in this process and to urge others to hop on the native habitat bandwagon.

It's a good idea to further your native plant education right at the beginning of a naturalizing project by joining your local native plant society chapter. You will find many smart people who care for the environment. Attend meetings, go on field trips, and participate in plant sales, workshops, and workdays. Volunteer to assist in the chapter booth at various outreach events. It's so educational to talk to attendees about native plants, but don't oversell—because as you now know, planting native plants does not mean a maintenance-free landscape. In Florida, join the Florida Native Plant Society (www.FNPS.org). To look for other native plant organizations see www.for-wild.org/hotlinks.htm.

For a more formal and structured education in local ecosystems, sign up for local master naturalist courses—no prior scientific training is needed. Classes cover core topics in ecology as a whole complex entity—geology, hydrology, weather, plants (native, exotic, and invasive), and wildlife including birds, mammals, butterflies, and other bugs. These courses focus specifically on ecosystems in your region and not on just general talking points about a subject—you learn exactly what you need to know to be a successful manager of a native landscape. The other important benefit is meeting the local experts who teach the courses so you will be more connected to local environmental issues and ongoing local initiatives. In Florida, the core topics are wetlands ecosystems, coastal ecosystems, and upland ecosystems—each core topic is covered by a 40-hour curriculum. Shorter courses cover additional, more specific topics that will also further your knowledge.

Once you have taken the core classes, you are expected to volunteer a certain number of hours as a master naturalist in state or local parks, schools, or other areas with natural habitats. As a master naturalist

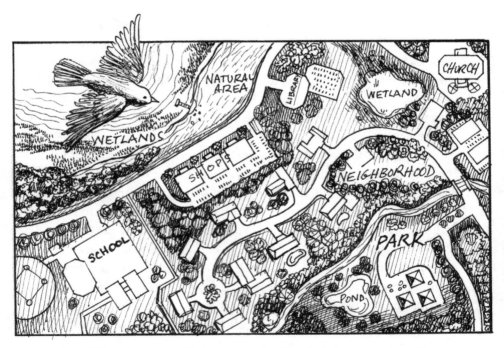

Doug Tallamy has proved that unpoisoned native plants in your yard provide much needed habitat services for wildlife. If the whole neighborhood is full of natives, the difference is huge. How can this bird not stop for a rest and a snack?

you can choose volunteer opportunities that are the best fit for your skills and lifestyle. With local budget cuts in place these days, your volunteer hours can make a huge difference for a small park, environmental center, or local school system. Schools and young people are a major leverage point when educating about using native plants. You'll reach more people and have a higher likelihood of impacting neighborhoods if the kids initiate family projects. In Florida see www.masternaturalist.ifas.ufl.edu/. Other states' programs are similar—for a listing, see the website of the Alliance of Natural Resource Outreach and Service Programs (www.anrosp.org). All in all, master naturalists are a force for nature.

Close to Home

Many communities own or maintain open lands for the use and enjoyment of residents. If this is the case for your own community, maybe some of the areas could be managed more sustainably by establishing native ecosystems around the fringes in the lesser-used areas. You could work from the inside by joining the community board of governors to have more influence over land management decisions and maybe help ease restrictive regulations about lawns. On a smaller scale, you could help community youth groups or schools build and maintain butterfly gardens. And who wouldn't want more butterflies? Maybe your community would qualify for a wildflower grant of some type to help fund the effort. In Florida, a good place to start looking for small grants is the Florida Wildflower Foundation (flawildflowers.org).

Perhaps a local retention pond needs attention. Find out whether it could be turned into a neighborhood project to clean up and plant appropriate natives at its edges. See chapter 10 for specific pond guidelines.

If there are roadways with extra-wide shoulders in your town or county, talk to the public works department to initiate no-mow areas where they could plant wildflowers instead of grass and mow only once a year. Local municipal districts also have lands around buildings such as town halls, courthouses, and libraries that probably have high-maintenance lawns that could be reduced by installing native butterfly

The Rule of "Ps"

When talking with politicians, people who work for government agencies, or HOA officers, follow the Rule of "Ps":

Be Prepared

Have your materials and handouts ready ahead of time. Your face-time may be severely limited, so this preparation can make the difference between making your point or not.

Be Polite and Respectful

Even if you disagree with a policy or a municipal worker thinks you're wasting time. Getting angry or antagonistic means that you may not be welcomed back in the future.

Deliver Praise

Compliment the workers or group for policies, laws, or actions that are steps in the right direction—no matter how small.

Be Punctual

If you've set up a time to meet someone, make it easy by meeting at his or her office (or other designated place) and be early for the meeting. Things can be a whirlwind of activity in government or agency offices, so don't be a hindrance to their operations.

Be Persistent

If your contact initially rejects your ideas but suggests a date when you can come back, don't let it slide; call back and be there. Or try talking to a different person with a slightly different responsibility. Or organize a grass roots group so you are harder to ignore.

Be Patient

Changing government policies can be a cumbersome process, so it may be a long time before anything happens even if your ideas are accepted.

This is an investment in not only your yard, but also everyone else's, and the whole community's ecosystems.

gardens and rain gardens. These could save taxpayer money because of less frequent mowing and they would also enhance the community and its habitats. Keep in mind that the initial building and establishment of native areas is only the start and they will need ongoing care, so plan for that with a "Friends of whatever township" group to coordinate the care, whether performed by public works department personnel or volunteers such as a youth group, garden club, master gardeners, or master naturalists.

Another public works type of project is to reduce the flow of stormwater into local waterways by cutting openings in curbs and installing large rain gardens to soak up the water. This effort would be a community-wide effort, with initial infrastructure changes being handled by the municipality, but a group of volunteers could plant natives appropriate for rain gardens. One community member who would want to be part of a stormwater initiative is the local riverkeeper or baykeeper, because containing stormwater is a big part of reducing water pollution. Also, these water-collecting swales make wonderful habitat that

CURBSIDE RAIN GARDEN

Public and private land managers can work together to reduce the flow of water into our precious waterways. Curbside rain gardens can accomplish this beautifully.

enhances the whole community. Find your local waterkeeper on this website: www.waterkeeper.org.

Churches and synagogues often have wide expanses of lawn that cost money to mow. Some of the lawn may be used for parking or events, but much of it is probably never used. You could present a plan to the congregation about becoming better stewards of their land and then help them get started on building butterfly gardens or groves of trees. Maybe they could build a meditation garden or natural cathedral.

Your Own Story

The story of how you are transforming your own landscape can be used as an example for others to follow. You don't need to be an expert with advanced degrees in ecology to tell your story—actually, your experience as an "average person" might resonate with more people. Telling your story works best if you document the process from the beginning with photos, sketches, and notes. At the outset, start a garden log, and take notes on what works well and what you would do differently. Sharing your experiences in how "things" went wrong is often more educational and memorable than sugarcoating everything and showing only the good parts.

To create the most compelling story, take plenty of "before," "during," and "after" photos of the process of going natural. Maybe you could perform a citizen science experiment with repeated counts of birds or butterflies, or both, over several days and during specific times during the day before you start planting natives and then again after you stop using pesticides and plant natives. One way to organize the science is to participate in the Great Sunflower Project, where you plant sunflowers and count the pollinators during certain times of the day. The group specifies how to do this and then collects pollinator data from citizen scientists across the country. Participating in this formalized study allows you to document and enumerate the real effects of building habitat on your property. If possible start your participation before beginning your native plantings to provide the best analysis of what happens after you plant a yard with natives (www. greatsunflower.org). Your citizen science experiment will make a compelling story.

Tips for Taking Photos of a Naturalizing Process

You do not need an expensive camera with huge lenses to take good photos that document landscaping projects. Many people have success using smart phones with picture-taking capability, but small point-and-shoot cameras may work better for landscape shots. It would be helpful to have close-up capability to record the bees and butterflies on native flowers. What you are aiming for here are photos with sufficiently high resolution to look good in a Power Point slide show, online in a blog, or in other social media. You will need photo-editing software with enough sophistication to resize, crop, rotate, adjust brightness and contrast, and balance the color.

Here are some tips for taking effective photos to document the process of going native:

• When you take "before" shots, find places to shoot from so you can frame each area of your landscape to give an overall view, without too much road in the foreground or too much sky. Mark the spots where you stand for these photos somehow, so that when you take follow-up photos after each of the various stages, your vantage point will be the same.

• Rake the leaves and clean up the debris before you take photos—even the "before" photo. This is especially important for the adjacent lawn areas where everything except turfgrass looks out of place. You may even want to mow the lawn first. What you want to avoid is distractions—no one will notice a neat lawn, but everyone will notice one covered with debris—natural or man-made.

• Time your photos so there is good light on the important parts of the landscape, but make sure your own shadow is not in the photo. You can avoid bright sun and shadows by shooting on a cloudy day when the light is flat. Many photographers like to take landscape photos early in the morning or late afternoon because of the interesting shadows and the lower levels of light, but the long shadows at these times of day might not be all that effective for your overall shots.

continued

- Pay attention to the horizon so it's horizontal in the photo. Yes, you can rotate the photo later, but that may cut off some of the important content.
- Take a lot of photos. Two or three repeats of each shot will increase the chances of getting at least one that is in focus. That said, learn how to use the focus function on the camera—your point-and-shoot camera may have an option to push the button down partway to see the squares on the screen of the focus area. Make your decisions on which photos to keep soon after you download them. Just save the best photos to your computer—delete the redundant shots so you won't be overwhelmed by volume when it's time to select the ones that best represent your projects.
- Create a separate folder on your computer for native projects so you will have one place to download the photos from your camera or phone.
- To make your story more compelling, take close-ups of flowers with their pollinators, and try to catch birds in the act of feeding on the berries, seeds, or bugs in your landscape. Find predators like toads, lizards, and snakes to show how well the ecosystem is working.

It's important to share photos of the butterflies and birds that grace your yard once you have planted natives. While social media, such as Facebook, Instagram, and Pinterest, play an important part in spreading the word, local newspapers and TV stations are always looking for interesting and photogenic "good news" stories. Another possibility is to volunteer to be a case study for a local native plant nursery that could use your story to sell more native plants. Invite native nursery experts to give presentations or to hold native plant sales right in your neighborhood.

Once you have your slide show put together, write some notes to use during your presentation. Do not read the Power Point slides to the audience, and it's best not to print out handouts of your presentation, but maybe a list of plants that you used would be useful. For more pointers on creating and delivering effective presentations see www. sky-bolt.com/PowerPointProblems.htm.

Now you're ready to contact local groups to see if they would like to share your story. Groups that are active in the area of native plants and working ecosystems, such as native plant society chapters, The Nature Conservancy, local riverkeepers, environmental centers, and local parks, are always looking for speakers. Groups that are not as active with native plants or naturalizing may provide a more important audience to reach. These could include community associations, garden clubs, garden festivals, Audubon Society chapters, Sierra Club chapters, libraries, civic organizations, and youth groups like scouts and 4-H. Once you are known as an available speaker, you'll have plenty of regional opportunities to tell your story.

Your native landscape will become an important oasis for wildlife, but as others in your neighborhood and in the broader community add natives to their landscapes, the habitat effect will become huge. Isn't it time to give back to Mother Nature?

Appendix I

Suggested Native Plant List

This short list of Florida natives that are easy to grow and care for is arranged by form: trees, shrubs, forbs, ferns, graminoids, and vines. Many of these plants are also native to much of the southeastern region of the United States. If a plant is a primary food for butterfly or moth larvae, it is listed as a "Butterfly host plant." This list is just a starting point; you should obtain other more complete plant references—both in print and online. Several are listed in the reference section of this book, but the following are three useful guides to choosing the best plants for your landscape:

- *Florida's Best Native Landscape Plants: 200 Readily Available Species for Homeowners and Professionals,* by Gil Nelson (University Press of Florida, 2003). Almost all the plants listed in this appendix are included in Nelson's book, because if a plant is not readily available in the trade, what's the point of suggesting it?
- The Florida Native Plant Society has a tool on its website for finding natives for your landscape. Select your county, the conditions, and properties desired such as providing wildlife food and cover. This tool will generate a list of suggested plants sorted by plant form. (www.fnps.org/plants)
- For South Florida, the website of the Institute for Regional Conservation, "Natives for Neighborhoods," provides a tool where you can type in your zip code to find appropriate native plants. (www.regionalconservation.org)

As stated in the text, your best bet for success is to build a relationship with reliable native plant nurseries in your area to help you make the right decisions and to ensure that plants you purchase are bred from local stock. If you are in Florida, go to www.plantrealflorida.org to find local native nurseries or nurseries that have a particular species in stock.

The USDA planting zones for each plant provide only a general guideline. A plant found in your planting zone may not work in your landscape because of its various other habitat needs. In this list, where a genus is listed without a particular species, the zones encompass more than one species.

Map showing North, Central, and South Florida. Courtesty of USDA.

Trees

Acer rubrum L., red maple (zones 3–10) This medium to large tree is dioecious and deciduous with good fall and early spring color. It's adaptable but prefers neutral to acidic soil. A good rain garden tree that does well in wet sites, but it also can do well in drier sites. Butterfly host plant. Maintenance: It tends to sucker at its base, has wide-spreading shallow roots, and reseeds freely. Older trees sometimes develop heartwood rot.

Betula nigra L., river birch (zones 4–9) This medium to large deciduous tree with shaggy bark provides year-round interest. It prefers acidic soil and adapts to wet or somewhat drier sites. Can be used in a rain garden and is often planted in groups of three or five. Butterfly host plant. Maintenance: This tree has no particular problems.

Celtis laevigata Willd., sugarberry (zones 4–10) A deciduous medium-sized tree, it can grow in either acidic or alkaline soils and also adapts to moist or dry habitats; drought tolerant. It grows quickly and provides good habitat for birds. Butterfly host plant. Maintenance: Sugarberry and other hackberries are allelopathic and may have a negative impact on plants growing nearby.

Cercis canadensis L., redbud (zones 4–9) This small deciduous understory tree is in the legume family and can grow in poor soils. Prefers well-drained acidic soils. Pink flowers appear in the spring before its heart-shaped leaves emerge. Not wind tolerant. Butterfly host plant. Maintenance: The beanlike seedpods turn brown in the winter and stay attached to the tree until spring, so if it's a lawn tree, pods can be messy.

Coccoloba uvifera (L.) L., seagrape (zones 10–11) This small tree or large shrub is evergreen and salt tolerant. It grows in poor sandy soil and is also drought tolerant. It's dioecious; its showy grapelike clusters of berries are borne on the female plants. It usually has irregularly shaped multiple stems and is often seen around sand dune areas used as a hedge and windbreak. Maintenance: Its large leathery leaves will need to be cleaned up on a regular basis from walkways and lawns, so plant where the leaf drop doesn't matter.

Diospyros virginiana L., persimmon (zones 6–11) This small to medium-sized deciduous tree is dioecious, with the females bearing good-sized fruits that are eaten by wildlife and humans alike. Be sure to include at least one male plant if you want fruit. It's adaptable to various habitats and has good fall color. Best planted at edges of wooded areas. Insect pollinated. Butterfly host plant. Maintenance: Fallen fruit attracts wasps and can be messy, so plant where this won't be a problem, or harvest the fruit as it ripens. Note: Unripened fruit is quite astringent.

Ilex spp., hollies (zones 4–11) More than a dozen hollies are native to Florida; most are evergreen, but winterberry (*I. verticillata*) is deciduous, leaving its striking red berries on bare twigs in the winter. Most are understory trees, but some like gallberry (*I. glabra*) are shrubs. Hollies are dioecious, so whichever species you choose, make sure at least one plant is male so the females can produce those famous berries. Hollies grow in a wide variety of habitats, so choose those that will work best in your situation. Maintenance: Even though most are evergreen, hollies will drop their leaves (which are hard and spiny in some species) all year long, so you will need to sweep them from walkways. Yaupon holly (*I. vomitoria*) sends up lots of suckers, so it will spread across your yard. You can save pruning until the holidays and use the trimmings for traditional decorations.

Juniperus virginiana L., eastern redcedar (zones 3–10) This medium-sized, evergreen conifer is a pioneer species that grows well on upland disturbed sites, at first growing into a perfect elongated cone shape. As it matures the crown becomes rounded or irregular. Often used as a screen, it is a good addition to a hedgerow, but give it room to spread. Offers good habitat value for its denseness and berrylike cones. Butterfly host plant. Maintenance: No particular maintenance is needed.

Liquidambar styraciflua L., sweetgum (zones 6–10) This large tree thrives in many habitats, but may grow faster in moist sites. Butterfly host plant. Maintenance: Plant away from human-use areas because of its abundant, hard, spiny seedpods (gumballs) and the resinous leaves, which can stain hardscape features and vehicles. In addition, it readily reseeds and sends up numerous root suckers at some distance from the tree.

Magnolia grandiflora L., southern magnolia (zones 6–9) This elegant evergreen tree prefers acidic soil and can grow in full sun or partial shade. Fragrant white flowers are showy, as are its bright red fruit. Birds eat the fruit. Butterfly host plant. Maintenance: Its leathery leaves drop throughout the year, so plant where the leaf drop doesn't matter, or raking will become an ongoing chore. Some pruning of suckers and water sprouts may be needed, but wait until the holidays so the trimmings can be used for wreaths and other decorations.

Magnolia virginiana L., sweetbay (zones 5–11) This large semievergreen tree will drop its leaves in the winter in cooler climates. The leaves' silvery undersides are exposed when they blow in the wind. The blooms are about half the size but more fragrant than those of *M. grandiflora*. Prefers moist or wet sites and tolerates periodic flooding, so it's a good choice for rain gardens. It tends to form thickets in damp places. Butterfly host plant. Maintenance: The leaves tend to drop all at once, so keeping them cleared is usually an annual chore if it's located where neatness counts. Trimming back suckers may be needed in some cases.

Nyssa spp., tupelos (zones 4–10) The tupelos are small to medium-sized deciduous trees, often with an interesting, gnarly growth pattern. They have good fall color even in the southern ranges. Prefer moist or wet slightly acidic soils. The flowers attract pollinators and birds, and other wildlife consume the berries. A good contrast tree in the landscape. *N. aquatica* is a good rain garden plant. Maintenance: No particular maintenance is needed. Note: On young trees the branches are perpendicular to the trunk and may interfere with nearby foot or vehicular traffic if you don't allow space for this growth pattern.

Pinus spp., pines (zones 3–11) The pines prefer acidic upland habitats and are often the pioneer woody plants in fields and meadows. Six species of pines are native to Florida, but none of them are good lawn trees because of their continuous needle drop and their preference for acidic soils. Most pines, such as the longleaf pine (*P. palustris* Mill.), are adapted to fire, but they and their pine needles are highly flammable. Butterfly host plants. Maintenance: Pine needle cleanup can be a constant chore unless the trees are in groves away from hardscape features. Plant away from buildings in fire-prone areas.

Quercus spp., oaks (zones 3–11) The oaks prefer acidic upland soils and range in size from large (80 feet tall and 130 feet wide for the live oak, *Q. virginiana* Mill.) to small (less than a foot tall) for the dwarf live oak (*Q. minima* (Sarg.) Small). Some grow quickly, but most do not, so choose carefully. Oaks provide excellent wildlife habitat value. Butterfly host plants. Maintenance: Most oaks reseed profusely, and in the spring their male catkins can make quite a mess.

Roystonea regia (Kunth) O. F. Cook, royal palm (zones 10–11) This tall palm is widely planted in South Florida and with good reason. Occurs naturally in moist to wet sites, but adapts well to more upland sites once established. What could be more stately than the straight, tall royal palm? Maintenance: Since palms cannot heal gouges in their trunks, do not grow turf right next to the trunk where lawn-care machinery can do damage. This palm is self-trimming, and its huge fronds, weighing 40 pounds or more, will fall when they are ready. Don't plant where something or someone could be hit by a falling frond.

Sabal palmetto (Walter) Lodd. ex Schult. & Schult.f., cabbage palmetto or cabbage palm (zones 8–11) This is Florida's (and South Carolina's) state tree, even though it is not a true tree botanically. It prefers moist, rich, somewhat alkaline soil but can adapt to other habitats. Salt tolerant. It's a medium to large tree and grows slowly; it will be shrublike for 10 years or more before it develops a trunk. The huge inflorescence is fragrant and attracts a wide variety of pollinators. The berries are eaten by birds and other wildlife. Butterfly host plant. Maintenance: It's normally sold as a field-grown tree with almost all its fronds trimmed away. At no other time should the fronds be trimmed back as severely, and it should never be topped because that will kill it. Since palms cannot heal gouges in their trunks, do not grow turf right next to the trunk where lawn-care machinery can do damage. Trim away only dead fronds that are drooping well below horizontal, and only if necessary for neatness.

Salix caroliniana Michx., Carolina or coastal plain willow (zones 5–11) This deciduous willow is the most common member of the genus in Florida, but a few other native willows could also work in your landscape. They attract pollinators with their early flowers and are a larval host for butterflies. *S. caroliniana* is naturally found in wet sites and is a good rain garden plant, but it may adapt to drier sites if you irrigate well during the establishment period. It roots easily and is one of the better candidates for building living fences. It is not wind tolerant. Maintenance: It often sends up many sprouts from the base of the trunk. The roots aggressively seek water, so do not plant it anywhere near septic or sewer pipes.

Taxodium spp., cypresses (zones 6–11) Bald cypress (*T. distichum* (L.) Rich.) and pond cypress (*T. ascendens* Brongn.) are large deciduous conifers that occur naturally in wet, acidic areas, but they can adjust to drier habitats, especially *T. distichum*. Do not use them as lawn trees because they tend to develop knees (gnarly, vertical root extensions) that will impede walking and mowing. Either would work as a rain garden tree. Butterfly host plants. Maintenance: No particular maintenance is necessary. The soft needles provide interesting fall color and disintegrate quickly.

Ulmus alata Michx., winged elm (zones 6–9) This elm is a deciduous, fast-growing, medium-sized tree with interesting corky extensions on its young branches. It grows best in moist acidic soils but is adaptable. Offers good habitat value and is a butterfly host plant. A few other elm species may also be available. Maintenance: May need corrective pruning while young to encourage a single leader for a stronger structure. Any of the elms may be susceptible to Dutch elm disease, but it's not normally a problem in Florida.

Zanthoxylum fagara (L.) Sarg., lime pricklyash, locally known as wild lime (zones 9–11) This thorny, small to medium, evergreen, aromatic tree prefers poor, alkaline soil but is adaptable. Use as a screen or in a hedgerow. It offers good habitat value and has interesting foliage. Butterfly host plant. Maintenance: It naturally produces multiple trunks, but you may wish to prune some of them out for looks or airflow.

Shrubs

Ardisia escallonioides Schltdl. & Cham., marlberry (zones 9–11) This evergreen, shade-tolerant shrub to small tree is attractive to pollinators and birds. Occurs naturally as an understory plant, but it will work as a screen or in a hedgerow. (Do not confuse with the invasive species in this genus, *A. crenata*.) Maintenance: It has brittle wood, so some pruning may be needed after high-wind events.

Avicennia germinans (L.) L., black mangrove (zones 9–11) This mangrove is a subtropical, salt-tolerant shrub in its northern range, but a medium-sized tree in frost-free areas. It plays an important role in protecting intertidal areas and shorelines and provides good structural habitat for birds and aquatic animals. It is the most cold hardy of the three true mangroves in Florida. Butterfly host plant. Maintenance: No particular care is needed once established. See chapter 10 for more on mangrove regulations.

Baccharis halimifolia L., eastern baccharis or groundsel tree (zones 3–9) This salt-tolerant, dioecious, semievergreen shrub grows just about anywhere, but it does better in moist habitats. The female individuals have showy white flowers with fluffy seeds in the fall. A good choice for a hedgerow. Butterfly host plant. Maintenance: It takes to trimming if necessary. Reseeds freely but is relatively short-lived, so you may wish to let some of those seedlings grow. The wood is brittle and may require pruning after high-wind events.

Callicarpa americana L., beautyberry (zones 6–11) This deciduous shrub lives up to its name with its unbelievably vivid purple berries that are eaten by a wide variety of birds. It tolerates poor soil but does better in richer environments. The gracefully arching canes can reach out to more than 6 feet from the main plant. Maintenance: If growing in poor soil, provide a topdressing of compost.

Capparis cynophallophora L., Jamaica caper-tree (zones 9–11) A tall, broad, evergreen shrub or small tree for South Florida that is both drought and salt tolerant. Recommended for hedgerows in areas with neutral to alkaline sandy soils, especially in coastal areas. Its beautiful blooms change from white to pink. Butterfly host plant. Maintenance: Its normal rounded shape reduces the need for pruning if given enough room. No particular care is needed, once established.

Cephalanthus occidentalis L., common buttonbush (zones 3–10) This tall, deciduous, multicaned shrub will form colonies or thickets along freshwater shorelines and grows well with constant inundation. Its Sputnik-shaped flower heads attract a wide variety of pollinators. It bears more blooms in sunnier habitats, but it will grow well in the shade. Butterfly host plant. Maintenance: If it spreads too much, the new offsets can be transplanted or pulled out. Some trimming may be needed for older shrubs as the canes break off.

Chrysobalanus icaco L., coco-plum (zones 10–11) This dense evergreen shrub grows in a variety of conditions from swamps to beaches, but it does best in rich soil in a sunny location; recommended for hedgerows. It bears fruit mostly in the winter but continues intermittently throughout the year. The fruit is noticeable and eaten by wildlife and humans alike. Maintenance: Germination of seeds is slow, but once established no particular maintenance is required.

Clethra alnifolia L., coastal sweet pepperbush (zones 3–9) This deciduous understory shrub prefers slightly acidic moist sites and will form thickets, particularly in wetter areas. Its highly fragrant flowers attract a wide variety of pollinators including hummingbirds. Maintenance: No particular maintenance required.

Euonymus americanus L., bursting-heart or American strawberry bush (zones 5–9) This tall, deciduous, thicket-forming shrub prefers rich, well-drained soil. It provides interest in the landscape with unusual dark pink and orange fruit. The canes stay green for several years and are mostly upright. Maintenance: No particular management is necessary.

Forestiera segregata (Jacq.) Krug & Urb., Florida swampprivet (zones 8–11) This large drought-tolerant, salt-tolerant, evergreen shrub can be used as part of a hedgerow. It grows best in moist rich soil but will adapt to other habitats. Attracts pollinators and birds. Butterfly host plant. Maintenance: It tolerates trimming well, but if you allow it to grow out to its natural size, no particular maintenance is needed.

Hamelia patens Jacq., scarletbush or (locally) firebush (zones 9–11) This cold-sensitive shrub becomes woody in frost-free zones but dies back to the ground after frosts. It prefers dry, sandy, alkaline soils but will also grow on limestone and humus-rich hammocks. In the frost-free areas it has a continuous blooming cycle and attracts hummingbirds and butterflies. Songbirds eat the berries. While it's drought tolerant, it grows better with regular irrigation. Butterfly host plant. Maintenance: Readily reseeds. Clear out dead plant material after die-back in its northern ranges.

Hydrangea quercifolia W. Bartram, oakleaf hydrangea (zones 7–9) This large deciduous shrub bears beautiful large white to pink flower heads, and its leaves turn reddish in the fall. Plant in hedgerows for its texture and beauty. It prefers rich, slightly acidic soils, and while it can survive droughts, it will look better with supplemental irrigation during the dry season. Maintenance: No particular maintenance is required if you've planned for its full size.

Ilex spp., hollies. This genus has a few shrubs, but see Trees for details.

Iva spp., seacoast and marshelders (zones 6–11) Several species of elders are native to Florida—all are low-growing, salt-tolerant, and drought-tolerant shrubs. They grow naturally on sand dunes and are excellent choices for beach stabilization. They spread by deep runners, so leave plenty of room for them to spread out. Maintenance: No particular maintenance is required—they stay low.

Licania michauxii Prance, gopher apple (zones 8–11) This slow-growing woody subshrub stays close the ground in poor soil with a maze of underground stems. It could be used as a ground cover and turfgrass substitute in hot sandy places with some salt spray. Maintenance: High mowing annually to keep down weeds while it becomes established.

Lyonia spp., staggerbushes (zones 8–10) These understory shrubs do best in moist acidic wooded areas. Several species occur in Florida and any of them should work well in the right environment. They add to the habitat with their flowers and fruit. Maintenance: No particular maintenance is necessary.

Morella cerifera (L.) Small (synonym: *Myrica cerifera* L.), wax myrtle (zones 7–11) This highly adaptable, salt-tolerant, evergreen shrub or small tree grows well in poor soils because its roots fix nitrogen. Dioecious. Provides food for winter songbirds with its prolific waxy berries. Good for screening or hedgerow. Rain garden plant. Butterfly host plant. Maintenance: It produces suckers, so plant where that won't make a difference or cutting back suckers will become an annual chore. For the least amount of maintenance, allow space for its adult size, but it does well when trimmed into a tidy hedge.

Myrcianthes fragrans (Sw.) McVaugh, twinberry or (locally) Simpson's stopper (zones 9–11) This slow-growing evergreen shrub or small tree is suitable for hedges or hedgerows. It tolerates alkaline soils.

It's drought tolerant but will do best if irrigated during dry periods the first few years after planting. Its fragrant flowers and colorful fruit are attractive to wildlife and humans. Maintenance: No particular maintenance is necessary after establishment.

Psychotria nervosa Sw., Seminole balsamo or (locally) wild coffee (zones 9–11) This evergreen understory shrub tolerates full shade. Its attractive fruits and shiny leaves create interest in the landscape and provide contrast in a hedgerow. It prefers well-drained neutral to alkaline soils. Attracts pollinators. Maintenance: No particular maintenance is needed.

Rhizophora mangle L., red mangrove (zones 9–11) This shrub or medium-sized tree has stiltlike roots and grows farthest out in the water compared to other mangroves. Will grow in either salt- or freshwater habitats, but occurs naturally only in salt water. Effective for controlling coastal erosion. Butterfly host plant. Maintenance: See chapter 10 for information regarding mangrove regulations. Once established, it's trouble-free.

Rhododendron spp., azaleas (zones 5–9) Azaleas that are native to Florida are deciduous and have showy flowers that are white, yellow-orange, or pink. They prefer rich, well-drained acidic soil and grow best as understory shrubs in partial shade. The fragrant swamp azalea (*R. viscosum* (L.) Torr.) is the most widespread in Florida but not often found for sale. Maintenance: No particular maintenance is required once established, but they will do better with an annual compost topdressing.

Rhus copallinum L., winged sumac (zones 4–11) This deciduous, dioecious, pioneer species often forms a thicket or colony. It can grow to more than 20 feet tall but stays short in poor soils. Found mostly in sandy acidic soils. It prefers full sun but is often found in the ecotone next to wooded ecosystems. The showy greenish-white flowers attract many pollinators; later, flowers on the female shrubs will mature into red fruits. It has good fall color, even in Florida. Butterfly host plant. (Note: This is not poison sumac, *Toxicodendron vernix* (L.) Kuntze.) Maintenance: It spreads via rhizomes, so if it produces suckers in unwanted spaces, it's easy to pull them up or transplant them. If you plant it where it can spread, no particular maintenance is necessary.

Sabal minor (Jacq.) Pers., dwarf or bluestem palmetto (zones 7–10)
   This tough palmetto shrub has leaves or fronds up to 4 feet across.
   If it grows in standing water, it can grow a trunk, but even in drier
   areas it can still grow to 10 feet tall. Showy flowers and berries on
   tall stalks. Butterfly host plant. Rain garden plant. Maintenance: If
   it's in an area where neatness counts, trim back the dead fronds and
   spent fruiting stalks every other year.

Serenoa repens (W. Bartram) Small, saw palmetto (zones 8–11) A long-
   lived palmetto shrub that can adapt to many habitats, including
   salty sites where it often turns silver—often called a silver palmetto.
   Berries are eaten by birds and other wildlife. The trunk is recum-
   bent. Highly flammable. Butterfly host plant. Maintenance: If it's
   in an area where neatness counts, trim back the dead fronds and
   fruiting stalks annually.

Vaccinium spp., blueberries and sparkleberries (zones 5–11) Species
   in this genus are shrubs that can be tall or short. They prefer acidic
   soils and full sun to partial shade. All provide good habitat value.
   Plant provenance is important for the blueberries—those bred from
   New Jersey stock will not do well in Florida. Maintenance: Unless
   they are planted specifically as edible crops, no particular maintenance is required. If you want to eat the blueberries, you may need a
   fine mesh or net cover to keep out the birds, but don't install it until
   after the pollinators have done their work.

Viburnum spp., viburnums (zones 5–11) The common name viburnum
   is applied to both deciduous and semievergreen understory shrubs
   that have flat or global flower heads with white florets that become
   black or purple berries. They prefer acidic, well-drained soils and
   full sun to partially shady habitats. Five species are native to Florida
   and all would make good additions to your hedgerows. They all offer good habitat value. Butterfly host plants. Maintenance: They can
   adapt to pruning but will probably do better unpruned and will require less maintenance if allowed to grow into their natural shapes.

Yucca spp., yuccas or Spanish bayonets (zones 4–11) Yuccas offer a
   spiky, coarse texture to your landscape with their showy white to
   pink flowers and interesting green fruit. Found naturally in dry
   sandy soils, but they adapt to other conditions as long as they are

well drained. They colonize by sending up new shoots from the main plant. The tips of their leaves are quite sharp and can be hazardous to people and animals. Butterfly host plants. Maintenance: If they overgrow their spots, you can cut off the taller shoots—be careful of their leaves.

Zamia integrifolia L.f. (synonyms: *Z. pumila* L. and *Z. floridana* Alph. de Candolle), coontie (zones 8–11) This is Florida's only native cycad (a primitive nonflowering plant with male and female individuals). It was nearly harvested to extinction for its starchy roots (it's also known as arrowroot and was used as an ingredient in animal crackers), but it has made a comeback (along with the atala hairstreak butterfly, *Eumaeus atala,* that depends on it for its larval food), because more people are planting it as a slow-growing, easy-care, and well-behaved short shrub. It can grow in full sun or deep shade and is drought and salt tolerant. Butterfly host plant. Maintenance: Keep vines and aggressive weeds away. Scale insects can be a problem.

Forbs

Allium canadense L., meadow garlic (zones 4–9) This tough perennial garlic, with its flat leaves and unusual inflorescence that includes both bulblets and flowers on stalks, occurs naturally in damp ditches, but it can also do well in drier sites and may already exist in damp places in a freedom lawn. It dies back in the summer and resprouts in late fall. Rain garden plant. All parts of this plant are edible; you may want to add it to your herb garden next to the chives. Maintenance: No particular maintenance is required, but it will spread if you allow the bulblets to drop from the inflorescences. It tolerates mowing.

Asclepias spp., milkweeds (zones 4–10) The milkweeds are a beautiful and important addition to a native landscape because they are the exclusive larval food for monarch and queen butterflies. Some species do well in moist habitats, while others work well in dry fields, so do your research before planting. Butterfly host plants. Note: Scarlet or tropical milkweed (*A. curassavica*) is widely sold, but it's not native to Florida and is harmful to monarch butterflies, especially in South Florida. If you have it, cut it to the ground in December. Maintenance: Once established, milkweeds do not require any particular care, and true butterfly gardeners will cheer when caterpillars of monarch and queen butterflies eat it.

Conoclinium coelestinum, blue mistflower (zones 6–11) This short-lived perennial occurs naturally in moist habitats and dies back in the winter. Its fuzzy blue or lavender flower heads attract many pollinators. Rain garden plant. Butterfly host plant. Maintenance: In moist conditions, it can spread, so give it plenty of room or be ready to divide it.

Coreopsis spp., tickseeds (zones 4–11) Tickseeds are meadow plants with mostly yellow flower heads; most are annuals. They are Florida's state wildflower. Most coreopsis species prefer moist, sunny habitats, but some do well in drier conditions. They attract a wide variety of pollinators. Maintenance: Will do well with an annual mowing in the winter. You may need to reseed to maintain their density in long-term meadows.

Eryngium aquaticum L., rattlesnakemaster (zones 3–10) This interesting member of the carrot family is best used at the edges of fresh to brackish bodies of water. Its unusual flower heads and basal leaves add good texture to shorelines. Attracts many pollinators. Maintenance: Once it's in place, it doesn't require any special maintenance as long as it's damp.

Erythrina herbacea L., redcardinal or coral bean (zones 8–11) This perennial dies back to the roots in areas that have frost, but it can become a small tree in frost-free regions. It's a drought-tolerant legume with showy red flowers and red poisonous fruit. It grows in dry rich soils, but it adapts to a wide range of habitats as long as they are well drained. The flowers attract pollinators, including hummingbirds, and birds and other wildlife consume the fruit. Maintenance: Removal of dead plant material in the winter where necessary.

Gaillardia pulchella Foug., Indian blanket (zones 5–11) This drought-tolerant, short-lived perennial or annual blooms profusely even in poor sandy soils. It grows best in full sun and is often used in meadows and roadside plantings. Attracts pollinators, and later in the season, the seed-eating birds. Maintenance: It will reseed, so use in areas where that won't be a problem. Tolerates annual mowing.

Glandularia maritima (Small) Small, coastal verbena (zones 9–11) This short-lived, salt-tolerant, evergreen perennial occurs naturally in coastal alkaline sandy soil but is adaptable. Its showy purple flowers attract pollinators. Butterfly larval host. Endangered in Florida. Maintenance: No requirements once established.

Helianthus spp., sunflowers (zones 4–11) At least 14 species of sunflowers are native to Florida. Some are annuals, while others are perennials. Sunflowers occur in a wide variety of habitats, from beaches, where a ground-hugging dune sunflower (*H. debilis*) decorates east coast sand dunes, to freshwater marshes and damp roadside ditches, where the swamp sunflower (*H. angustifolius* L.) makes a show in the fall. Other sunflower species are found in more neutral habitats, so know what you're getting to make the right choice for your habitat. Attract pollinators and seed-eating birds and other wildlife. Butterfly host plants. Maintenance: Some sunflowers are allelopathic, which may have a negative effect on plants around them. Use sunflower trimmings as path mulch—don't add them in great quantities to your compost pile.

Hibiscus coccineus Walter, scarlet rosemallow or (locally) scarlet hibiscus (zones 7–11) This wetland perennial puts on quite a show in spring and summer with its huge red flowers. It dies back in the winter, but if conditions are right it will increase the number of shoots each year, and seeds that are not eaten will float and plant themselves around the shoreline. Butterfly host plant. Maintenance: Collect the seeds if it becomes too rambunctious.

Ipomopsis rubra (L.) Wherry, standingcypress (zones 5–9) This biennial has bright red flowers attractive to hummingbirds and butterflies. Great for dry meadows and is salt-spray tolerant. Reseeds. Maintenance: Can tolerate annual winter mowing at a high level.

Iris savannarum Small, Addisonia (formerly *I. hexagona* Walter), dixie iris (zone 7–10) The most widespread of Florida's native irises, works well along freshwater shorelines with its beautiful blue/purple flowers. Usually evergreen, but it may die back in cooler regions. Its thick rhizomes intertwine, making it a good choice to stabilize shorelines. Maintenance: It may need to be cut back for the winter where neatness matters, and in some habitats, it can spread.

Lachnanthes caroliana (Lam.) Dandy, Carolina redroot (zones 6–11) This is an easy-to-grow and well-behaved perennial as long as it's wet and acidic. The white to cream flowers attract a wide variety of pollinators. Dies back in the winter. Yes, the roots are bright red, but don't pull them out to see. Butterfly host plant. Maintenance: No particular maintenance.

Liatris spp., blazing-stars (zones 6–11) More than a dozen *Liatris* species are native to Florida. Most are short-lived perennials that die back each winter. They can occur naturally in wet or damp meadows or in sandy uplands. They are attractive to butterflies and other pollinators. Maintenance: No particular maintenance is necessary, but you may need to replant every few years to renew your population.

Lobelia cardinalis L., cardinal flower (zones 3–10) This short-lived perennial is a beautiful addition to acidic damp or wet garden areas. Its red tubular flowers attract hummingbirds and butterflies, but it's not usually a good rain garden plant in Florida because of the long dry season. Maintenance: Unless your conditions are just right, you'll need to replant to retain the population.

Monarda punctata L., spotted beebalm or (locally) dotted horsemint (zones 3–10) This tough bunching perennial has an unusual flower structure that is attractive to humans but particularly so to pollinators. It is tolerant of salt spray and can occur on the backsides of sand dunes, but those plants are shorter and their bracts are pinker than those grown in moist, salt-free habitats. This is a wonderful addition to your butterfly garden or meadow. It may be more short-lived in more southern regions. It has the same oil as thyme and oregano, so you can add it to your edible garden. Maintenance: It has a rangy habit and stems can lean over as it grows. If it is growing along an edge, prune the stems near the edge back somewhat in early summer. Old stalks turn brown and may need to be cut back if growing in a managed area of the landscape, but deposit them in a brush pile so birds can find those seeds and so overwintering bugs can complete their life cycles. Reseeds to some degree.

Phyla nodiflora (L.) Greene, turkey tangle fogfruit (zones 6–11) This widespread plant grows coast to coast and in all parts of Florida. It's a great ground cover and serves well as a turfgrass substitute. You probably already have this plant growing under your feet. Attracts pollinators. Butterfly host plant. Maintenance: No particular maintenance needed, but if it grows beyond its bounds, trim it back. (You can root the trimmings to add to your population.)

Pontederia cordata L., pickerelweed (zones 4–11) A clumping, emergent perennial with a showy purple spike of flowers that attracts pollinators. Soil can be acidic to neutral, but it must be wet. Pickerelweed works well by itself or with other freshwater shoreline plants. Various waterfowl eat the seeds. Maintenance: No particular maintenance is required as long as the site stays wet.

Rudbeckia spp., black-eyed Susan (zones 2–10) *R. hirta* is the most widespread and most widely available of the nine *Rudbeckia* species native to Florida, but other species are also worthy additions to your landscape. It's a ruderal plant and occurs naturally in meadows, roadside ditches, and other disturbed habitats. It attracts pollinators and seed-eating birds. Most black-eyed Susans are short-lived perennials, but they usually self-sow if the conditions are right. Butterfly host plants. Maintenance: Needs full sun to thrive, so annual mowing to maintain a meadow ecosystem is necessary. While they can adjust to drier conditions, they will do better with some irrigation during droughts.

Sagittaria spp., arrowhead or duck potato (zones 3–11) These colony-forming aquatic perennials are normally found in wet ditches and pond shorelines. Thirteen species are native to Florida, but they are found throughout the continent. They produce tall flower spikes and bloom over an extended period each year. The fruits and starchy tubers are eaten by many animals. Butterfly host plant. Maintenance: Can be aggressive, so plant where you need shoreline stabilization.

Salvia coccinea P. J. Buchoz ex Etlinger, blood sage or (locally) tropical sage (zones 7–11) An annual or short-lived perennial, it is a member of the mint family. It may die back after a heavy frost but will usually grow back from the roots. Its beautiful tubular red flowers attract butterflies, bees, and hummingbirds. It grows in full sun or partial shade. Grows best in poor neutral to slightly alkaline soils, but adapts to many habitats. Butterfly larval host plant; seeds attract birds. Maintenance: Reseeds freely. Pull or transplant seedlings that sprout in inconvenient places. If neatness counts, cut back the frost-killed tops.

Saururus cernuus L., lizard's tail (zones 4–11) This striking perennial is a colonizing wetland or emergent plant with showy white flower spikes that droop. It dies back in the winter. It prefers acidic soils and sunny to mostly shady habitats. Maintenance: No particular maintenance as long as it is wet and has room to spread, otherwise some thinning may be necessary. Removing invasives such as wild taro (*Colocasia esculenta*) that compete for the same habitat can be an ongoing problem.

Sesuvium portulacastrum (L.) L., seapurslane (zones 6–11) A fleshy, salt-tolerant, drought-tolerant ground cover that occurs naturally on dunes and alkaline soils. The small lavender flower is attractive, but the plant's hardiness is its best asset. Butterfly larval host. Maintenance: No particular maintenance is necessary if given room to spread; otherwise trimming back from sidewalks may be necessary.

Sisyrinchium angustifolium Mill., narrowleaf blue-eyed grass (zones 3–11) This dainty member of the iris family is a bunching, short-lived perennial with showy pale blue flowers in the spring. Use as a turfgrass substitute in a lawn, in short damp meadows, or at the edges of native areas, but not so close to a lawn that it will be mowed with the turfgrass. Maintenance: Reseeds. Can take mowing and light foot traffic.

Solidago spp., goldenrods (zones 3–11) Goldenrods do not cause allergies—they have big sticky pollen grains that are carried away by their pollinators, so the pollen is too heavy to fly into your nose. They are mostly fall-blooming perennials that work well for meadows; they spread by bunching or via rhizomes to form wide-spreading colonies. In South Florida, the wand goldenrod (*S. stricta* Aiton) can bloom throughout the year. Some are salt tolerant and some are drought tolerant, while others do better under irrigation. Most have some allelopathic tendency to keep other plants at bay. Butterfly host plants. (Two other genera are also called goldenrods, *Euthamia* and *Bigelowia;* you rarely find them for sale, but they may volunteer in your meadow.) Maintenance: Throughout most of their range, the stalks die at the end of the season, so you may wish to remove them from your meadow area at the end of the winter. They can tolerate an annual mowing in the winter.

Stokesia laevis (Hill) Greene, Stokes' aster (zones 8–9) This low-growing and bunching perennial has showy lavender flower heads that attract pollinators. Good for borders or edges. Does best in sun or partial shade in neutral to acidic soils. Maintenance: Flower stalks turn brown after blooming, so deadheading may be called for if neatness counts or if you wish to reduce reseeding. Keep other vegetation from flopping over it.

Symphyotrichum spp., asters (zones 3–11) The asters occur in many different habitats, and if you develop a meadow or butterfly garden, it's likely that at least one of the two dozen native asters will volunteer there. Some are annual and others are perennial, but most will bloom from late summer into early winter and will attract many late pollinators. Butterfly host plant. Climbing aster (*Ampelaster carolinianum* (Walter) G. L. Nesom) belongs to a different genus, but it may be the one that is most often sold by native nurseries. It prefers wet soil and will scramble up and over nearby vegetation. Maintenance: Will withstand annual mowing in a meadow or manual cutting back, but it's not necessary for the plant. Will reseed.

Zephyranthes spp., rain lilies (zones 7–9) These bulbaceous perennials are in the amaryllis family. They occur naturally in wet meadows and ditches but can grow well in drier habitats. Three rain lilies are native to Florida, but the most abundant is the atamasco lily (*Z. atamasca* (L.) Herb.). Normally they are short-lived, but colonies can last for many years in the right conditions. They tend to bloom in the spring a few days after a heavy rainfall, but by the middle of summer they will die back. The grasslike leaves are not particularly noticeable when they are not blooming. They work well in short, damp meadows or in roadside ditches. Maintenance: It can reseed, but how can you object to a beautiful little lily growing in your lawn? It can survive in mowed areas.

Ferns

Acrostichum danaeifolium Langsd. & Fisch., giant leather fern (zones 9–11) This robust evergreen fern requires wet or moist habitats with rich soil. In South Florida, it can get large enough to use as a low hedge. Spreads by rhizomes and spores. Golden leather fern (*A. au-reum*) may also be available but occurs mostly in southwest Florida. Maintenance: If fronds become ragged, they can be cut back, but don't do this more than once a year, because this practice will reduce its vitality.

Osmunda regalis L., royal fern (zones 3–10) This magnificent large clumping fern deserves its common name. Its fronds have fully separated, doubly pinnate leaves, making the fern appear lacy. The fertile fronds appear only at the top of its main sterile fronds, so later in the season, after the fertile parts have fallen away, the remaining fronds look cut off. Plant only in habitats that are moist to wet. Fronds die back in the winter. Maintenance: May need to irrigate this fern if planted in drier sites.

Osmundastrum cinnamomeum (L.) C. Presl. (synonym: *Osmunda cinnamomeum* L.), cinnamon fern (zones 3–11) A large clumping fern, it makes quite a statement in damp or wet habitats. It will grow well in full sun if it has reliably wet soil; if the soil dries out for part of the year, it should have full or partial shading. Good for rain gardens that are partially shaded. The fertile frond is the color of cinnamon. In Florida, it sends up fertile fronds in both spring and fall, and its sterile fronds appear in the spring and keep growing until late fall when they die back. Maintenance: It's best to keep weeds and vines from overrunning it.

Woodwardia spp., chain ferns (zones 3–11) These ferns form colonies in wooded or partially shaded areas. While they occur naturally in wet sites, they can adapt to drier locations as long as they have some shade. Use as a ground cover in your groves once there is some shade. The stiff, fertile fronds usually persist through the winter, but the sterile fronds die back where there is frost. Maintenance: No particular maintenance, but it's best to keep vines and other vegetation from overrunning the area.

Graminoids

Andropogon spp., bluestem grasses (zones 7–11) These are tough bunching grasses that can grow in acidic, poor soil. Because of their bluish leaves and showy inflorescences, they are a great choice for a meadow or to fill in between natives while you're waiting for them to grow. Butterfly host plant. Maintenance: In fire-prone habitats, they should be cut back toward the end of winter.

Eragrostis spp., lovegrasses (zones 3–11) A large number of lovegrass species occur in Florida, but not all are native, so be careful with your selection. Most do best in loamy, slightly moist soils. The stems often arch over giving them a fountain or weeping form—use them as edge plants to highlight this form. Butterfly host plant. Maintenance: They could be cut back, but it's not necessary unless they are in fire-prone habitats. Divide when they grow too dense.

Juncus effuses L., common rush (zones 3–10) This adaptable rush grows as an emergent plant, a shoreline plant, and an upland plant. If you have an unmanaged moist acidic area in your landscape, there's a good possibility that you already have a stand of this common plant. Very useful for holding shorelines and as an attractive bunching, spiky plant in all but the driest landscape. Works well in rain gardens. Maintenance: Old stalks turn brown in the winter and do not decompose quickly, so in more civilized landscapes comb out the old stalks with your gloved fingers because new stalks will already have begun to emerge. Use the stalks as a tough pathway mulch.

Muhlenbergia capillaris (Lam.) Trin., hairawn muhly (zones 4–11) This easy-to-grow grass is a tough but beautiful bunching grass with pink flower heads and a favorite in native landscapes. It is salt tolerant and drought tolerant (once established). Small seed-eating birds will consume the seeds. Butterfly host plant. Two other Florida species, gulfhairawn muhly (*M. filipes* M.A. Curtis) and cutover muhly (*M. expansa* (Poir. Trin.)) are sometimes sold as *M. capillaris*, but any of the three are good additions to your landscape. Maintenance: In locations where neatness is important, old stalks can be cut back or combed out with your gloved fingers late in the winter, but if you live in a fire-prone area, cut to the ground in winter.

Rhynchospora colorata (L.) H. Pfeiffer, starrush white-top (zones 7–11) This lovely small sedge naturally occurs in wet places and along shorelines and roadside ditches. It is somewhat salt tolerant. It may adapt to somewhat drier habitats if shady. You may wish to include it in a damp meadow or rain garden, or even use as a lawn substitute in damp areas. Unlike most sedges, it is insect pollinated—the white bracts attract the pollinators. Maintenance: It colonizes, so give it space. Tolerates mowing, but does better with only an annual mowing.

Scirpus cyperinus (L.) Kunth, woolgrass (zones 3–9) This is an important bulrush for holding shorelines in freshwater habits. Its flower heads are showy. Can get large and it can spread, so leave enough room for its growth. Butterfly host plant. Other native bulrushes are placed both in this genus and also in *Schoenoplectus*. *Schoenoplectus californicus* (C.A. Mey.) Soják and *Schoenoplectus robustus* (Pursh) M.T. Strong are salt tolerant. Be sure you know exactly which bulrush you are buying. Maintenance: No particular maintenance except to make sure they stay wet.

Spartina spp., cordgrasses (zones 3–11) The cordgrasses are the major components of salt marshes all over the east and gulf coasts. Five species are native to Florida—all are deep-rooted, tough, and salt tolerant. Highly flammable. Butterfly host plant. Maintenance: No particular maintenance is required if planted in appropriate sites.

Tripsacum dactyloides (L.) L., eastern gammagrass or (locally) fakahatcheegrass (zones 5–11) is a tough, large bunching grass that is somewhat salt tolerant. Its unusual inflorescence adds interest in the landscape and offers good habitat value. Butterfly host plant. Maintenance: In a managed landscape, cut back at the end of winter; otherwise it requires no particular maintenance after establishment.

Uniola paniculata L., seaoats (zones 6–11) This tough, salt-tolerant, drought-tolerant, spreading grass has a massive root system that allows it to survive in the ever-shifting sand dune environment. It occurs naturally on beaches and sand dunes but grows well in other sunny habitats. It is illegal to dig it up or harvest seed in Florida because of its importance in holding dunes, so purchase from trusted sources. Maintenance: It needs no maintenance once established.

Vines

Gelsemium sempervirens (L.) Aiton f., evening trumpetflower or Carolina jessamine (zones 7–10) This is a fast-growing, evergreen, winter-flowering vine that can be used on trellises and fences or as a ground cover in sunny and partial shade areas. Its showy flowers are also fragrant. It roots readily. Poisonous to livestock. Maintenance: If it's used as a ground cover, it tends to climb vertical obstacles in its path. Even though it's a fast grower, it's relatively easy to control.

Ipomoea spp., morning-glories (zones 8–11) These plants are garden favorites for their showy flowers. About half of the two dozen species that occur in Florida are natives. Two species do well out on the sand dunes—beach morning-glory (*I. imperati* (Vahl) Griseb.) and bayhops or (locally) railroad vine (*I. pes-caprae* (L.) R. Br.)—but most species appreciate more fertility and moisture. Most morning-glories are vines, but swamp morning-glory or (locally) water spinach (*I. aquatica* Forssk.) is an invasive floating plant. Butterfly host plants. Maintenance: Most will need severe trimming to contain their growth to a confined area. In addition to growing vigorously and rooting at every node, many morning-glories also reseed profusely.

Lonicera sempervirens L., trumpet honeysuckle or (locally) coral honeysuckle (zones 4–10) This long-lived vine provides excellent habitat value with its beautiful red tubular flowers that attract hummingbirds and butterflies and orange berries that are eaten by a wide variety of songbirds. It blooms best if allowed to climb a fence or trellis, but it can also serve as a ground cover. Butterfly host plant. Maintenance: If neatness counts, trim back the vines yearly after the hummingbirds have left for the season.

Mimosa strigillosa Torr. & A. Gray, powderpuff or (locally) sunshine mimosa (zones 8–11) This vining ground cover is evergreen in frost-free climates but tends to be deciduous in its more northerly range. It's a legume and can grow well in poor, sandy soils because its roots fix nitrogen, but it prefers a slightly acidic soil in sunny or partial shade area. Makes a beautiful turfgrass substitute with its pink powderpuff flower heads, and it withstands light foot traffic. Attracts pollinators. Butterfly host plant. Maintenance: Once it's established, an annual mowing at the highest setting will probably be needed to keep down the weeds at least until it forms a thick mat.

Passiflora spp., passionflower (zones 6–11) In most of its range these herbaceous vines die back in the winter, but in frost-free zones they're evergreen. They sprout pretty much anywhere within several yards of the original plant in the spring. A dozen species occur in the wild in Florida, but only half of them are native, so be sure that any you acquire are natives. They attract pollinators and are the larval food for several butterflies, including Florida's state butterfly, the zebra longwing (*Heliconius charithonia*). Maintenance: If new sprouts pop up in inappropriate places, they can be transplanted, but do so early in the year for the best success rate.

Pentalinon luteum (L.) B.F. Hansen & Wunderlin, wild allamanda (zones 10–11) This long-lived perennial vine is woody. Its showy flowers and glossy foliage make quite a show in full or partial sun. It can grow in poor, sandy soil and is somewhat salt tolerant. Attracts pollinators. Butterfly host plant. Maintenance: No particular care is needed after establishment except for trimming it back where neatness counts.

Appendix II

Types of Mulch

A wide variety of organic and inorganic materials can be used for mulching. Sources of plant material for mulching are vast, and many are on hand on your property or in your neighborhood. If your target habitat is nutrient poor, you'll want to go easy on nutrient-rich organic mulches, or use gravel instead of organic mulches that may add too many nutrients. Also, if your landscape is in a fire-prone area, most organic mulches are flammable and should be used only outside the 30-foot clear zone around buildings.

Each type of mulch has its pros and cons as they relate to sustainability. Here are some considerations about commonly used mulches.

Chipped Tree Trimmings

This is a mix of shredded wood and green leaves depending on the season and whether live trees were shredded, but chipped tree trimmings are the tree parts that have been run through a chipper. As a mulch, it consists mostly of nicely chopped wood mixed with leaves and some thin branches that slide through the shredder. This mulch will last for a year or more as a garden or pathway mulch. If it is used in areas that are not disturbed, a thick layer of wood chips can form a crust, so in those areas, use no more than a 2-inch layer unless you're attempting to kill the weeds. It will eventually decay and become part of the soil.

Because nothing has been added to it, the look is quite natural, and if leaves fall on it, no removal is necessary—it all blends together. For

Should You Layer Anything under the Mulch?

Much as been written about layering, or the lasagna method of landscape mulching, but is it a good idea?

Newspaper or Cardboard

It has been widely recommended to place a layer of corrugated cardboard or several layers of newspaper under mulch to better stop the weeds. But it's been shown that this is rarely worth the effort in a natural habitat because this layer does not work as well as, say, wood chips in suppressing the weeds, and the soil under the paper can become anaerobic in wet conditions or hydrophobic in dry conditions. Also, if the mulch on top of it becomes dislodged, it can become an unsightly mess.

Geotextiles

You can purchase giant rolls of woven or unwoven weed barrier cloth with various guaranteed lifetimes at local hardware stores or garden centers. Save your money, especially for natural areas. Geotextile will degrade in the landscape, and roots of nearby plants will soon claim it as their own, which will increase your maintenance chores, disrupt the landscape when you need to remove it, and reduce the habitat value for many important soil inhabitants such as toads and native bees. On the other hand, geotextiles are useful in the construction of dry wells to keep soil from intruding into the catchment space.

beds that are in full view, you may want to reduce the rustic look by pulling out or burying the sticks as you lay down the chips. This is one of the most sustainable mulching solutions because the tree trimmers save gas by dumping in the neighborhood; you save gas by not having to drive somewhere to pick it up; you save money and someone else's gas by not having it delivered; and the landfills are not used. The production of bagged mulch, no matter what type, uses more energy in its packaging and delivery.

Compost

Unfinished compost, in which you can still see the shapes of some of the original ingredients, provides a soil-enriching mulch. In this state, the microbes are still working to decompose the materials and may extract available nitrogen from the soil to live. This suppresses weed seeds from germinating. Compost moderates the temperature or moisture of the soil below because it is organic and dark in color. Since its texture is similar to that of the soil, it provides less of a physical barrier than coarser mulches. Compost is probably best used in the landscape as a topdressing around plantings and on lawn areas.

Leaves or Shredded Leaves

Of course leaves are Mother Nature's own mulch. As leaves fall from trees and shrubs, they mulch the surrounding areas. It's best to let the leaves remain under the trees or shrubs from which they fall—they supply just the right mix of nutrients. When leaves fall on lawn or hardscape areas, rake them into the surrounding beds, or save them in a large pile in an out-of-the-way location in your landscape. If the leaves are large or leathery, you may wish to shred or compost them before using them as mulch. You could use a lawn mower as a leaf shredder. Shredded leaves don't last as long, but they may stay in place better than whole leaves. Some people collect their neighbors' bags of leaves in the fall as they put them on the curb for pick-up. This is a good way to build up a large supply to use throughout the year, especially if your trees are still small.

Fallen leaves are great to use in compost piles. Use them as a dry or brown ingredient.

Pine Needles

Pine needles make such a long-lasting and good-looking mulch that they are harvested from tree farms and sold as pine straw, but if you have pines in your neighborhood, you can gather your own. It's been shown that while the pine needles are quite acidic, the soil under a pine-needle mulch becomes only slightly more acidic. A waxy or resinous coating on the needles makes pines more drought resistant. It also makes pine-needle mulch shed water to some degree and resist decomposition more than other materials. Pine needles make a durable mulch for paths, and if you use them in garden beds or around trees they will not form a crust like some other mulches.

Be aware of invasive weeds included with the purchased bales—Japanese and Old World climbing ferns (*Lygodium japonicum* and *L. microphyllum*) have been found in some of the pine-straw bales from South Florida.

Hay or Straw

Hay consists of grasses and forbs that have been allowed to go to seed before mowing and gathering. Straw generally does not include the tops or seed heads, but just the stalks, so it contains fewer weed seeds and would be preferable instead of hay in places where you don't want more seeds. In a meadow, where a greater variety of seeds would add to diversity, hay with all its seeds might be preferable. It is effective as a mulch, but don't pile it too thickly or it can become anaerobic and start to smell sour. In a native bed, the look won't be natural, but it could be covered with a thin layer of a more natural-looking mulch such as pine needles, leaves, or wood chips if desired.

Pine Bark or Other Bark

Bark's purpose is to protect the tree from injury and to prevent water loss, so it contains waxy materials to repel water. Use only a 2- or 3-inch layer of bark mulch to allow air into the soil around tree roots. As mulch, bark products usually last longer than other organic materials because of their water-repellent chemicals. Bark nuggets may be easier to handle and they tend to stay in place better than the larger bark chunks unless a lot of water is flowing through the landscape. Don't use bark for mulching rain gardens or bioswales—it tends to float away. Bark is usually a byproduct from lumber mills and generally a sustainable product. This is the least flammable of the organic mulch types.

Shredded Wood

Melaleuca is a sustainable choice because using this mulch can help the effort to reduce these invasive trees in Florida's ecosystems. Shredded eucalyptus is also a reasonable choice, but because it is farmed, using this mulch does not necessarily help the effort to clear it from wild areas. Cypress is probably Florida's most popular mulching material—often dyed in several colors. It used to be a byproduct from lumber mills, but now whole cypress forests are being ripped out to accommodate demand. So, while this may be a good mulching product, it's definitely not sustainable because the high demand has outstripped the supply.

Sawdust

A byproduct from lumber mills, the small particles pack together and often cause anaerobic conditions if held in a pile. You'll notice a sour smell if this happens. As a mulch, sawdust reduces nitrogen in surrounding soils more than other mulches. This means that it is a good weed suppressant, but not necessarily good to use around new seedlings or newly planted natives. Don't use sawdust from chemically treated wood.

Gravel

Gravel is sometimes recommended for low-maintenance succulent gardens, firewise landscaping, and nutrient-poor sites. Although it does help retain soil moisture to some extent, gravel has several negatives as a mulch: it's not much of a weed deterrent in Florida, plus you'll never get rid of it in the landscape once you lay it in. Rocks, big and small, retain and reflect the heat long after the sun has set, so a layer of rocks can turn a sunny spot into an oven. Gravel can be thrown by power mowers or lofted by hurricane-force winds. On top of that, it's difficult to keep gravel clear of leaves and other debris. This creates another maintenance chore—using a rake or leaf blower to keep it clear.

Shredded Rubber or Shredded Tires

Don't use shredded rubber. Some studies have shown that rubber leaches harmful and persistent chemicals into the soil. Rubber mulch is highly flammable, and it does not add nutrients to or improve the structure of the soil beneath it.

Plastic Sheeting

Plastic is not recommended for native landscapes. When it's used as a mulch, plastic is impenetrable by even the most vigorous of Florida's weeds, but it also disrupts soil ecosystems and would not be recommended for natural landscapes. Many agricultural operations use plastic sheeting stapled to the soil between vegetable rows. In order to have it work well, they use drip irrigation to water the plants because the plastic doesn't allow water to penetrate. Any plastic heats the soil and in fact is recommended if you wish to solarize your soil to kill plants, weed seeds, nematodes, and other microbes. See chapter 4 for details on solarization.

Glossary

Acidity. Acidity is measured on the pH scale of 1 to 14, where pH refers to the potential of Hydrogen. The acidity of the soil determines the rates of uptake of various nutrients from the soil. A pH of 7 is neutral. Substances with pH below 7 are acidic, while those above 7 are alkaline, or basic. Most of Florida's soils are moderately acidic to neutral, but in much of South Florida, the underlying limestone creates an alkaline environment. It's important to test your soil, including its acidity, for a better chance of choosing the right plants for your site.

Adventitious roots. Roots that form on stem tissue are called adventitious roots. Some plants readily form roots, while others are more reluctant. If you're using cuttings as a propagation method, the formation of adventitious roots will allow that stem to become a new plant—a clone of its parent.

Aggressive. A plant that spreads easily (maybe too easily) in the landscape is aggressive. Many exotic aggressive plants have become invasive, but a native aggressive plant is not, by definition, invasive—it belongs in the ecosystem no matter how exuberant it is, but that doesn't mean you can't pull it out if it's creating too much chaos in your landscape. Also see **Invasive**.

Alkaline. See **Acidity**.

Allelopathic. Plants that release one or more herbicidal chemicals into the soil that have direct harmful effects on other plants are allelopathic. This is a natural adaptation to reduce competition from other species. Some examples of exotics that have allelopathic effects are Australian-pines (*Casuarina* spp.) and melaleuca (*Melaleuca quin-*

quenervia), but native plants can be allelopathic as well, including sunflowers (*Helianthus* spp.), sycamore (*Platanus occidentalis*), and hackberry (*Celtis* spp.).

Angiosperm. The angiosperms or flowering plants have vascular tissue for transporting water and food and produce seeds after the ovule (egg) is fertilized and develops in an enclosed ovary. Angiosperms make up 80 percent of the green plants in the world and express the most variation. See **Gymnosperm**.

Annual. A plant that usually completes its lifecycle (germination, growing, flowering, and setting seed) within one year is an annual. In frost-free zones, some annuals can live much longer than a year. See **Biennial** and **Perennial**.

Auxin. A type of plant hormone, auxin controls growth patterns. Auxins produced in terminal buds suppress growth of side buds and stimulate root growth. Pruning a newly planted tree removes some of its natural auxin, slowing root regeneration. Indole acetic acid (IAA) is a common natural auxin. Commercial rooting hormone products are usually synthetic auxins.

Biennial. A plant that usually takes two years to complete its lifecycle is a biennial. Normally it will germinate and grow only leaves in the first year and store its energy in a swollen root structure of some type. The second year it will emerge from dormancy to flower and set seed. Because of the long growing season in Florida, many biennials complete their life cycles in one year. See **Annual** and **Perennial**.

Biomass. The amount of living matter, in the form of organisms, present in a particular habitat, usually expressed as weight per unit area or as the carbon, nitrogen, or caloric content per unit area. It can also be used to describe the weight of plant materials and animal waste that can be used for fuel.

Bioswale. See **Rain garden**.

Bract. A reduced leaf or leaflike structure that subtends the flower or flower head. In some species, such as flowering dogwood (*Cornus florida*), starrush white-top (*Rhynchospora colorata*), and spotted beebalm (*Monarda punctata*), it's the bracts, not the petals, that are showy.

Bugs. Entomologists classify true bugs as those belonging to the Hemiptera, an order of insects characterized by their sucking mouthparts such as aphids. Informal use of the term "bug" refers to various members of the arthropod phylum (animals with exoskeletons) that includes the six-legged insects, the eight-legged spiders and mites, scorpions, the crustaceans such as sowbugs and pillbugs, and the many-legged centipedes and millipedes. With apologies to the entomologists, this book uses the informal terminology.

Bunch grass (or bunching grass). A member of the Poaceae, or grass family, that grows in clumps rather than spreading via stolons or rhizomes. Other graminoids such as rushes (*Juncus* spp.) could also fill the same role in the landscape.

Caliper. Tree trunk caliper (trunk diameter for saplings) is measured 6 inches up from the root flare on trees with caliper of 4 inches or less. For saplings larger than 4 inches in diameter, caliper is measured at 12 inches above the ground. Mature tree measurements are dbh (diameter at breast height or 130 centimeters above ground—a little less than 4½ feet). Since trunks are seldom perfectly round, the largest diameter is used as the measurement. Tree professionals and ecologists use a special measuring tape with conversion of circumference to diameter marked on the tape.

Cambium. The living tissue in a woody plant that is located just under the bark. It is the growth of this layer of wood that creates the annual rings. If a tree is girdled—with a gap cut out of the bark around the entire trunk—the cambium cannot function and the tree will usually die within a year. Palms do not have cambium and therefore do not produce true wood with annual rings.

Cane. A cane is a stem of a shrub that arises from the ground. Some brambles such as blackberry (*Rubus* spp.) also have canes. The primocane sprouts one year with only leaves, it persists through the winter, and then it becomes a floricane the next year when it bears flowers and fruit.

Canopy. The tops of the trees in a forest or wooded area form a canopy. Canopy trees in a grouping are the ones that will grow the tallest and produce the most shade. A dense canopy is characteristic of most forests and blocks most direct sunlight from the forest floor. A thin or broken canopy is characteristic of most woodlands; it allows more sunlight in and therefore supports a more diverse variety of plants and animals below, in the understory.

Climax community. A stage in ecological development in which a community of organisms, especially plants, is stable and capable of perpetuating itself. With no outside disturbances, a climax community will not be succeeded by a different set of plants—it will have reached its ultimate equilibrium. Fire, flood, or other disaster will disturb the succession and the process may start all over again. Fire climax communities are found in much of Florida.

Coir (coconut coir) (pronounced "core"). This is a byproduct of the coconut industry and is made from the husks. It has good water retention qualities and is a sustainable substitute for peat moss. It is not acidic and has some nutrient value as opposed to peat moss, which is highly acidic with virtually no nutrients and is never sustainable. Coir has many uses, from pressed starter pots, sterile soilless medium, and woven matting to filling for erosion logs.

Compost. Compost is a mixture of organic materials such as garden and kitchen waste, leaves, and grass clippings that are decayed in a controlled environment such as a bin or a pile, and the word also applies to the act of composting, as a verb. The wider the variety of products in a compost pile, the richer the nutrients are likely to be, but for nutrient-poor areas where you are planting natives, limit compost materials to local, native products to better mimic the natural environment. A topdressing of compost applied outside the root-ball of a recently planted native just at the beginning of a growth period will improve the soil and entice the roots to grow outward.

Compost extract. To make compost extract, place a shovelful of compost in a bucket, fill with rain barrel water, and stir occasionally for several hours. Use as liquid fertilizer for seedlings. This is not compost tea brewed with molasses in an artificially aerated container, which can contain harmful levels of bacteria.

Cotyledons. These are the leaves that are formed inside the seed and are also called seed leaves. The cotyledon leaves of most plants have a different shape than the true leaves that develop later. If there is one cotyledon leaf, the plant is a monocot; but if there are two, it is a dicot.

Cultivar. A plant that has been developed for the horticultural trade through intentional hybridization or selective breeding, or by taking advantage of accidents of nature. Cultivars don't normally breed true with open-pollinated seed and are usually reproduced asexually by cuttings or divisions so their special characteristics are retained.

Deadheading. The practice of cutting off flowers before they drop their seeds. This is commonly done in manicured landscapes to force more blooming and keep them neat, but in a native habitat garden, at least some of the flowers should be allowed to set seed to feed the seed-eating wildlife, especially the songbirds. On the other hand, if a plant has been too prolific, deadheading can reduce next year's population to some degree.

Deciduous. A plant that loses its leaves in the fall or winter and sprouts a whole new set in the spring. See **Evergreen**.

Detritus. A combination of dead plants and animals, plus their waste products, in various states of decay. Detritus is naturally found in the leaf litter on the forest floor and in the bottoms of ponds, lakes, and other waterways. Various animals, bacteria, and fungi feed on detritus and contribute to decomposition. See **Eutrophication**.

Dioecious. A species is dioecious if individual plants bear all male flowers or all female flowers. Maples (*Acer* spp.) and hollies (*Ilex* spp.) are examples of dioecious plants. Make sure you plant at least one male-flowered specimen of a dioecious species so female plants can produce berries or seeds.

Dicot or dicotyledon. A flowering plant that has two cotyledon leaves preformed in the seed is a dicot. When its seed germinates, the two seed leaves are the first to emerge. The first true leaves normally have a completely different shape from that of the cotyledons.

Drip line. The area around a tree or shrub defined by where water would drip to the ground from its outermost branches. The area inside this ring is known as the drip zone. The root zone of a healthy, well-established tree usually extends 30 percent beyond its drip line or more.

Ecology. The study of the relationship of organisms to each other and to their environment. Organisms and their environment are known as an ecosystem. (When people say they are taking an action for the good of the ecology, they are misusing the term.)

Ecosystem. A complex interrelationship of organisms (plants, animals, fungi, and bacteria) in the substrate where they live and die.

Ecotone. The transitional area between two types of plant communities. For instance, the area between a meadow and a forest produces an ecotone in which exposure to direct sunlight causes the trees in the forest edge to produce many more branches along their trunks, and many understory shrubs, vines, and herbaceous plants also grow there. Ecotones can be maintained either by man-made interventions or by naturally occurring physical processes or conditions including fire, salt spray, elevation, or hydrology. Ecotones often support a greater diversity of both plants and animals than either of the adjoining ecosystems.

Edge feathering. A wildlife-friendly process of replacing straight forest edges with broad undulating lines weaving in and out, with pockets of dense thickets offset by more open meadow areas. See chapter 7.

Edge-Feet. A linear measure along the edge of a human-centered landscape feature such as a lawn, driveway, or path and its intersection with a natural area such as a meadow or a wooded area. This term was coined for use in this book.

Emergent wetland plants. Plants that grow from the bottom of a body of water and emerge past the surface. Some examples are cattails (*Typha* spp.), pickerelweed (*Pontederia cordata*), and some rushes (*Juncus* spp., *Scirpus* spp.).

Epicotyl. The stem portion of a plant embryo in a seed that is located above the cotyledon(s) and will bear the true leaves.

Erosion-log. A long roll of organic material used for erosion control. It is usually staked in place across the slope; plants are installed into or next to "logs" so they will grow on the slope or shoreline as the "logs" decompose. The material most often used is coconut coir, but sleeves or socks are also available that can be filled on-site with compost, straw, or other organic material.

Eutrophication or eutrophy. The process in which an overly nutrient-rich body of water or stream fills in and becomes a wet meadow. It is a natural process but often quickened by pollution runoff (including fertilizers) or too much organic plant matter. Results of eutrophication include sedimentation of organic plant matter and dense algal blooms that may cause hypoxia (the lowering of oxygen in the water), which kills aquatic wildlife including fish. Unnaturally high eutrophication rates in waterways can be reduced when fertilization of lawns and plants near wetlands is kept to a minimum.

Evergreen. A plant that stays green throughout the year, though it may, like the southern magnolia (*Magnolia grandiflora*) and most pine trees (*Pinus* spp.), drop its leaves throughout the year. Some species are semievergreen and keep their leaves all year in some climates but not others. See **Deciduous**.

Exotic. A plant from another part of the world. In Florida, if a plant wasn't here 500 years ago (before the Europeans started to bring plants from their home countries), it is exotic or non-native. This is not a perfect definition since indigenous peoples regularly moved plants, and plant ranges continue to change naturally on their own, but it is verifiable and the one most often used.

Fence effect. Birds that eat berries and then perch on fences or in hedges will deposit perfectly fertilized seeds at the base. A higher population of berry-producing plants growing along a fence or hedge is called the fence effect. This term was coined for this book.

Fix nitrogen. See **Nitrogen fixing**.

Floating plants. Plants that float on the surface of a body of water. Some examples of floating plants that are rooted in the bottom are spatterdock (*Nuphar advena*) and American white waterlily (*Nymphaea odorata*). There are also free-floating plants with no roots in the bottom such as the invasive water hyacinth (*Eichhornia crassipes*).

Florida-friendly law. This law (Section 373.185(3)), passed in 2008, states that no organization or government body can prevent a homeowner from using "Florida-friendly" landscaping practices. www.fyn.ifas.ufl.edu

Forbs. Herbaceous flowering plants with broad leaves—not grasslike and not ferns or fern allies.

Freedom lawn. A lawn that is free from pesticides (including herbicides), free from over-irrigation, and free from fertilizers is a freedom lawn. Whatever grows is mowed during its growing season, and it is allowed to go dormant at other times.

French drain. French drains absorb and direct water to a distant point. Modern French drains are usually built using a porous, cloth-covered flexible pipe. French drains are also known as blind drains because the water enters through percolation and not open channels, and most often they are not noticeable in the landscape. Traditionally, French drains consisted of a trench filled with rocks, gravel, sand, or other permeable media. Sometimes the trench was also lined with tiles.

Girdle. A process used to kill trees by peeling a 3-inch strip of bark all the way around the circumference of the tree near the base. This disrupts the flow of nutrients in the cambium layer and the tree is likely to die the next year. Some vigorous trees will grow new bark and jump the gap and then need subsequent treatments. Girdling does not work on palm trees because they have no cambium layer.

Graminoids. Grasses and grasslike plants including rushes, sedges, and others.

Ground covers. Plants that range in height from less than 1 inch to 3 feet and provide dense soil cover, retard weed growth, and prevent soil erosion. They can be woody or herbaceous, clumping or running, evergreen or deciduous. While turfgrass is a ground cover, many other far more sustainable choices are available for landscapes.

Grove. A grove consists of trees, shrubs, and perennial ground covers that grow together in their own small ecosystem. See chapter 9.

Gymnosperm. Gymnosperms or conifers are vascular seed-bearing plants with seeds produced after fertilization usually borne on exposed surfaces of reproductive structures such as the female cones. See **Angiosperm**.

Hardening-off. A procedure used to better prepare seedlings for life in the ground, to acclimate plants to the outdoors. Because seedlings may be grown in a protected environment, introducing them slowly to the elements of wind and intense sun and less frequent irrigation increases their viability after transplanting into the landscape.

Hardscape. The nonplant features in the landscape such as benches, pergolas, patios, fences, and paved walkways.

Hat-racking. The process of chopping all the branches of a tree or shrub at the same height. Some trees, such as the exotic crape myrtle (*Lagerstroemia indica*), are subjected to this poor pruning technique each year. This practice weakens the tree and should be replaced by wiser pruning methods.

Hedgerow. Not to be confused with the typical sheared hedge created from one species of plant such as privet, a hedgerow consists of a variety of shrubs and small trees that are planted far enough apart so that they can grow into their natural shapes, but close enough so they form a wall of vegetation that forms a buffer or screen. See chapter 9.

Herbaceous. Plants that do not produce wood are herbaceous or non-woody.

HOA (home owners association). Many communities have HOAs that decide on management of community-owned lands. Some also have rules and restrictions on the plants that individual homeowners may or may not plant in their own yards. See **Florida-friendly law**.

Hypocotyl. The stem portion of a plant embryo in a seed that is located below the cotyledon(s).

Inflorescence. The part of the plant that bears multiple flowers, including all its bracts, branches, and flowers. Usually refers to compound flower heads.

Infructescence. The part of the plant that bears multiple fruits, including all its bracts, branches, and fruits. See **Inflorescence**.

Integrated Weed Management. The use of more than one weed removal and/or weed prevention method in a coordinated way. An example would be to physically remove as much of a deep-rooted perennial as possible (maybe several times) and then to poison the new sprouts as soon as they emerge for maximum effectiveness of the herbicide.

Invasive plant. An exotic plant that has escaped from cultivation and outcompeted native plants in native ecosystems to such a degree that it has adversely affected and altered the native habitat. Although native plants may be rambunctious multipliers and take over various habitats, they are not, by definition, invasive. The terms "aggressive" and "invasive" are not used interchangeably in this book. Florida Exotic Pest Plant Council maintains two lists of the most invasive exotic plants on its website (www.fleppc.org). Plants listed in Category I are the most invasive: they are altering native plant communities by displacing native species, changing community structures or ecological functions, or hybridizing with natives. Category II plants are somewhat invasive, but they have not yet significantly altered Florida plant communities to the extent exhibited by Category I species. These species may become ranked Category I, in the future. Many other states have their own EPPCs. See chapter 3 for more details.

Lawn tree. In urban/suburban landscapes the lawn tree is a common feature—a tree surrounded by a vast sea of lawn. This situation is not good for the lawn and it's not good for the tree. Read chapter 9 to find out how to incorporate a lawn tree into a sustainable grove. This term was coined for use in this book.

Layering. (1) A method of rooting a cutting without removing it from the parent plant. Soil layering forces a branch to make contact with the soil so it will root. Air layering is a method of inducing root formation with no contact with the soil. See more details in chapter 6. (2) A method using paper or cardboard under mulch to keep weeds at bay; this is not recommended for native landscapes. See appendix II for details.

Legume. A plant belonging to the bean family (Fabaceae). Legumes are important in soil building because most of them have a symbiotic relationship with root bacteria that take in nitrogen from the air and transform it to a nitrate essential for good plant growth. The process is called "fixing" nitrogen. This adaptation allows legumes to grow in poor soil. See **Nitrogen fixation**.

Limb-up. A pruning practice whereby the lower limbs of trees are trimmed back to the trunk. This is called for in areas where the low branches interfere with human or vehicular traffic and also in a firewise landscape to reduce ladder fuels. On the other hand, getting rid of lower branches usually increases the maintenance chores because more weeds grow with increased light and exposure. Some trees naturally shed their lower branches.

Littoral. The littoral zone is an ecotone that extends from the normal high-water mark at the shoreline out to a depth where sunlight reaches the bottom of the water body. If there are tides, it will include the intertidal area between the high tide line and the low tide line. This zone can be miles wide as in a salt marsh or mangrove swamp; it can also be a narrow band if the shoreline is a steep slope at the edge of a deep lake.

Living fence. A specialized hedge that has pliable canes of living shrubs or trees woven into a trellis-like fence structure. For details on how to create a living fence, see chapter 9.

Living shoreline. A combination of tough, native species such as grasses, rushes, and shrubs planted along the shoreline or on barriers or berms of rock, gravel, or sand. Living shorelines allow water flow around the vegetation, but the shoreline is protected from wave action. The scale can be large or small and configured in various ways depending on the situation.

Meristem. A meristem is a region in a plant where there are undifferentiated cells. This is where growth can take place. In a stem, meristematic cells occur at each node (where a bud can form)—normally these cells form a new branch or flower, but with the help of a rooting hormone, they can also develop into roots. These are literally the stem cells.

Microclimates. Growing conditions on your property depend on the amount of sun in different seasons, drainage conditions, and proximity to heat-retaining elements such as bodies of water, foundations, large rocks, and paved surfaces. Another thing that affects microclimate is wind circulation—hedgerows and buildings affect the flow of air in a landscape. As you become familiar with the microclimates in your landscape, you can make better decisions on what to plant where.

Monocot or monocotyledon. An angiosperm or flowering plant that has one cotyledon leaf preformed in the seed. When it sprouts, this seed leaf emerges first. Monocots include palms, grasses, irises, orchids, rushes, and sedges. See **Dicot**.

Monoculture. A situation where only one type of plant grows. Usually it's an artificial environment like a St. Augustine lawn (*Stenotaphrum secundatum*) or a weeping fig hedge (*Ficus benjamina*), but it could also be natural like the sawgrass prairie (*Cladium jamaicense*) in the Everglades.

Mulch. Mulch consists of nonsoil materials laid on top of soil. This can happen naturally as leaves and small branches fall to the ground in a grove of trees and shrubs. In maintained landscapes, various materials are laid on top of soil to reduce weed populations, moderate temperature fluctuations, and preserve moisture.

Native plant. A plant is native if it is indigenous—occurring in natural associations in habitats that existed prior to significant human impacts and alterations of the landscape. The definition in Florida and the rest of the New World is a plant that grew here before the onset of colonization by Europeans. See **Exotic** and **Regional native**.

Nitrogen fixation or nitrogen fixing. Plants require nitrogen to grow, but they can't make use of the nitrogen gas in the air directly. (Air is 78 percent nitrogen.) Nitrogen-fixing soil bacteria and fungi produce ammonia byproducts containing available nitrogen that can be absorbed by the plants. Legumes and some woody plants, such as wax myrtle and alder, harbor symbiotic bacteria or fungi in their roots that use the nitrogen gas to produce ammonia. Nitrogen (N_2) + hydrogen ($8H_2$)—> ammonia ($2NH_3$) + hydrogen(H_2). Plants with nitrogen-fixing organisms do better in low-nutrient soils than other plants and tend to be ruderals or pioneer plants.

Node. The area on a stem where a branch, leaf, or bud occurs.

Non-native plant. See **Exotic**.

Non-point-source contamination (or pollution). Pollution that comes from many diffuse sources, including fertilizers and pesticides from agricultural and residential lands, and nutrients from wastes: livestock, pet, and human—from nonfunctioning septic systems. As runoff moves over impervious surfaces and over the ground, it dissolves natural and man-made contaminants and transports them to oceans, streams, rivers, wetlands, lakes, and ground water. Aggregated non-point-source contamination is by far the leading and most widespread cause of water-quality degradation.

Organic. Anything that's alive or has been alive is made up of organic materials. For example, when organic material is advised for your soil, it could include compost, dead leaves, wood chips, manure from herbivores, and worm castings. J. I. Rodale coined another use of the word "organic" in the 1940s when he started *Organic Gardening Magazine* and wrote about farming without synthetic chemicals.

Peat moss. Peat moss is partially decomposed sphagnum moss. It takes centuries to form under pressure in a bog environment and is acidic and sterile when mined—the pH ranges from 3.5 to 4.5. It is not farmed, and harvesting peat is not a sustainable practice. Use coconut coir instead.

Perennial. A plant that has a life cycle of more than two years. Trees and shrubs would fall into this category, but normally the term is used for herbaceous perennials that do not develop wood. Normally, herbaceous perennials die back or go dormant for part of the year. See **Annual** and **Biennial**.

Perlite. This product is used to lighten the soil in container gardens and as a sterile medium for starting seeds. Perlite, an extremely absorbent medium, is made from a type of volcanic glass that becomes porous when it is heated and expands to as much as 20 times its original volume.

pH. See **Acidity**.

Phloem. Phloem is made up of vascular cells that transport nutrients such as sugar and amino acids. Nutrient movement can start at the leaves for storage in the roots or return from the storage roots up to new growing areas. This movement is called translocation. Phloem cells are soft with sieve-like cell walls so the movement can be directed. They usually combine with hard xylem cells to form vascular bundles. See **Xylem**.

Photosynthesis. The process of converting light energy into storable energy (food). Photosynthesis is unique to plants, algae, and cyanobacteria. In plants, photosynthesis happens mostly in leaves or in green stems. It combines carbon dioxide (CO_2) and water (H_2O) with energy from sunlight to form sugar ($C_6H_{12}O_6$) and oxygen gas (O_2). Respiration is the equal and opposite chemical reaction, and all organisms, including plants, respire. For most vascular plants, the water is supplied by transpiration and the carbon dioxide is available from the air. Almost all life on earth is dependent on photosynthesis for energy.

Pot-bound. See **Root-bound.**

Potting up. When plants grown in pots outgrow their original pots, they can be placed in larger pots to allow more growth. Growers sometimes wait too long before potting up and end up with pot-bound specimens; for woody plants, this can mean winding roots that can be deadly to the plant if allowed to persist.

Propagule. A general definition is any plant part that can give rise to a new individual plant, usually seeds (including sprouted seeds in a protective structure as in mangroves), spores, and cuttings.

Provenance. Plant provenance is the origin of the parental stock. When you purchase native plants you need to be aware of their origins, because you'll have much better success with local stock. In Florida the soil doesn't freeze; a five-month wet season starts in June and a seven-month dry season starts in November. Florida natives have adjusted to this climate over time. A tree bred from stock from New England—where the soil freezes and an average of 3 or 4 inches of rain falls each month—will not do well in Florida even though it may be the same species.

Rain garden or bioswale. A natural or constructed low area in the landscape where stormwater from roofs, roads, and driveways collects. Plants suitable for a rain garden can withstand days of inundation and months of drought. See chapter 10 for more details.

Radicle. The part of the plant embryo in a seed that will become the main root.

Regional native. A plant that is naturally occurring within a general region (e.g., Florida) but not locally is a regional native. For example, the eastern purple coneflower (*Echinacea purpurea*) naturally occurs in one county in Florida north of Tallahassee in the Florida Panhandle. It qualifies as a "Florida native" and is widely sold in all of North Florida as a native. If you plant it in Jacksonville in northeast Florida, it may grow successfully even though it would not naturally occur there. It is a regional native for the rest of North Florida, and some native plant enthusiasts would not include it in a restoration project outside its natural region nor recommend it for landscape use as a native.

Respiration. The chemical reaction in which living organisms take in oxygen gas (O_2) and break down sugar ($C_6H_{12}O_6$) to get energy to sustain life and then release water (H_2O) and carbon dioxide (CO_2). Photosynthesis is the equal and opposite chemical reaction.

Rhizome. A horizontal, underground stem that can produce new shoots and roots to generate new plants that are clones of the parent stock. Some plants have rhizomes that can also store sugars or starches. Aggressive rhizomatous plants are useful in blocking out undesirable plants; however, they are also difficult to eradicate because any piece of rhizome left in the ground could produce a whole new plant. Many ferns (e.g., *Woodwardia* spp.) and graminoids (e.g., *Spartina* spp.) have rhizomes.

Riparian zone. The strip of land adjacent to streams or rivers. This zone can be wide such as a floodplain or narrow like a stream bank in an otherwise dry ecosystem. Riparian vegetation varies with the type of aquatic ecosystem and supplies significant regional habitat value for a wide variety of wildlife.

Root-bound. A plant is root-bound if the roots are tightly packed or circling inside a pot and also possibly growing through the drainage holes in search of more soil. Take care when installing such a plant because it is already highly stressed. See chapter 5 for details on dealing with a root-bound or pot-bound plant.

Root flare. The place at the bottom of a tree trunk where the roots begin to grow outward. The root flare should be situated above the soil line when planting a tree. Palms don't have root flares and neither do woody plants that have been started as cuttings.

Root-prune. Root-pruning a tree or shrub a month or more before transplanting allows it to adjust to fewer roots and increases the success rate of the transplant. Use a sharp shovel to cut a circle around the tree—sink the shovel into the soil right up to the top of the blade. Depending on the size of the plant, the circle might be 12 to 24 inches out from the trunk—this will be the size of the root-ball. Root-pruning cuts the surface roots and encourages the tree to develop more roots close to the trunk. Root-pruning is not effective for most palms because they will generate all new roots upon transplanting.

Rooting hormone. See **Auxin**.

Ruderal (ruderals). The literal meaning is "of rubble." Ruderal species germinate quickly and thrive in sunny disturbed landscapes. Plants that grow well in ruderal areas are ruderals, including some of our favorite native plants such as black-eyed Susans (*Rudbeckia* spp.).

Runner. See **Stolon**.

Scarify. In gardening, two different procedures can be described with this term: (1) When you scarify a seed with a hard seed coat you create a gap in the coat by nicking it with a sharp blade or abrading it with sandpaper or an emery board. This mimics how a seed would naturally be abraded in the gizzard of a bird or other animal's digestive system. It allows water to soak in to promote faster germination. You would do this only for hard-to-germinate seeds. (2) The term is also used to mean dethatching a lawn by raking or some other means to remove the underlying dead grass tissues— the thatch.

Seed bank or soil seed bank. Plants produce a lot of seeds, but some do not germinate right away and become dormant in the soil—they are added to the soil seed bank. When conditions are right, they will emerge from dormancy and sprout. The conditions could be a disturbance like your digging up a plant or pulling a weed, or the seeds might need to experience cold (stratification), warm temperatures, fire, or rain.

Shovel-pruning. A form of asexual propagation in which you dig out extra cane(s) of a shrub and plant in a new location as a separate plant. For a large shrub it's wise to root-prune those canes before the pruning. See chapter 6 for details.

Softscape. Softscape refers to the ever-changing plant materials in the landscape. The plants are the dynamic features of the landscape. See **Hardscape**.

Snag. A dead tree left standing in the landscape to provide good habitat for birds and other wildlife. You would do this only where no one would be hurt when it finally falls. You can create snags by "planting" logs vertically in the landscape.

Solarization. A technique used to kill weeds with heat, without chemicals. During the hottest part of summer, lay clear plastic sheeting on an area in full sun that has been closely mowed, cleared of plant material, and watered. Weigh down the edges of the plastic with soil, bricks, or boards to make a good seal. Let it sit for six weeks or more. See chapter 6 for details.

Stolon. An aboveground horizontal stem emanating from a plant that will produce a new plant. Plants with stolons form colonies. Also called a runner.

Stoma, pl. stomata (or stomates). The stomata are the pores on leaves and/or stems of plants that control the flow of water by means of guard cells that expand or collapse depending on heat, humidity, and soil moisture. When they are open, water quickly evaporates from the leaf tissues as part of the transpiration process. For most plants, the vast majority of the stomata are on the undersides of the leaves.

Stratification. The cold treatment necessary for some seeds before they germinate.

Succession. The process in which plant communities change through time after physical events (disturbances or formation of new land such as barrier island accretion). Starting with a bare landscape there will be a series of plant species and communities that will be dominant for a period of time until a climax community is achieved. Soil type and climate are some of the determining factors in which plants will grow. Other limiting factors like salt spray, fire, mowing, and grazing can stop the progression of plants.

Sucker. A vigorous shoot growing vertically from a surface root of the parent plant or from a low spot on the trunk or cane. Also see **Water sprout**.

Surfactant. The word is a blend of surface-active-agent. A surfactant reduces the surface tension of liquids and enables water and oily substances to mix. An example is a detergent or soap. Surfactants are used with herbicides and pesticides to help the plant poison stick to its targeted plant or to help reduce waxy plant coatings for better absorption.

Swale. A naturally occurring or constructed low spot in the landscape where precipitation and other water can collect. See chapter 10 for information on swales and rain gardens.

Thatch. (1) A layer of dead stems and roots of grass and other plants that accumulate near the soil surface in a lawn. When thatch is more than half an inch thick it prevents moisture, oxygen, and nutrients from penetrating the soil. In lawns cared for sustainably, thatch is rarely a problem. (2) Roofing material comprising reeds or palm fronds. (3) "Florida thatch" is a type of palm (*Thrinax radiata*) that is often used for thatching roofs.

Transpiration (transpire). Water is absorbed from soil into the roots and drawn through the vessels (xylem) by the loss of water from leaves through evaporation. The rate of transpiration is determined by the amount of water in the soil, humidity, temperature, and whether the plant's stomata are open or closed. Less than 10 percent of the water pumped through the plant is actually absorbed into the plant's tissues or used in photosynthesis. Transpiration increases local humidity and cools the plant's tissues and the surrounding air.

Vermiculite. Derived from rocks containing large crystals of the minerals biotite and iron-bearing phlogopite, also known as mica. These rocks are mined, then heated to produce the wormlike strands that are broken into smaller flaked pieces to produce a moisture-holding medium often added to commercial potting mixes.

Viviparous. When seeds germinate while still on the parent plant to form a propagule without a period of dormancy, that plant is viviparous, and the process is called vivipary. Both red and black mangroves in Florida are viviparous and produce propagules that are already growing when they fall from the parent plant.

Water sprouts. Vertical, fast-growing tree branches that sprout from horizontal branches or from a trunk if the tree has fallen. It's generally a good idea to prune back these sprouts because they can weaken the whole tree structure, making it more prone to wind damage, but on the other hand, plants that easily form water sprouts are good candidates for constructing living fences.

Whip. A young tree sapling that is 3 to 6 feet tall and has not developed any significant side branches. Whips can be purchased as bare-root plants or potted plants. These are the best stage to plant because they adapt well and start growing quickly without much extra irrigation or other attention. In addition, they are usually quite inexpensive, allowing you to purchase more trees for your landscape.

Wildland. A natural area with no buildings. It's possible that it's a virgin land where no human intervention has occurred, but more likely, it is second or third growth (successional) forest, scrub, or marsh that has reverted to its natural or near natural state after man-made disturbance such as mining, farming, or ranching.

Xylem. Xylem cells become lignified (hardened) as they mature, forming hard hollow tubes. They form the center of the vascular bundles of woody plants, with phloem cells on the outside—together they form the cambium. This is where water flows from the roots up through the plant to the stomata in the leaves where the vast majority of it evaporates into the air during transpiration. See **Phloem** and **Transpiration**.

Resources

Native Plant Resources

Online

Atlas of Florida Vascular Plants lists *all* the plants in the state with distributions, and most listings include several photos for identification. This site is the authority used by this book on whether a plant is native to Florida or not. www.florida.plantatlas.usf.edu.

The website of the Florida Association of Native Nurseries (FANN) helps you find nearby native nurseries, and you can also search for nurseries with specific plants in stock: www.plantrealflorida.org

The Florida Department of Transportation (FL DOT) has published a study on the value and ecosystem services of roadside wildflowers, including an extensive resources list on this topic. www.dot.state.fl.us/research-center/Completed_Proj/Summary_EMO/FDOT-BDK75-977-74-rpt.pdf

The Florida Wildflower Foundation provides grants and education about Florida's native wildflowers. www.flawildflowers.org

The Florida Wildflower Growers Cooperative has authentic Florida wildflower seeds for sale with instructions on the best time to plant them. www.floridawildflowers.com

The Institute for Regional Conservation's (IRC) Natives for Your Neighborhood page allows you to generate a list of plants and plant habitats for South Florida. There are also guidelines for creating a pine rockland and rockland hammock. www.regionalconservation.org

The Florida Native Plant Society includes information on Florida's native plant communities and recommended natives by county on its website. Local chapters hold native plant sales, educational meetings, and field trips and participate in outreach events. Each year there is a statewide conference with two days of field trips and two days of educational sessions. www.fnps.org (50 percent of the royalties from this book will be paid directly to this organization.)

Most states have native plant societies. The American Horticultural Society website has a page that lists all the NPSs: www.ahs.org/gardening-resources/societies-clubs-organizations/native-plant-societies.

The University of Florida's Institute of Food and Agricultural Sciences (UF/IFAS) (Florida's extension service; other states have their own extension programs):

> Resources about native trees and their care for both South and North Florida: www.edis.ifas.ufl.edu/eh157 and www.edis.ifas.ufl.edu/ep007.

> IFAS bulletin on saw palmetto: www.plantapalm.com/vpe/misc/saw-palmetto.pdf

The Wild Ones: Native plants and natural landscapes. Healing the Earth one yard at a time. This group promotes the use of natives and has a Seeds for Education grant program and many resources on its website: www.wildones.org

Books

Huegel, Craig N. 2012. *Native Wildflowers and Other Ground Covers for Florida Landscapes*; 2015. *Native Florida Plants for Shady Landscapes*. Gainesville: University Press of Florida.

Nelson, Gil. 2003. *Florida's Best Native Landscape Plants: 200 Readily Available Species for Homeowners and Professionals*. Gainesville: University Press of Florida; 2000. *The Ferns of Florida*; 2013. *The Trees of Florida*. Sarasota: Pineapple Press.

Osorio, Rufino. 2001. *A Gardener's Guide to Florida's Native Plants*. Gainesville: University Press of Florida.

Wunderlin, Richard P., and Bruce Hansen. 2015. *Guide to the Vascular Plants of Florida*. Gainesville: University Press of Florida.

Plant Removal Resources (Invasive Exotics and Other "I Don't Want It" Plants)

Online

Florida Exotic Pest Plant Council (FLEPPC) is a nonprofit organization of professional land managers, researchers, consultants, and others who share the objective of supporting the recognition and management of invasive exotic plants in Florida's natural areas. It maintains two lists of exotic plants: The 2013 Category I list comprises the 76 most invasive plants in Florida, and the Category II list adds another 75 potentially invasive plants. The lists are updated every two years. Many states have EPPC organizations, which are listed on the "links" page of the FLEPPC site. www.fleppc.org

Florida Fish and Wildlife Conservation Commission website includes information on invasive plants and animals and is the organization that grants permits for sterilized Asian carp for waterweed control. www.myfwc.com/.

The University of Florida's Institute of Food and Agricultural Sciences (UF/IFAS):

Solarization: www.edis.ifas.ufl.edu/in856.

University of Georgia, et al. *Invasive Plants of the Eastern United States: Identification and Control*, a downloadable book from www.invasive.org/eastern/

Books

Chace, Teri Dunn. 2013. *How to Eradicate Invasive Plants*. Portland: Timber Press. Although this book does not differentiate between aggressive and invasive, it does include photos of many of the worst invaders in the country.

Sustainable Landscaping

Online

811: To find out what's underground, call 811, or in Florida go to the 811 website for details. www.Sunshine 811.com

Alabama extension perennial care: www.aces.edu/pubs/docs/A/ANR-0566/ANR-0566.pdf

Linda Chalker-Scott provides extensive scientific literature research, including the following:

Horticultural myths: www.informedgardener.com

Summary of mulches: www.hriresearch.org/docs/publications/JEH/JEH_2007/JEH_2007_25_4/JEH%2025-4-239-249.pdf

Florida Fish and Wildlife Conservation Commission provides guidelines and extensive resources list for creating wildlife habitat at home. www.myfwc.com/viewing/habitat/

Florida Wildflower Foundation

Developing wildflower meadows: www.flawildflowers.org/resources/pdfs/pdf10/FloridaWildflowersPlanningandPlanting.pdf

Model resolutions for no mow roadsides: www.flawildflowers.org/resolution.php

Florida State Government: Florida-Friendly handbook provides useful guidelines for creating an overall landscape plan. The extensive Florida-friendly plant list includes only about half natives, but it still provides useful information on design, size, and the best conditions for good growth. www.swfwmd.state.fl.us/publications/files/FFL_Plant_Selection_Guide.pdf

The website of the International Society of Arboriculture has general information on trees and also a location tool for finding a certified arborist near you. www.treesaregood.org

University of Florida, Institute of Food and Agricultural Sciences (UF/IFAS)

IFAS resource on landscape design: www.edis.ifas.ufl.edu/mg086.

IFAS website about planting palms: www.edis.ifas.ufl.edu/ep001

detailed resource on trees and shrubs: www.hort.ufl.edu/woody/.

web pages on planting shrubs: www.edis.ifas.ufl.edu/ep391 and www.edis.ifas.ufl.edu/ep390

resources on growing wildflowers: www.nfrec.ifas.ufl.edu/programs/wildflowers.shtml

Fire in the Wildland-Urban Interface: Selecting and Maintaining Firewise Plants for Landscaping by J. Douglas Doran, Cotton K. Randall, and Alan J. Long www.edis.ifas.ufl.edu/fr147

Books

Chalker-Scott, Linda. 2008. *The Informed Gardener*; 2010. *The Informed Gardener Blooms Again*. Seattle: University of Washington Press. These books cover some of Linda's Horticultural Myths in detail.

Stibolt, Ginny. 2009. *Sustainable Gardening for Florida*. Gainesville: University Press of Florida. This book covers compost, mulch, rain barrels, rain gardens, best planting practices, integrated pest management, living shorelines, and planning for hurricanes and fires.

Waterfront and Wetlands Gardening

Online

Chesapeake Bay Foundation has information and a variety of resources for waterfront management: www.cbf.org.

Florida Department of Environmental Protection (FL DOT)

A 40-page book for waterfront landowners and others: www.dep.state.fl.us/water/nonpoint/docs/nonpoint/wpog-book-final.pdf

A 68-page booklet: *Best Management Practices for Protection of Water Resources in Florida*. 2002. www.dep.state.fl.us.

Information by zip code on proper disposal procedures for household hazardous waste: www.dep.state.fl.us.

A 16-page brochure on regulations and procedures for trimming mangroves: www.manatee.ifas.ufl.edu/seagrant/pdfs/Mangrove_Trimming_Guidelines.pdf

Florida's water management districts offer a 60-page booklet, *Waterwise Florida Landscapes*: www.floridayards.org/landscape/SJRWMD_Waterwise.pdf

Hillsborough County, Florida, has an adopt-a-pond program through which residents can sign up to take care of a stormwater retention pond in the county: www.swfwmd.state.fl.us.

Maryland's Department of Natural Resources has information on that state's living shorelines program: www.dnr.state.md.us.

University of New Hampshire offers a 93-page book on lakefront landscaping: www.extension.unh.edu/resources/files/resource001799_Rep2518.pdf

The National Oceanic and Atmospheric Administration's (NOAA) habitat website has detailed information on living shorelines and other wetlands restoration: www.habitat.noaa.gov.

Stroud Water Research Center has done the science of streamside buffer plantings: www.stroudcenter.org.

U.S. Department of Agriculture (USDA): Information on dune restoration, including specifics on plants to use—adapted for Florida's coasts: www.nrcs.usda.gov/Internet/FSE_DOCUMENTS/nrcs141p2_014932.pdf

The U.S. Geological Survey website has information about waterfront management: www.usgs.gov.

Wildlife Habitat Resources

Online

National Wildlife Federation has a habitat certification program for landscapes, schools, and even whole towns or communities: www.nwf.org

The Butterflies and Moths of North America (BAMONA): online moth and butterfly handbook, including the larval and nectar plants for each butterfly and moth species: www.butterfliesandmoths.org/

Books

Daniels, Jaret C. 2000. *Your Florida Guide to Butterfly Gardening: A Guide for the Deep South.* Gainesville: University Press of Florida.

Huegel, Craig N. 2010. *Native Plant Landscaping for Florida Wildlife.* Gainesville: University Press of Florida.

Minno, Marc C., and Maria Minno. 1999. *Florida Butterfly Gardening: A Complete Guide to Attracting, Identifying, and Enjoying Butterflies.* Gainesville: University Press of Florida.

Tallamy, Douglas W. 2007. *Bringing Nature Home.* Portland: Timber Press.

Index

Page numbers in *italics* refer to photos and illustrations; the letters *pl* following a page number denote a plate.

Walter's viburnum, 159, 175
Water hyacinth, *38*, 239
Watering saucer, 72, *75*, 75–77, 92, 164
Wax myrtle, 40, 165, 175, 179, 212
Wedelia, 44, *45*
Weed(s): regulations, 22, 145; weed-
    ing strategies, 13, 15, 18, 22, 26, 35,
    38, 38–40, 46–67, 79, 81–84, 89–94,
    101–4, *103*, 120–25, 130–33, 137–43,
    139, 148–52, 166, 191–92, 227–28, 241
Weeping fig, 34, 166, 243
West coast dune sunflower, 3–4, 190
Whip, 69, 167, 250; reasons for planting,
    34–35
White fringetree, 40
Wild allamanda, 226
Wild coffee, 213
Wild garlic, 26, 175, 215, 6pl
Wildland(s), 251; damage to, 37, 193;

fire-prone, 23, 29, 33, 127, 153, 207, 223,
    227; as inspiration, 3–4, 11, 14–15, 120
Wild taro, 41
Willow: Carolina, 208–9; tea, 112–13
Winged elm, 43, 160, 209
Winged sumac, 213
Wisteria spp.: *W. floribunda*, 44–45; *W.
    frutescens*, 45; *W. sinensis*, 44–45
Woodwardia spp., 128, 222, 4pl
Woolgrass, 224

Yucca spp., 214

Zamia spp.: *Z. integrifolia*, 40, 41, 129,
    137, 157, 215, 3pl; *Z. floridana* and *Z.
    pumila* (see *Z. integrifolia*)
Zanthoxylum fagara, 209
Zebra longwing butterfly, *6*
Zephyranthes spp., 175, 221, 6pl

GINNY STIBOLT is a lifelong gardener and earned a Master of Science degree in botany at the University of Maryland, but gardening is different in Florida. She's been writing about her adventures in Florida gardening since 2004. In 2006, she changed her landscaping style after joining the Florida Native Plant Society to include more native plants and more natural areas in her yard. She wrote *Sustainable Gardening for Florida* and *Organic Methods for Vegetable Gardening in Florida* with Melissa Contreras. In addition, she blogs for the websites Native Plants and Wildlife Gardens (www.nativeplantwildlifegarden.com), Florida Native Plant Society (www.fnpsblog.org), and her own blog, Green Gardening Matters (www.greengardeningmatters.com).